God's
Strategy
in
Human
History

God's Strategy in Human History

Roger T. Forster &
V. Paul Marston

HIGHLAND BOOKS

ISBN: 0 946616 55 8

BIBLE VERSIONS

For a work like this, it seemed preferable to use a translation of the
Bible which followed closely the structure of the original, rather
than a free rendering. For this reason it seemed best to adopt the
Revised Version (R.V.) of 1881, and (unless otherwise stated) **bold
print in this work always indicates direct quotation from the
RV.** It was decided, however, that in order to give the text a modern
appearance, archaic word endings would be dropped, "thee"
changed to "you," etc. In the interest of consistency this has been
done without changing word order or grammar.

Where other versions have been cited, the abbreviations used are
as follows.

Authorized Version (AV)
Revised Standard Version (RSV)
New English Bible (NEB)
Jerusalem Bible (JB)
J. B. Phillips — no abbreviation
Septuagint (LXX)

The Septuagint (LXX) is the Greek translation of the Hebrew Old
Testament, completed in the second century B.C. The LXX was the
version in common use in apostolic times. The New Testament
writers sometimes quoted it, and it may help us to understand something of the implications of various Greek expressions used by them.

Printed in Great Britain for
HIGHLAND BOOKS
Broadway House, The Broadway
Crowborough, East Sussex
by Richard Clay Ltd, Bungay, Suffolk

Contents

FOREWORD TO THE ORIGINAL EDITION

It is a sign of grace on the part of the authors of this book that they should invite an impenitent Augustinian and Calvinist to write a foreword for it. There are several reasons for my ready acceptance of their invitation, but there is one which outweighs all others, and that is the thoroughly exegetical character of what they have written.

There is a great danger, when once we have adhered to one particular school of thought or adopted one particular system of theology, of reading the Bible in the light of that school or system and finding its distinctive features in what we read. One reader may tend to do less than justice to those texts which stress man's responsibility; another will be inclined to modify the force of those which emphasize eternal election. The remedy for this is to bear resolutely in mind that our systems of doctrine must be based on biblical exegesis, not imposed upon it. The authors of this work bear this in mind, and make a special point of asking what the Scriptures really say. They do this by means of a study of key words and key passages in context.

This is not to say that I am convinced by all their arguments; perhaps my heart, like Pharaoh's, has been "strengthened"! That, however, is not important; what is important is that the reader is provided with evidence on which he can form his own judgment.

A study of the following pages will impress on the reader that the initiative in saving grace rests with God; that the election of believers is "in Christ"; and the election implies not that some are elected and the others consigned to perdition, but that some are elected so that others through them may receive the divine blessing.

F. F. BRUCE, M.A., D.D.
*Rylands Professor of Biblical
Criticism and Exegesis,
University of Manchester*

INTRODUCTION TO THE 1989 EDITION

The issues which first led us to research and write *God's Strategy in Human History* remain as alive today as they ever were.

There has, for example, been some recent work on issues of providence and human freedom with which we would find much to sympathise, e.g. in the writings of Richard Rice *(God's Foreknowledge And Man's Free Will*, 1985) and Norman Geissler and Clark Pinnock (in *Predestination & Freewill*, Ed. D. & R. Basinger, 1986). There has been some other interesting work concerning which we might wish to be more critical, such as that of Paul K. Jewett *(Election and Predestination,* 1985), which we believe fails to explore the essential consistency of the Wesleyan approach, and glosses over the novel peculiarities in Augustine's system noted in our Appendix (it also seems strange to claim, as does Jewett, that the Greek Church Fathers 'ignored' Augustine's ideas on predestination, when his system was so novel and was invented after most of them had died). These and other publications show the continuing interest in this ever-relevant subject. We value some of the further contributions being made, but have not found any reason to change our understanding of the key concepts of Scripture which we present in *God's Strategy in Human History*.

On the words dealt with in our word studies, there is now available the complete version of Kittel's *Theological Dictionary of the New Testament,* and Colin Brown's *Dictionary of New Testament Theology.* Would these make us wish to revise our treatments? Their entries on 'elect' (Kittel iv p192, Brown 1 p533 are interesting and Christ-centred, whilst those on 'righteousness' and 'justification' (Kittel ii p192, Brown iii p352) add a wealth of detail to those concepts – but in neither case would we wish to alter the points made in our own word studies which focus on more specific issues. Their entries on 'foreknowledge' (Kittel i p715, Brown i p696) repeat the all too common assertion that in Rom 8:29, 11:2 and 2 Pet 1:20 the word means 'choose beforehand'. We have rejected any such implication for this word in these verses – its usual meaning of 'know beforehand' makes more sense in each case. It is therefore noteworthy that neither Kittel nor Brown can cite a single reference from all the wealth of Greek secular or apocryphal literature, in which 'choose beforehand' (rather than a straightforward 'know beforehand') is an accepted meaning for this word. This encourages us in the belief that the interpretation of the word in our word study on it is basically correct, and that it is important to the understanding of this aspect of God to recognise it.

We believe, then, it to be entirely proper for this new English edition of *God's Strategy in Human History* to carry the same text and message as the American printings have always carried. This explores the biblical concepts of a God of love, who wants to co-operate with whoever will accept his love, in the conflict to bring that love into its final victory in God's own universe. We found these ideas exciting when we first wrote about them. We still do!

Roger T. Forster
V. Paul Marston
January 1989

ACKNOWLEDGMENTS

The responsibility of anything said in this book remains that of the authors alone. We would, however, like to thank Dr. G. R. Beasley Murray, Mr. Geoffrey Bull, Rev. A. Morgan Derham, Mr. T. Harpur, Dr. and Mrs. A Kinnear, Rev. G. W. Kirby, Dr. Leon Morris, Mr. F. N. Martin, Dr. T. Martin, Cannon Alan Neech, Rev. K. F. W. Prior, Dr. A. Skevington Wood, Mr. Alan Storkey, Dr. Steven Travis, and many other fellow Christians, for reading all or part of the manuscript and offering encouragement or useful criticism. We thank especially four scholars who spared us time to make penetrating and constructive criticism in detail: Professor F. F. Bruce, Mr. H. L. Ellison, Rev. Derek Kidner and Mr. D. F. Payne.

PART ONE

The Nature of the Conflict

Introduction

This is a study of what the Bible says about God's strategy throughout human history. It deals with the conflict between good and evil, but it is not a series of homilies on how to struggle on in Christian living. A conflict, of course, has individual battles, but also maneuverings and campaigns that may go on over a considerable period. It is this general sweep and strategy of God's action throughout history which this book seeks to portray from the Bible.

Set in such a context, a number of topics that might otherwise seem boring or mysterious become interesting and clear. What was God's purpose in his special dealings with Israel? What is his purpose in the church today? Is there a meaning to history? This book looks at these important topics in context. It contains a detailed interpretation of Romans 9-11, showing how groundless are some people's fears over this passage. It deals with "problem" subjects like predestination, election, and foreknowledge—attempting to put these into their Biblical context of God's future plans. It attempts, in short, to explore a number of subjects all too often overlooked today.

Let us say at once that we find it tremendously exciting to be able to grasp a little of God's purposes in history. It enables us to see the whole movement of which we are a tiny part, the whole history into which our lives fit. Day by day we begin to discover how our actions, sufferings, and attitudes have repercussions for eternity. We realize the great future destiny God has in store for his children. The authors are conscious that such profound subjects are dealt with all too briefly. Nevertheless, it is to be hoped that the material presented may help the inquiring believer in his own reflections and studies.

AN
OUTLINE OF
THE BOOK

This outline may serve as a guide to the reader as he progresses through the book, to help him to understand where it is going.

First, in Part 1 we look at the nature of the spiritual conflict. What are the battlefields, the combatants, and the weapons used? Without these clear in our minds it would be difficult to examine the history of the conflict and God's strategy in it. We should understand how man may be a battlefield and/or a combatant. We need to realize that God's weapons and methods are different from ordinary methods of human conquest. We have to think, also, about just how real the conflict is.

The second part moves on from the nature of the spiritual conflict to consider its whole history as it has affected humanity. In short, it considers "God's strategy in human history." This began, of course, with Adam. It was, however, in Abraham and the Hebrew nation that God's coordinated plan of attack and rescue developed. The second part of the book, therefore, concerns itself with the history of Israel and the significance of God's dealings with them. Why did God choose Abraham? Why was Israel the chosen nation? What was their function in God's strategy and plan? The book develops their history with these questions in mind, and goes on to look at the position of the Hebrew nation since Christ. Some lessons about God's foreknowledge, sovereignty, and the general patterns of his dealings may be drawn at this point. This second part of the book then finishes with an account of God's revealed strategy for the future. God's plan for Christ and the predestiny of the church are vitally connected with the future culmination of the conflict and the final overthrow of the forces of evil. God's final design for the human race is one of goodness and peace in a universe to which harmony has been restored.

The third part contains six studies of concepts vital to understanding God's methods. These studies may be read individually, either before or after reading the rest of the book, and it is intended that they should add color and background to it. Finally, an appendix contains a discussion of the historical origins of many current ideas on God's will, man's will, and such topics. This is not strictly necessary to the theme, but it may help us to understand more clearly the influences that condition our thinking, and how they measure up to the Bible.

Man a Battlefield—Job

Spiritual warfare is the subject of a well-known passage of Scripture, Ephesians 6. We use this passage, therefore, to guide our thoughts at the start of this and the two subsequent sections.

To begin with, let us note the last part of verse 11: **Put on the whole armor of God that you may be able to stand against the wiles of the Devil.**[1] This gives us a clue as to the identity of the master mind behind those who take counsel against the Lord and his anointed, to throw off his rule.[2] This role of Satan is seen very clearly in the book of Job. This issue turns on the devil's charge that people love God solely because he has shown them some special favor: **Does Job fear God for naught? Have you not made a hedge about him, and about his house, and about all that he has on every side?**[3] Satan is saying that God's kingdom is based on expediency and that just as some people worship Satan to gain power and favor, so others worship God because he is more powerful. God takes up this challenge of Satan, and a battle is declared—the battleground being the soul of faithful Job.[4]

The most obvious temptation for Job is the temptation to revolt and godlessness—to **renounce God and die.**[5] Job did not do this, and so Satan's prediction was confounded.[6] The devil still has, however, a more subtle line of attack. How will Job stand up against an appeal by his friends to seemingly orthodox traditions?[7] Surely Job has heard that a man suffers only because of his own unfaithfulness?[8] The fundamental assumption in all the speeches of Job's three comforters and young Elihu is that it is *God* who binds up, who smites and heals[9] and who enters into judgment,[10] and even then he is punishing wicked Job less than he deserves.[11] They fail to understand that Job is not suffering because God wants to chasten him[12] or because of his own sin, but because in the conflict against Satan the latter is allowed to afflict one of God's blameless and upright servants. The comforters and young Elihu remain convinced that it is God who is afflicting Job, and that he is doing so because of Job's sin.[13] "God is so holy," they say, "that he does not even trust the angels;[14] whereas man is abominable and corrupt,[15] a mere worm.[16] God is so high that a man's righteousness can never bring pleasure to him."[17]

Notice how misled these four were, who imagined themselves to be proclaiming God's truth. They believed that God was too exalted for Job's righteousness to be of any account with him. The Lord in a sense (to use a human analogy) staked his reputation on Job: **Have you considered my servant Job? for there is none like him in the earth, a perfect and upright man, one that fears God and eschews evil; and he still holds fast his integrity, although you moved me against him to destroy him without cause.**[18]

These words not only show us God's pleasure and confidence in Job, but the reasons for Job's sufferings become clearer. It was not God but Satan who instigated and effected Job's misfortunes. It was Satan who first suggested that Job suffer materially and physically.[19] Further, although Satan suggested that God should "put forth his hand" there is no indication that God did so. God says: **you moved me against him to destroy him** but there is no indication that he complied with the request. Rather, he said: **he is in your hand; only spare his life,** and it was Satan who destroyed Job's possessions and health. It is enlightening for us to see that God was in no sense, either directly or via Satan, the cause of Job's afflictions. God allowed Satan's actions but this is another matter. We must be clear exactly what we mean if we say that God "could have stopped" Job's suffering. We may indeed accept that he had the sheer power to stop or even destroy Satan. The problem is that in this case, even as Satan sank under God's wrath and destruction, he would have gone with a sneer on his lips as though to say, "I told you so." Such a "solution" would have left forever unanswered Satan's accusation that God's kingdom was based (like his own) on force and expediency. It was not lack of power that prevented God from crushing Satan—it was a matter of princple. It is, perhaps, comparable to the moral restraint that makes it impossible for God to lie.[20] Satan's accusations must be answered, and they cannot be truly answered by a force that crushes the accuser. They can only be fully answered by the method God adopts, by allowing Satan to remove Job's privileges. He must show that the servant in whom he trusts loves him for himself and not for what he can get out of him.

In this particular instance[21] it seems that God allowed Job to be afflicted to prove to Satan that someone could love him without any reward and even in the midst of misunderstanding about him. Was God's confidence in Job vindicated? If we read through the book we find that Job, like his friends, mistakenly ascribed his misfortune to God. Yet Job remained certain of his own innocence and cried out for an opportunity to bring his case for trial. He seems to have felt that something had somewhere gone wrong. There had been an anomaly in the justice of the universe. We see, therefore, that Job did not understand the situation he was in. Satan had ruined Job's fortunes and, through the comforters, had multiplied Job's doubt and confusion. Would Job, as Satan had predicted, renounce God to his face?[22]

Job, however, vindicated his master's trust. He said: **though he slay me, yet will I wait for him: Nevertheless I will maintain my ways before him . . .**[23] Job would serve God, come what may. God showed, through him, that his kingdom was not based on the obedience of expediency but the obedience of love.

It is instructive to set out in detail a comparison of what God says and what is said by the comforters and young Elihu:

(a) God has confidence in his servants.

God says: **Have you considered my servant Job? for there is none like him in the earth . . .** (Job 1:8; 2:3)

But the comforters say: **He puts no trust in his servants . . .** (Eliphaz in 4:18)

Can a man be profitable unto God? . . . Is it any pleasure to the Almighty that you are righteous? Or is it a gain to him, that you make your ways perfect? (Eliphaz in 22: 2, 3)

If you are righteous what give you him? Or what receives he of your hand? (Elihu in 35:7)

(b) Job is perfect (i.e., complete) and upright.

God says: **. . . a perfect and upright man . . .** (Job 1:8; 2:3)

But the comforters say: **If you were pure and upright surely now he would awake for you, and make the habitation of your righteousness prosperous.** (Bildad in 8:6)

Behold God will not cast away a perfect man. (Bildad in 8:20)

Remember, I pray you, who ever perished being innocent? Or where were the upright cut off? (Eliphaz in 4:7)

I have heard the voice of your words, saying, I am clean without transgression; I am innocent neither is there iniquity in me: . . . in this you are not just. (Elihu in 33:8-12)

What man is like Job, who drinks up scorning like water? Which goes in company with workers of iniquity and walks with wicked men. (Elihu in 34:7)

How then can man be just with God? Or how can he be clean that is born of a woman? (Bildad in 25:4)

What is man that he should be clean? And he which is born of a woman that he should be righteous? (Eliphaz in 15:14)

For you say, My doctrine is pure, And I am clean in your eyes. But Oh that God would speak . . . Know therefore

that God exacts of you less than your iniquity deserves. (Zophar in 11:4-6)

(c) Job's attitudes to God and to evil are right.

God says: One that fears God and eschews evil. (Job 1:8; 2:3)

But the comforters say: Yea, you do away with fear, and restrain devotion before God. (Eliphaz in 15:4)

Is it for your fear of him that he reproves you, That he enters with you into judgment? Is not your wickedness great? Neither is there any end to your iniquities. (Eliphaz in 22:4, 5)

(d) The innocent do suffer "without cause."

God says: and he still holds fast his integrity although you (i.e., Satan) moved me against him to destroy him without cause. (Job 2:3)

But the comforters say: If you were pure and upright; surely now he would awake for you. And make the habitation of your righteousness prosperous. (Bildad in 8:6)

Know therefore that God exacts of you less than your iniquity deserves. (Zophar in 11:6)

Remember, I pray you, who ever perished being innocent? . . . they that plow iniquity, and sow trouble, reap the same. By the breath of God they perish. (Eliphaz in 4:7-9)

For Job has said, I am righteous, . . . notwithstanding my right I am accounted a liar; my wound is incurable though I am without transgression. What man is like Job, who drinks up scorning like water? . . . For he has said it profits a man nothing that he should delight himself with God. Therefore hearken unto me, you men of understanding: Far be it from God, that he should do wickedness: . . . For the work of a man shall he render unto him, And cause every man to find according to his ways. (Elihu in 34:5-11)

(e) Job's affliction is caused by Satan and not by God.

The truth is: So Satan went forth from the presence of the Lord, and smote Job with sore boils from the sole of his foot unto his crown. (Job 2:7)

But the comforters say: Therefore despise not the chastening of the Almighty. For he makes sore, and binds up; He wounds and his hands make whole. (Eliphaz in 5:17, 18)

Know therefore that God exacts of you less than your iniquity deserves. (Zophar in 11:6)

Is it for fear of him that he reproves you, that he enters with you into judgment? (Eliphaz in 22:4)

Behold, God is mighty and despises not any . . . He preserves not the life of the wicked; but gives to the afflicted their right. (Elihu in 36:5, 6)

Yea, he would have led you away out of distress into a broad place, where there is no straitness; and that which is on your table should be full of fatness. But you are full of the judgment of the wicked. (Elihu in 36:16, 17)

(f) Job's words are acceptable to God.

God says: My wrath is kindled against you (Eliphaz) and against your two friends: for you have not spoken of me the thing that is right, as my servant Job has. (Job 42:7)

But the comforters say: And how long shall the words of your mouth be like a mighty wind? (Bildad in 8:2)

Should not the multitude of words be answered? And should a man full of talk be justified? (Zophar in 11:2)

For your iniquity teaches your mouth, and you choose the tongue of the crafty. (Eliphaz in 15:5)

How long will you lay snares for words? (Bildad in 18:2)

And I have heard the voice of your words saying, I am clean without transgression . . . in this you are not just. (Elihu in 33:8-12)

Job speaks without knowledge, and his words are without wisdom. Would that Job were tried unto the end because of his answering like wicked men. For he adds rebellion unto his sin. (Elihu in 34:35-37)

Therefore does Job open his mouth in vanity; he multiplies words without knowledge. (Elihu in 35:16)

What lessons can we draw from the story of Job? It is true that God sometimes allows sickness or catastrophe to come on someone as a "chastening," but not all suffering is to be thus explained. The comforters seem to imagine that God is determining everything that happens in the world.[24] If they were right in this, then it would be logical to expect suffering always to be either for punishment or for chastening. If everything happened as God willed, and if he is just, then the innocent could never suffer. "Who ever perished then being innocent?" asked Eliphaz, and on his own presuppositions it would be difficult to disagree with him—Job must be guilty. But in fact there is a battle involved, and thus it may often happen that one of God's perfect and upright servants suffers.

It was not God but Satan who instigated the sufferings of Job. Nevertheless, God could use Job's sufferings to bring him to a deeper relationship with himself. The principle is that "in everything God works for good with those who love Him, who are called according to His purpose."[25] Whatever disaster may strike and however bad the situation may be, God wants to work in that situation for good. He wants his servants, moreover, to cooperate with him in doing this. It is therefore important that we react rightly to situations of suffering or tragedy.

We may remember the incident when Jesus and his disciples saw the tragic sight of a man born blind.[26] Sin is the ultimate cause of all suffering and sickness, and the disciples tried to raise the theological question: **Rabbi, who did sin, this man or his parents, that he should be born blind?** They were trying to unravel the causal chain linking suffering ultimately to sin. Jesus' reply indicated the futility of such questions. The man's blindness was not a result of his own sins and neither was it a result of those of his parents. It would have been pointless to have tried to unravel its causes. The real question should not be: "What caused the suffering?" but rather: "How can I cooperate in doing the works of God in this situation?" or in other words: "How does God want in this instance to work for good with those who love him?"[27] Christ did not see suffering as an intellectual challenge but as a need and opportunity to show the works of God in healing. Sometimes a person may be suffering because he has sinned. More commonly, however, the causes of suffering are too complex to unravel. Our task should be to seek to cooperate with God in alleviating it. We see, therefore, that our reactions to suffering are important.

Also of importance is our attitude when we ourselves suffer. If Job had "cursed God and died," he would neither have received blessing himself nor been a channel of blessing to others. Job did not curse God and neither was he content with pious platitudes. He was real with God in the situation, and therefore God commended his words. Job confessed his doubts, his confusion, and yet he knew he had not done the wickedness his friends imagined. God commended this, and then commanded Job to play the man and answer his questions.[28] It is important in times of trouble for us to be open for him to reveal more of himself to us. Many people, like Job, have found a deeper experience of God through suffering. This does not mean that God necessarily brings such sufferings, but that he is ready to exploit any situation to bring in blessing. We read, further, that **the Lord turned the captivity of Job, when he prayed for his friends . . .**[29] As Job turned from his own needs to those of others and began to cooperate with God to bring in blessing, he found that his bondage to despair began to lift. Thus it often happens that as a person becomes a channel for blessing, his own burdens seem lightened. At the end of the book Job may have realized something of the conflict that had been going on, for through prayer he himself became a participant in the battle.

Job, therefore, was a battlefield in which God proved to Satan that his servants could love him for himself, and not merely for what he could give them. Perhaps, as a result of his experience, Job began himself to realize what was happening, and actually participate, through prayer, in the bringing in of blessing.

NOTES
1. Ephesians 6:11
2. Psalm 2
3. Job 1:9, 10
4. From Job's point of view, of course, it was a struggle to maintain his faith in the face of incomprehensible circumstances. During his troubles he was quite unaware of Satan's role. This, perhaps, explains

why most of the book of Job omits reference to Satan. It is only from the divine standpoint of chapters 1-2 that we see Satan's activities.

5. Job 2:9
6. Job 2:5
7. Job 8:8, 9; 15:10; 20:4
8. Job 4:7, 8; 8:8-20; 20:4, etc.
9. Job 5:18
10. Job 22:4, 5
11. Job 11:6
12. Job 5:17
13. Job 8:4-6; 11:5, 14; 15:5; 22:4; 25:4; 34:7-11, 37; 36:6, 7
14. Job 4:18; 15:15
15. Job 4:17; 15:16
16. Job 25:6
17. Job 22:3. A verse that may come to mind at this point is Isaiah 64:6—"All our righteousness is as filthy rags." It is unfortunate that one often hears this verse quoted without any regard for context, and we must be careful here. Those in Isaiah who say: "All our righteousness is as filthy rags" go on in the next verse to accuse God of hiding his face from them. This latter is, we note, explicitly denied by God in Isaiah 65:1, 2 where he says that he is not hiding but rather is offering himself to them. (We might also compare Isaiah 63:17 with 65:12 where the Lord affirms that it was not his doing but their own choice to reject his call and go against his wishes.) There is, then, no reason to suppose that the Lord endorses these people's extreme position over human sinfulness. It is not even a guard against spiritual pride, for God accuses these same people of a "holier than thou" attitude (65:5).

None of this is to deny that salvation is "not of works lest any man should boast," but it is to affirm that God's attitude to his servants' righteousness is different from that often supposed.

18. Job 2:3
19. Job 1:11; 2:5
20. Hebrews 6:18. To use a human analogy we might ask "Can a Christian commit fornication?" The answer to this is Yes if we mean physical ability, but No as far as moral obligation and consistency are concerned.
21. In other cases of suffering, of course, God may have different reasons for having to allow it.
22. Job 2:5
23. Job 13:15; see also 27:1-7
24. see (e) above and Job 11:7-10; 20:23-29; 24:10-18; 25:1-6; 32:12, 13; and 36:5-14
25. Romans 8:28 RSV. The AV rendering "All things work together for good" seems unlikely here. A number of important early manuscripts contain an additional nominative "God," which strongly indicates one of the other renderings. The idea is not one of "things" somehow working impersonally together, or even of God somehow working them together. The idea is of God co-working with those who love him, as Athanasius said: "to all who choose the good, God works with them for good." Thus the RSV renders: "in everything God works

for good with those who love him." The NEB renders: "in everything, as we know, [the Spirit] cooperates for good with those who love God." Since the Spirit is also the subject in verses 26 and 27 this seems the most likely rendering of all. (See also F. F. Bruce's commentary on Romans.)

The word "work-together" (*sunergeō*) is not used much in the New Testament, but there are some verses of interest in this context. In Mark 16:20 we find that as the disciples preached the Lord "worked together" with them. In 1 Corinthians 3:9 Paul says that "we are God's fellow workers . . ." In 2 Corinthians 6:1 he again describes himself as "working-together" with God.

There are, therefore, a number of points in favor of the RSV or NEB rather than the AV or RV:

(a) There are early manuscripts that contain the extra word "God" to put it beyond doubt.

(b) There is nothing else in Scripture to indicate that all things somehow work for good, whereas the idea of Christians as God's "fellow-workers" is well attested.

(c) The preceding two verses of the passage in Romans 8, speak precisely of such a co-working in prayerful intercession between the Christians and the Holy Spirit. This makes the RSV (or even more the NEB) much more natural in development.

On a practical level it may often be a cause of doubt and despair for a Christian when tragedy or disaster strikes, if he has to try to convince himself that "things" are somehow working for his best good. They may, indeed, not be, and Satan rather than God may be behind them. Nevertheless, what any Christian *can* be sure of is that God will be there—wanting to work-together with him and with other believers, to bring good out of the situation.

26. John 9:1
27. John 9:3; compare Romans 8:28 RSV or NEB and see note 25 above.
28. Job 40:7
29. Job 42:10

15

3

Man a Combatant—Daniel

Job was primarily a battlefield. Ephesians 6 explains further how we may be more than unwitting individual battlefields. God wants us to understand that we form part of the larger battle, and actually fight in it: **For our wrestling is not against flesh and blood, but against the principalities, against the powers, against the world rulers of this darkness, against the spiritual hosts of wickedness in the heavenly places.**[1]

From the book of Daniel one obtains a vivid picture of how man can participate in the struggle against such spiritual hosts of wickedness. For three weeks Daniel, a prayerful man of God, set himself to **understand and to humble himself before his God.**[2] His prayers were heard, but for three weeks God's messenger was prevented from reaching him by the "prince of Persia." Only when Michael assisted the messenger were Daniel's wrestlings in prayer answered.

Who is this Michael, and who are the other spiritual combatants? Much of the book of Daniel is concerned with the history and destiny of the chosen nation Israel.[3] Through them God was to prepare for the coming of the Messiah, the "anointed one" who was to be the redeemer. Michael is the prince of Israel[4] and he becomes involved in spiritual conflict with the other two angels: the prince of Persia and the prince of Greece.[5] These two *principalities* may well be "world rulers of this darkness" mentioned in Ephesians. They seem to be powers who seek to manipulate other nations playing a part in the history of Israel. In chapter 9 are predicted the activities of another **prince that shall come,** whose people will destroy the city soon after the **anointed one** is **cut off.**[6] There are, we discover, spiritual battles underlying world politics, and through Israel and their Messiah, God works for the extension of his Kingdom of Light.

We see in Daniel the angels as combatants. We see also the important messianic figure, the one whom we know to be Christ. Closely associated with this messianic figure is the role of the **saints of the Most High.** In Daniel 7:13 **one like unto a son of man** is presented to the Ancient of Days, and is given a kingdom and a dominion. Yet in verse 18 it is the **saints of the Most High** who receive the kingdom. Then again there is war between the **horn** and the **saints**[7] who eventually triumph[8] and receive the kingdom.[9] So the book of Daniel shows us that the war and the kingdom belong both to the Messiah and to his saints. Through prayer Daniel himself is part of the conflict. Man is a combatant in the battle.

NOTES
1. Ephesians 6:12
2. Daniel 10:2-12
3. See also part two of this book
4. Daniel 10:21; 12:1; Jude 9
5. Daniel 10:13, 20
6. Daniel 9:26. This prince may be the spiritual prince of Rome, for it was the Romans who destroyed Jerusalem in A.D. 70.
7. Daniel 7:21
8. Daniel 7:23
9. See Daniel 7:27

4

Weapons, Methods, and Banners—The Church

Man is a combatant. In Ephesians 6 we also find how the saints fight and with what armor: **Finally, be strong in the Lord and in the strength of his might. Put on the whole armor of God . . .**[1] These words show that we fight in God's strength and God's armor. Paul goes on to compare various parts of Christian character with the different sections of a soldier's armor. It is instructive to our understanding of "the armor of God" to see the Old Testament stimulus of Paul's ideas on it; Isaiah 59 reads: **And he saw that there was no man, and wondered that there was no intercessor: therefore his own arm brought salvation unto him; and his righteousness, it upheld him. And he put on righteousness as a breastplate, and a helmet of salvation upon his head . . . And a redeemer shall come to Zion, and unto them that turn from transgression in Jacob.**[2] This is the **armor of God.** It is God's armor because it is worn by the Messiah as he comes to bring redemption. It is also the armor that should be worn today by the body of Christ on earth, the church.[3] In the book of Daniel we saw how the saints entered into the battle, and that when the kingdom was given it was given both to the Messiah and to the saints. In Ephesians we find that the battles of the Messiah and of his body the church are the same, for *we* fight in his armor and **in the strength of his might.** The Christian soldier is not fighting a lone battle against the forces of evil, but as a part of the body of Christ is using Jesus' own armor.

The actual weapons mentioned in Ephesians 6 are well known: the girdle of truth, the breastplate of righteousness, the shoes of the preparation of the Good News of peace, the shield of faith, the helmet of salvation and the sword of the spirit. Only one of these weapons is for attack, and it is particularly important to note. What is the Christian's sword? We know that to have a "shield of faith" means that faith is our shield, and our "helmet of salvation" is comprised of salvation. It seems, therefore, that to have a "sword of the spirit" means that we use a sword comprised of spirit. The apostle further clarifies this by adding that this "spirit" (or "breath") is the word of God.[4] The whole phrase in Ephesians 6:17 might be literally rendered: "the breath[5] which is the saying of God." Our sword is the breath which is the saying of God. This may also be the breath with which Christ shall slay the wicked: **he shall smite the earth with the rod of his mouth, and with the breath (spirit) of his lips shall he slay the wicked.**[6] This is taken up in Revelation 19:15: **And out of his mouth proceeds a sharp sword, that with it he should smite the nations: and he shall rule them with a rod of iron: and he treads the winepress of the fierceness of the wrath of Almighty God.** The sharp sword[7] comes out of Christ's mouth, for his weapon is the truth he speaks. To us Christ's words are spirit and life,[8] for the living application of Christ's revelation in our lives brings life, feeds, and cleanses.[9] But his sword of truth is two-edged, and to the wicked it is destructive.

We have already seen how Satan used the weapon of words through the mouths of Job's comforters. Twice at the end of the book of Job the Lord judges them for their words and commends Job for his. Words are a weapon, but how does Satan use them? We are told that **he was a murderer from the beginning, and stood not in the truth because there is no truth in him. When he speaks a lie, he speaks of his own: for he is a liar, and the father thereof.**[10]

Even at the beginning of human history the devil used a lie in the garden of Eden to seduce mankind into death.

Yet though the devil uses words perversely, he is afraid to stand in the truth, which reveals him as he is. Words of truth are like light, in that both reveal an object or person for what it or he is. Those whose deeds are evil are afraid to come into the light.[11] Through the weapons of truth and light Christ will finally reveal evil for what it is, and in doing so will destroy it. In the full revelation of what it is, evil shrivels up and is destroyed. Paul links light with words of truth in his expansion of Isaiah 11:4, a verse we have already mentioned: **And then shall be revealed the lawless one whom the Lord Jesus shall consume with the spirit of his mouth, and shall destroy with the brightness of his coming.**[12]

The "sword of the spirit" is given to us, as well as to Christ, but how should the ordinary Christian use it? Paul says: **And take . . . the sword of the spirit which is the word of God; with all prayer and supplication praying at all seasons in the spirit.**[13] Through praying in the Holy Spirit we learn how to use the spiritual weapon of the sayings of God. We learn to praise, we learn to use the name of Jesus, we learn when and how to speak God's message to a person, and how to apply a verse of Scripture in our lives. There is, of course, no virtue in quoting Scripture for the sake of the words themselves—for the devil himself did this in tempting Christ.[14] It is not the words as such, but the illuminating power they have as we apply them correctly in our lives. Christ himself used a verse in this way as he replied to the Devil's "proof text." This is the power of Scripture, as the Holy Spirit applies it in lives.

We see, therefore, that in Ephesians (as in Daniel) prayer occupies a key place in the fight. Through prayer the Christian learns to use his weapons. Through prayer we support and intercede for each other.[15] Yet Paul makes it clear that it should be prayer **in the Spirit.** We should let the Holy Spirit direct our prayers so that God may use us according to his overall strategy.

This has given us some insight into the weapons of warfare. But can we find out more about these and the methods of fighting used by the forces of the Lord of Hosts?

Another book in the Bible clearly presents the picture of the battles, the Revelation. In Revelation 4 and 5 we read of a throne from which come peals of thunder, lightning, etc. It is set right in the middle of the elders, the creatures of the earth, the angels, and every created thing. Everyone is waiting for a person who would be worthy to open the scroll concerning man's destiny.[16] Then John hears that the "lion from the tribe of Judah" has overcome and is worthy. He looks around for this "overcoming lion," perhaps expecting something like the one in 1 Peter 5:8, only bigger! What he in fact sees is a little lamb (*arnion*) which looks as if it has been killed. This is the symbol of God's power and armies throughout the book of Revelation, and the word is used in this way 27 times. Can we imagine any militant nation marching out to conquer under the banner of a lamb that looks as if it has been killed? Yet this is God's emblem, and by the end of Revelation the lamb is seen to be on the same throne as the Father himself.

If this is the leader of God's armies, what can their weapons be like? **And there was war in heaven: Michael and his angels going forth to war with the dragon[17] and the dragon warred and his angels; and they prevailed not . . . for the accuser of our brethren is cast down, which accuses them before our God day and night. And they overcame him because of the blood of the lamb and because of the word of their testimony; and they loved not their life even unto death.[18]** Throughout history the armies of the world have used weapons of ever increasing power and violence. Swords and bows have been replaced by guns and napalm. The weapons of God: truth, martyrdom, and the blood of his lamb, are of a totally different order from any of these. They do not destroy by violence, but by revealing the depravity and ugliness of evil for what it is—thus leading to its destruction. So the blood of the martyred saints and prophets itself becomes a weapon: in drinking it the wicked become drunk for their own destruction.[19] Time and again in Revelation there is war between the forces of good and the forces of evil, for example, Revelation 17:14—**These shall war against the Lamb and the Lamb shall overcome them,** for he is Lord of lords and King of kings; and they also shall overcome that are with him, called and chosen and faithful. The conquerors are the Lamb and those who are called and chosen and faithful. These last are the faithful saints, called and chosen in Christ. We remember that these saints fight in the same armor as did Jesus the Messiah, for they fight in the armor of God and the strength of his might. We will later see how their chosenness also depends on being part of Christ's body, for they are chosen in him. (See section 15)

To return to Revelation, we find two great images of evil: the Beast and the Harlot.[20] We may regard the Beast as perversion of the truly masculine, representing love of power for its own sake, a "might is right" philosophy which is typical of monsters. The Harlot represents perversion of the truly feminine, a desire for material things, a worship of pleasure, etc. God's answer to these things is a slain lamb. What can this represent but innocence, suffering, and death —and through them the victory?

NOTES

1. Ephesians 6:10, 11; compare Philippians 4:13: I can do all things in him that strengthens me. Only in the Lord do we have strength.

2. Isaiah 59:16-20

3. Compare Isaiah 59:16, 17 and Ephesians 6:13-17

4. The Greek word *which* in the phrase "sword of the spirit which is the word of God" is neuter. This suggests that the phrase: "which is the word of God" refers to the spirit. The spirit *is* the word of God.

The expression "the word of God" should not be confused with the title "Word of God" given to Christ (e.g., John 1:1, Revelation 19:13) for Christ is called by the Greek term *"logos* of God" whereas in Ephesians the term is *"rhēma* of God". There is no *distinct* line between the meanings of these two Greek terms, but it would seem that *rhēma* means a saying, and is included in the more philosophical term *logos*.

5. Breath or spirit; the Greek word *pneuma*, like the Hebrew *ruach*, can be translated as spirit, breath, or wind.

The word is commonly taken in Ephesians 6:17 to mean the Holy Spirit, but nothing in the Greek text would necessitate this. In fact the language implies that the "spirit" or "breath" in this verse *is* the "word of God."

6. Isaiah 11:4

7. See also Revelation 1:16; 2:12, 16

8. John 6:63
9. John 6:63; Matthew 4:4; Ephesians 5:26
10. John 8:44
11. John 3:19
12. 2 Thessalonians 2:8, AV. We have used the AV to emphasize that the word *pneuma* can mean either breath or spirit. The AV renders it "spirit of his mouth" but the RV, RSV, JB, and NEB all render it "breath of his mouth." It seems, in fact, to be the *truth he speaks* which consumes the evil.
13. Ephesians 6:17, 18
14. Matthew 4:6, 7
15. Ephesians 6:18
16. Revelation 5:3, 4
17. Revelation 20:2 shows that this dragon is Satan.
18. Revelation 12:7-11
19. Revelation 16:6; 17:6; 18:24; 14:8
20. F. F. Bruce gave us the suggestion that, in view of the background of the time, the Beast is the Roman empire in its military ruthlessness, the Harlot is the city of Rome in its commercial prosperity—persecuting the saints in the one guise or the other.

God's Glory in the Battle—Jesus

This is the marvelous thing about God. It is at the name of Jesus (which means *Jehovah is Savior*) that every knee shall bow. This is the name above every name.[1] The throne of God does not contain a roaring lion, but a slain lamb. Failing to understand this, many Christians have misunderstood what is the glory of God.

Eliphaz and his friends seem to spell out the greatness and glory of God in terms of his supposed emotional detachment about human "righteousness," coupled with his absolute sovereignty in bringing healing or sickness. God is so high and holy, says Eliphaz, and Job in comparison so wicked, that his "righteousness" could bring God little or no pleasure.[2] Moreover, he adds, it is God who makes sore and binds up, who wounds and heals.[3] Thus, according to Eliphaz, all Job's present sufferings are the outworkings of God's glorious power, and if he seeks God he will get all he wants.[4] (Such interpretations are not confined to comforters of Job's day.)

Are our ideas of the glory of God that he should lord it over people, exercise authority, and appear as a benefactor? This, according to Jesus, is the type of glory sought by the kings of the Gentiles.[5] Is it possible that God himself should be merely a bigger version of a heathen despot? When put thus, Christians would surely unite in condemning the notion as blasphemous rather than glorious.

There is a tragic context to these words of Jesus about the kings of the Gentiles. While he is thinking of his coming suffering and the cup he must drink,[6] his closest friends are arguing about which of them is greatest. Many great human leaders might have said: "You can all stop arguing because I myself am so incomparably greater than any of you." Jesus did something totally different from this. He tried to explain that in the kingdom of heaven everything is upside down—or rather right side up! They call him Master and Lord quite rightly, for so he is,[7] but in the kingdom of heaven this means that he voluntarily makes himself the greatest servant of all: Jesus came to them and knelt to wash their feet. The greatness and glory of God is precisely that he gives himself freely to us his creatures who are but dust—it is not in lording it over people. Jesus was the **effulgence of his glory, and the very image of his substance.**[8] Being the express image of God's person, Jesus showed us what God is like. True Christian orthodoxy, therefore, lies in looking at Jesus' example and words, rather than following the path of Job's traditionalist comforters. We learn from Jesus what the glory of God is.

Jesus was glorified when he ascended into heaven, but he himself also seems to refer to his crucifixion as the time of his glorification: **The hour is come, that the Son of man should be glorified. Verily, verily I say unto you, Except a grain of wheat fall into the earth and die, it abides by itself alone . . . what shall I say? Father, save me from this hour. But for this cause came I unto this hour. Father, glorify your name . . . I, if I be lifted up from the earth, will draw all men unto myself . . .**[9] When therefore he (Judas) **had gone out, Jesus said, Now is the Son of man glorified, and God is glorified in him; and God shall glorify him in himself, and straightway shall he glorify him . . .**[10] Jesus, facing the cross, looked to it as the time of his glorification. The glory of the Lamb of God is that he is a "lamb as though slain" and that he has conquered by becoming like a grain of wheat which dies to give life. Let us never imagine that the glory of God is anything like that of the rulers of the Gentiles.

Further, the two books (Daniel and Revelation) most obviously concerned with the glory and majesty of God, are the two in which the battles between good and evil are seen the most clearly. God does not directly determine everything that happens (see also the next section) and his glory partly lies in the fact that he triumphs in spite of this. The forces of evil put the Messiah Jesus to death. God foreknew that it would happen[11] and God delivered him up to them,[12] knowing and intending what would happen. But they alone did the act. **Yet it pleased the Lord to bruise him** and through his sin offering to save the world. This is typical, in a sense, of his whole working with us and the human race. The righteous are not wafted away leaving the wicked to suffer. God allows the righteous, like Job or for that matter like Jesus himself, to stay in situations where he knows they will suffer. Yet through suffering and love the victory is achieved. God may sometimes even use the forces of evil as "chasteners." An example of this is found in Habakkuk, where God chastened Israel through the evil Chaldeans, whose motto "might is right"[13] was the philosophy of the Beast! Yet there are usually the righteous, the just, who are living **by their faith** even in persecution or difficult times.[14] Habakkuk finally understood how the righteous were to live even in times of trouble, and that the wicked would burn themselves out in judgment. This is God's way with evil. How unsearchable are his judgments and how inscrutable are his ways! God does not waft away the righteous from suffering, but is willing to be right there with them in the midst of it.

NOTES
1. Philippians 2:9, 10
2. See also note 17 to section 2.
3. Job 5:17, 18
4. Job 5:8 *et seq.*
5. Matthew 20:25-28; Mark 10:42-45; Luke 22:24-27
6. Matthew 20:22
7. John 13:13
8. Hebrews 1:3; James 2:1
9. John 12:23, 24, 27, 28, 32
10. John 13:31, 32
11. Acts 2:23 and 1 Peter 1:20 both give this thought, but many versions obscure it in the latter verse. We have given reasons for believing the RV to be correct in section 18, pp. 193, 194.
12. Acts 2:23
13. Habakkuk 1:11
14. Habakkuk 2:4

6

Fight or Fake?

This section may, to some people, seem a parenthesis, but the issue it deals with is vital to the meaning of this book. The problem arises because there are Christians whose views amount to a belief that everything that happens is God's direct will and the whole conflict is therefore a fake.[1] Their views may be expressed in various ways, but the basic idea is the same. They may, for example, say that men are responsible for breaking God's commandments but that nevertheless whatever men do is his will being enacted. They may say that Satan's revolt and the ensuing "conflict" are part of God's will and design. Some would even go as far as to say that God deliberately ordains all the suffering and sorrow in the world. They would reject the point made so well by C. S. Lewis: that suffering is the price that had to be paid for freedom and love to exist at all.[2]

Were we to find any support in Scripture for such teachings on God's "sovereign will," what is said in this book would have to be considerably modified. It is necessary, therefore, to examine what exactly the Bible says on these matters. Is God's will always done?

In the New Testament there are only two Greek roots from which come the words for God's *will* and God's *plan*. One root is *thelō*, which means wish, will, or desire. The second root is *boulomai*, from which come such words as *counselor* (*bouleutēs*; Mark 15:43; Luke 23:50); *taking advice* (*bouleuomai;* Luke 14:31); and *plan* or *wish* or *would* (*boulē* and *boulēma;* Luke 23:51; Acts 5:38; 27:42, 43; 17:20, etc.). The Bible makes it clear that both God's *will* and God's *plan* can be opposed and rejected by men. Let us take the words in turn and examine scriptural use of them.

GOD'S PLAN
REJECTED
(Greek root: *boulomai*)

We discover that an individual can reject God's plan for him: Luke 7:30—**But the Pharisees and the lawyers rejected for themselves the counsel (*boulē*) of God, being not baptized of him. . . .** Human beings, of course, could not thwart God's ultimate plan for the world, but they both can and do thwart his plan that they, as individuals, should have a part in it. The Pharisees could not prevent God's ultimate plan from achieving its end. The new heaven and new earth will come, whether they want it or not. In this sense we may well cry, "Hallelujah, the Lord our God, the Almighty, reigneth."[3] But what they can do is to opt out personally of the new creation to come. God ordains that the new heaven and earth will come. He does not ordain which particular individuals will accept his plan for them to have a part in it.

How, then, are we to take verses like: "My counsel shall stand, I will do my good pleasure"?[4] If we were to take them to mean that every detail of God's plan was always enacted then they would flatly contradict Luke 7:30. We must, therefore, take them to refer to the broad outlines of what will be accomplished, not to details about what part each individual will play in it. There seems to be no other way to interpret Scripture consistently.

We must now look briefly at a passage containing the root *boulomai,* over which there has sometimes been misunderstanding. It is Ephesians 1:9-12: . . . **having made known unto us the mystery of his will, according to his good pleasure which he purposed in him unto a dispensation of the fulness of the times, to sum up all things in Christ, the things in the heavens, and the things upon the earth; in him, I say, in whom also we were made a heritage, having been foreordained according to the purpose of him who works all things after the counsel (*boulēn*) of his will (*thelēmatos*) to the end that we should be . . .**

This has sometimes been thought to be saying that absolutely all events are directly determined by God's will. We must, therefore, examine it carefully.

Let us look first at the word in this passage rendered as "works" in the RV. It comes from the root *energeō,* which we may keep in mind by representing it with the little-used English word "energize." Its general sense may be illustrated by James 5:16—"The energizing prayer of a righteous man avails much." It does not convey an impression of irresistible directive power, but rather one of stimulation. There is, in fact, more than one source of such energizing. Compare the following:

(a) "I also labor, struggling according to the energizing

of Him who energizes in me in power . . ." (Paul in Colossians 1:29)

(b) "The lawless one . . . whose coming is according to the energizing of Satan, with all power . . ." (2 Thessalonians 2:9; see also 2:7).

The same teaching is found in Ephesians:

(c) ". . . the purpose of the One who energizes all things after the counsel of His will . . . and what the exceeding greatness of His power to us-ward who believe, according to the energizing of the strength of His might, which He energized in Christ . . . I was made a minister, according to the gift of that grace of God which was given me according to the energizing of His power . . . according to the power that energizes in us . . ." (Ephesians 1:11, 19, 20; 3:7, 20)

(d) ". . . sins; in which in time past you walked according to the course of this world, according to the prince of the power of the air, of the spirit who now energizes in the sons of disobedience; . . ." (Ephesians 2:1, 2).

Both God and Satan are *energizing*, and Christians must turn on to the right *energy*. Thus Paul says: "Work out your own salvation with fear and trembling for God is energizing in you both to will and to energize for His good pleasure."[5] God energizes in us, but we ourselves must plug in to the energy in order to work out our own salvaging process.

The connotations of "energizing" in Ephesians 1:11 are not, perhaps, adequately conveyed to us by translations like the RSV: "who *accomplishes* all things according to the counsel of his will." We must, therefore, bear this in mind as we think further about the verse.

The second thing we must consider in Ephesians 1:11 is what the phrase "all things" refers to. In verse 10 Paul refers to the "all things" (*ta panta*) which are to be headed up in Christ. He next clarifies what these things are (things in the heavens and on the earth). He then refers (verse 11) to God *energizing* in the "all things" (*ta panta*). Surely we must suppose that the all things God energizes are the same as the all things to be headed up in Christ. It does not mean "all events" or "all that happens" but "all creation."

The thought is similar to that in Colossians 1:16-20 where we find that the "all things" were created and consist in Christ, that Christ will have preeminence in them, and that all things will be reconciled in him. Eventually the all things will be reconciled and headed up in Christ, but in the meantime God energizes them according to his plan—presumably moving them in this direction. This is what Ephesians 1:11 seems to mean. There is certainly no reference to God determining all events, and no indication that everyone acts according to his plans.[6]

There is, then, no inconsistency between Ephesians 1:11 and the clear teaching of Luke 7:30 that an individual may reject God's plan for him. While God's plans for the universe will certainly succeed, an individual may none the less reject God's plans for the part he himself will play in this.

An individual can reject God's good plans for him, but does God ever deliberately plan that a person should be lost? We know, of course, that Christ is the propitiation not only for our sins, but for those of the whole world.[7] We know that God does not delight in the death of the wicked but would rather he repented.[8] It will not surprise us, therefore, to find Peter saying of God's plan: **The Lord is not slack concerning his promise, as some count slackness; but is long-suffering to you-ward, not wishing (***boulomai***) that any should perish, but that all should come to repentance.**[9]

God's plan does not specify that particular individuals should perish. If a man perishes it will be because he has rejected God's plan for him.

GOD'S WILL DEFIED
(Greek root: *thelō*)

We also find that God's will can be, and is, defied by man. Thus we read:

(a) Matthew 23:37; Luke 13:34—**How often would I**

have gathered your children together, even as a hen gathers her chickens under her wings and you would not!

(b) Matthew 12:50; Mark 3:35—For whosoever shall do the will of my Father which is in heaven, he is my brother, and sister, and mother.

(c) Matthew 7:21—Not everyone that says unto me, Lord, Lord, shall enter into the kingdom of heaven; but he that does the will of my Father which is in heaven.

(d) John 7:17—If any man wills to do his will, he shall know of the teaching, whether it be of God, or whether I speak from myself.

(e) 1 John 2:17—And the world passes away, and the lust thereof; but he that does the will of God abides for ever.

From these verses we can see that not all men do God's will. If everyone were acting according to God's will then presumably they would all live forever and enter God's kingdom. This would amount to universalism, which we know to be unscriptural. Thus we must conclude that men can and do refuse to do God's will.

Not only unbelievers but also Christians may, on occasion, reject the will of God as well as his commandments:

(f) 1 Thessalonians 4:3—For this is the will of God, even your sanctification, that you abstain from fornication. (See also 1 Peter 2:15; Hebrews 10:36).

(g) 1 Thessalonians 5:17-19—Pray without ceasing; in everything give thanks: for this is the will of God in Christ Jesus to you-ward. Quench not the spirit . . .

Christians do sometimes quench the Spirit. Some men actually *fight* against the Spirit. God, who wills that all men should be saved, and come to the knowledge of the truth,[10] sends his Spirit to convict their hearts,[11] but they *reject* his plan for them,[12] and *resist* the Spirit's urgings to repent. Scripture says of them:

(h) Acts 7:51—You stiffnecked people and uncircumcised in heart and ears, you do always resist the Holy Ghost: as your fathers did, so do you.

But can they continue to resist the Spirit, or does there come a time when they have no choice but to repent? Let us note that those accused here by Stephen of "resisting the Holy Spirit," although "cut to the heart," promptly murdered him. History shows, moreover, that many of this council stayed unrepentant all their lives. Their resistance to the Holy Spirit and rejection of God's plan for themselves was a permanent thing.

It is clear, therefore, that whichever word for "will" or "plan" we consider, there are Scriptures showing that God's will can be, and is, defied by man.[13] Nothing in Scripture suggests that there is some kind of will or plan of God which is inviolable.

Some Christian writers seem to have been unable to accept this, and have therefore found themselves facing a difficult problem. If, as they believe, everything that happens is God's will, then the unrepentance and perishing of the wicked must also be God's will. Yet God himself says it is *not* his will—so how can they reconcile this?[14] The most obvious approach is for them to try to distinguish the two different senses of the word *will*. Consider the following passage from a well-known commentary on Romans:

> It is true, God would not men should perish as touching His *signified will*, for He offered unto man a law, promises, threatenings, and counsels, which things, if he had embraced, he had surely lived. But, if we have respect unto that mighty and effectual will, doubtless we cannot deny, but God would have men to perish.

The phrase "signified will" presumably means here *will-as-revealed-to-man*, and the phrase "effectual will" means *will-as-carried-into-effect*. The argument in this passage, therefore, is that verses like "God is not willing that any should perish" show us God's "will-as-revealed-to-man" but the fact that many *do* perish shows us God's "will-as-carried-into-effect." We are thus presented with a supposed "signified will" which is the complete opposite of his supposed "effectual will." His "signified will" is that he "would not men should perish"; his "effectual will" is that he "would have men to perish." Now as far as we can see there would be only two possibilities if this view were correct. One would be that God is lying: he tells us (or "signifies") that he wants to save everyone but in fact has no such wish. The other would be that God really does at the same time actively want to save them and not to save them. In short, either God would be a deceiver or he would be a God of contradiction and chaos. Neither of these conclusions would be acceptable to any Christian, but there would seem to be no other possibilities if the commentary we quoted were correct.

But is there, in fact, the slightest basis in Scriptural language for distinguishing in this manner between a signified and an effectual will? We can discover nothing in Scripture which shows that God has an effectual or any other kind of will that men should stay unrepentant and so perish. If one is prepared to abandon any presupposition that God's will is always done, and accept the simple Bible teaching that a man perishes because he rejects God's plan for him and does not do the Father's will, then the whole elaborate apparatus of signified and effectual wills[15] becomes unnecessary.

At this point it might be helpful to mention a rather different distinction of two types or aspects of the will of God: this distinguishes his "permissive will" and his "active will." It is often said, for example, that it is only God's permissive will that people should suffer. Could this distinction be applied to the present problem? Could we say that it is only God's permissive will that men should perish, but his active will to save them? It is difficult to comment on this suggestion, for it is not clear exactly what it means. If we speak of God's permissive will, then he is presumably permitting something. What exactly is it? Is it that he permits men to continue on the road to hell when he could transfer them to the road to life? Is it rather that he permits them to choose which road they want and permits that choice to stand? Or is it that he permits the world to carry on when he could annihilate it? The first of these interpretations would again be contradicted by God's repeated statements that he does not want people to perish. One of the other two versions might be better, but one could wish for a clearer statement of what exactly is meant.

Let us, therefore, consider whether the Scriptures themselves give a hint of two aspects to God's will—and if so, what they are. We know that one clear aspect of God's will is his unwillingness that any should perish and his desire that all men everywhere should repent and come to a knowledge of the truth. Is there another aspect? A good clue may be found in the moving words of Psalm 32. David begins by saying: **Blessed is he whose transgression is forgiven, whose sin is covered . . . I said, I will confess my transgressions unto the Lord; and you forgave the iniquity of my sin . . .** The Lord replies in verse 8: **I will instruct you and teach you in the way which you shall go: I will counsel you with my eye upon you. Be you not as the horse, or as the mule, which have no understanding: whose trappings must be bit and bridle to hold them in, else they will not come near unto you.**

Why did God allow David to sin and then forgive him when he confessed it? Why not simply stop David from sinning in the first place? Was it God's permissive will to allow him to sin? Well, in a sense, yes. But the reason was that God does not want mule-like servants who have to be forced to obey him all the time. He wants those who will freely[16] accept his instruction and counsel. He wants relationships of mutual affection and love, not those based on some kind of force. God *could* bridle unbelievers, tinker with their wills and hearts, and turn them into automata (or mules), so that they have to do what he says. But if he did this it would still not achieve his purpose of developing free relationships such as he desired with David. We could, then, set out two aspects of his will as:

(a) He wants all men to be saved and to come to a knowledge of the truth.

(b) He doesn't want a set of bridled mules; he wants, therefore, to leave men free to accept or refuse his plan to give them the free gift of salvation.

This, however, might still be misleading. These two "aspects" are really part of the same will. God wants all men to repent and enter a free love-relationship with himself. But, if he "forced" men to repent, then their allegiance would not be freely given—they would no longer be truly *men* but mules. He would not have "saved" men, but made mules out of them. God created man in his own image and desires men to be conformed to the image of his son.[17] This divine wish will be unfulfilled in those who perish through unrepentance, but it would be no better fulfilled in them if they were transformed into mules. There is a sense in which transformation into mules is just another way of perishing. God prefers to endure with much long-suffering those fit only for destruction, for at least there is then the opportunity for some to respond to his call to receive mercy and enter a love-relationship with him.[18] Thus the fact that some perish is quite consistent with God's desire that all should be saved. They are complementary expressions of a single will to save *men*.

The reason, we discover, for God not saving all men is not that he doesn't really want to. It is not a great mystery; it is not part of his "inscrutable will." It is simply that if he were to force them, they would no longer be men. He would have failed to achieve anything of his purpose. There is no contradiction, or even paradox, between the perishing of men and God's desire to save them. They are both necessary expressions of one and the same will to form relationships of love, sharing, and understanding with *men*.

This is the only conclusion we can see that reconciles Scriptures. In any event, there are Scriptures that make it clear that both God's "will" and His "plan" can be defied by individuals. Yet because of various influences, these Scriptures sometimes get neglected. What are these influences?

One may be the emotional appeal: "Surely God would not be sovereign if everything were not directly determined by him." Yet we must be careful of such appeals, for this word *sovereign*, used so prolifically by some Christians, is not used once in the entire Authorized Version of the Bible. This is not to deny that the Lord is indeed King of kings, but it may help us to remember that the reign of God (and of the Lamb) neither makes humans into automata, nor makes the battle a fake in which God directs both sides. Other versions than the AV (e.g., the NEB) do sometimes use the word *sovereign*. In the Old Testament, however, there seems to be no Hebrew word that might be strictly translated "all-mighty" or "omni-potent"; the nearest are perhaps *Yahweh Sabaoth* (Lord of Hosts) and *El Gibbor* (Mighty God). Only in the New Testament is there a word *pantokratōr* that might be strictly translated as *all-powerful*. Even this word is used only a total of ten times, nine of which come in that book of battles, the Revelation.

But how may we understand this "all-powerfulness" of God? For a concept like the *love* of God the Bible gives us human analogies (for example, the human father-son relationship). For a concept like *almightiness* we can have nothing comparable in the human realm. Care is needed, therefore, in surmising its meaning, and we must certainly take into account the implications of other statements made in the Bible. Whatever our conclusions about the meaning of almightiness, it clearly cannot mean that God's will or plan is irresistible, since the Bible says that they are not.

Further light on the word *pantokratōr* or *almighty* may be shed by Hebrews 2:14. There the power (*kratos*) of death is said to have been in the possession of the devil. It was, it implies, a central part of the great war that Christ himself had to die on the cross to wrest power from Satan's grip. Whatever we understand, therefore, by "all-powerful," it cannot be undiscerningly taken to imply that there are no powers but God in his universe. God's rightful dominion[19] is obviously the whole universe, but parts of it are, in practice, usurped by other agents to whom he has given some independence of will and delegated authority.

It is with such background in mind that we must approach such a difficult and little used word like "all-powerful," and it would be unwise to build any key doctrines on this word alone. Yet an appeal to God's sovereignty seems to have exerted great influence on some people.

A second appeal seems to be influencing those who say that they would "have nothing left" were God not sovereign in the totalitarian way they imagine: they must believe that God is willing everything. Surely though, if God really is determining everything, and yet children are starving and being bombed with napalm, then all that we have learned from Jesus about God's love for the world is pious delusion. For example, it would then be the Father's will that many of these little ones should perish.[20] We must admit that we find it strange that anyone should be unhappy that God does *not* act in this way. We should expect anyone rather to be unhappy in believing that he did.

A third influence is the appeal that God's glory would be denied if it were possible for something to happen contrary to his will. Yet as we have already seen, Christ taught us that the glory of God does not consist in lording it over people, but in his own sacrifice.[21] If we really grasped Christ's revelation that God's glory is the cross, and ourselves learned to glory in it,[22] then the glory of God could never again be confused with the glory sought by the natural minds of the rulers of the Gentiles, or, indeed, by the "world ruler" himself.

A fourth influence may be the often made accusation that those who do not believe God's sovereignty to be of this absolute form are teaching that salvation is "of works." But if a man owes a million pounds and someone offers to pay it for him, who has saved him if he accepts? Well, in one sense he has "saved himself" (and in this sense Peter urges sinners to "save themselves" in Acts 2:40). But one would obviously be more likely to say he was saved by his benefactor. He has in no way worked for or earned his salvation simply by accepting a free offer. How, then, may one regard the claim that if we are free to reject or accept God's free offer of salvation then we earn it by accepting? It is surely not a "work" to accept a free offer (either of salvation or of a million pounds), and a person who accepts a free gift has not earned it. As C. H. Spurgeon wrote: ". . . faith excludes all boasting. The hand which receives charity does not say 'I am to be thanked for accepting the gift'; that would be absurd." When Paul talks of this he says: "Now to him that works, the reward is not reckoned as of grace, but as of debt."[23] The suggestion that it is "works" to accept an undeserved offer must surely be rejected.

A more subtle form of this argument is the appeal to the Christian's own practice. The question may be asked: "To whom do you give the credit for your conversion—yourself or God?" But again, to use our analogy, it would be a foolish man who would strut about patting himself on the back simply for accepting an offer to pay his debt. His attention would surely not be focused on his acceptance of the offer, but on the offer itself and on the love that leads the offeror to fulfill it if he accepts. We, of course, thank and praise God for his Love, for his offer, and for his fulfilment of that offer to us. The fact that others have refused similar offers does not make our own less precious. Moreover, all this talk of "credit" is not Christ-like. A shepherd girl offered the heart and love of Solomon would be too taken up with wonder and love to think of "credit." The heavenly bride will be gazing on Christ, not wondering if she ought to receive credit for accepting his amazing offer of love. A concern with credit would only be the concern of such as those "rulers of the gentiles" of which Christ spoke. It may remind us of that Pharisee who was careful to ascribe all the credit to God: "God, *I thank thee* that I am not as other men."

Christ's kingdom of love is one in which the greatest is the servant of all. It is founded through and through on love and not on flattery or desire for credit. Yet an appeal to such things has sometimes influenced the thinking of even the most spiritual men. How careful we must be to leave aside emotional questions and look to the Bible for teaching on God's sovereignty.

The last influence we might mention is another appeal to the Christian's own practice: "Don't you pray that people will be converted? This means that you recognize in your heart that they will be converted only if God wills it." This is subtle, but not convincing. We pray that the Holy Spirit will powerfully convict people of their own need, of God's love and judgment. We do not pray that he will override their own decision processes and force them to believe. Obviously Christians believe that other people's decisions may be *affected* by their own actions—otherwise why should they preach? No man lives in a vacuum; this is true both in the physical and in the spiritual-psychic realms.[24] As we pray we ask the Holy Spirit to utilize and interpret our prayers,[25] and thus we join the battle against the principalities and powers in the fight to influence men. God's conviction of a man's heart can powerfully stimulate him to a decision for repentance—but the Bible nowhere indicates that God negates a man's own choice.[26] On the contrary, God is prepared to say: **When I called, you did not answer; when I spoke, you did not hear; but you did that which was evil in my eyes, and chose that wherein I delighted not.**[27] God leaves man with free choice. He does not "force" repentance on a man who chooses a path that does not delight him.[28] If it has been our practice to pray that God will do the latter, then our practice should change, not our theology. Our theology should be the same on our knees as in a Bible study.

These, then, may be some of the appeals that can influence us, but we should be careful not to let them prevent us from accepting the teaching of Scripture that God's will can be and is defied by men. There is a resistance movement against God in his world. When we see this we can begin to discover how God wants us to take part in his battle strategy.

NOTES

1. Some would go as far as to state specifically that there is no real conflict between God and Satan. Thus Calvin: "Satan also, himself . . . is so completely the servant of the Most High as to act only by His command." (Commentary on Romans)

2. See *The Problem of Pain* and *Mere Christianity* by C. S. Lewis, and also section 14 of our own book *That's a Good Question*.

3. Revelation 19:6

4. Isaiah 46:10, LXX uses *boulē* and *bouleuomai*.

5. Philippians 2:13; the RV reads: "for it is God which works in you both to will and to work, for his good pleasure."

6. The "all things" of verse 11 cannot refer either to "all events" or to "all people." If it referred to all events then verse 10 would be saying that all events will be "headed up" (or "united" as RSV in

Christ—which means nothing. If it referred to all people then we must suppose from verse 10 that the lost and even Satan himself will be united in Christ—which is unbiblical. We must therefore conclude that all things in verse 11 refers to "all creation"—which is to be headed up in Christ.

7. 1 John 2:2; John could hardly have put this more plainly; see also John 1:29; 3:16; Titus 2:11

8. Ezekiel 18:23

9. 2 Peter 3:9

10. 1 Timothy 2:4

11. John 16:8

12. Luke 7:30

13. The Bible clearly says that God's will is not always done by men, and those who have denied this have faced considerable difficulties in "interpreting" the verses that show it. The first Christian leader to teach that God's will is always done and is never impeded by the will of any creature seems to have been Augustine. The difficulties he faced in interpreting some of the verses we have quoted are illustrated in our appendix.

14. Some, of course, do not even try to reconcile the two, but simply say that there are "two sides to the truth." "On the one hand," they say, "man is responsible, but on the other hand God is sovereign and determines everything that happens."

We must be careful here. First let us note in what form the contrast is usually stated. Alongside God's supposed determination of all events is set "man's responsibility," or perhaps "man's own view of his conversion." Now the Bible undoubtedly does imply man's responsibility, but it is not the prime difficulty here. The point is that God himself says that man *can* (permanently) reject his will and plan for him, and refuse to follow it. God does not say merely that man thinks he can do this, but that he can and does do so. Thus if we are to set up "two sides to the truth" then the real antithesis must be:

(a) Man can and does reject God's will and plan for him.

(b) God determines all events and his will is always done.

This is plain contradiction, and if we are to allow such contradictions in our thinking then almost any doctrine can be read into the Bible on the basis of isolated verses—being heralded as a new "side to the truth."

In a recent IVP book *Arguing With God*, Hugh Silvester well says: "Once the Christian admits that there is a real and complete contradiction in his thinking he can give up his claim to talk sense and may logically make any statement he chooses, however outrageous" (p. 47). Yet, in spite of the many useful features of his book, it is not clear that Mr. Silvester himself escapes the criticism. Later on he tells us that "a thorough examination of the Bible usually finishes up with two apparently irreconcilable statements:

1. Man is responsible for his actions.

2. God orders or ordains all things" (p. 71).

Even if this is not contradiction (which is debatable), statement 2 is certainly in plain contradiction to God's own assertion in the Scriptures that man can and does defy his will and plan. For Mr. Silvester to go on to tell us that "on a practical level there is no difficulty" leaves as much contradiction as ever.

The choice, in fact, is simple. We must either give up any form of reason and accept plain contradictions as "sides to truth," or else we must abandon statement 2 (or b) as being (as it stands at least) inconsistent with Scripture.

15. This "apparatus" not only includes the supposition of two diametrically opposite "wills" of God. It must also suppose an "effectual calling" and a non-effectual one, an "unconditional election" and one which we need to "make sure" (2 Peter 1:10), and so on.

16. It is, of course, nonsense to say that God could create men who were free, but force them to do his will. It is no use having recourse to Jesus saying: "All things are possible to God," for he said this in the context of rich men entering the kingdom of heaven. God can perform miracles and do what is impossible to man; but the words "force a man to freely do God's will" do not state an impossibility. They do not, in fact, state anything at all, for they are a meaningless word series, and the addition of "God can" in front of them does not remove their meaninglessness. Hugh Silvester well says: "God is all powerful but that does not mean that He can do anything. He cannot make $2 + 2 = 5$ and He cannot make it raining and not raining in the same moment at the same place . . . When we say God is all-powerful we mean He can do all things that can be done, which doubtless includes many things that are impossible to man. But we do not mean that He can give a hydrogen atom and a helium atom the same atomic structure. Even God could not create free men without at the same time creating men who were able to rebel." (*Arguing With God* p. 60, 61)

See also section 18 which contains further comment on this.

17. Romans 8:29

18. Compare Romans 9:22

19. The word *kratos* in the New Testament seems to imply "dominion" in a majority of references, e.g., 1 Peter 4:11; 5:11; Jude 25; Revelation 1:6. Dominion is ascribed to Christ and God, whose right it is to rule.

20. Matthew 18:14

21. See above pp. 24, 25, and Matthew 20:25-28; Mark 10:42-45; Luke 22:24-27; John 13:12.

22. Galatians 6:14

23. Romans 4:4; see also section 20 which shows the importance of understanding the rabbinical ideas which Paul is here attacking.

24. See also Stafford Wright in *What Is Man?*

25. Romans 8:26

26. Even in revivals one hears of many who are convicted and smitten by God's Spirit, but later lapse back in unbelief.

27. Isaiah 65:12

28. The early church leaders and teachers coined the term "free-will" to represent the Bible's teaching that God allows man a choice of whether or not to obey him. In the appendix we have shown the apparently unanimous teaching among early church leaders for the first 300 years that man had been given this "free-will." It is important to note that the arguments which we have presented in this section are

by no means novel or new, but coincide with some of the earliest Christian arguments against heretics of those days. Irenaeus (c. 130-200 A.D.), for example, cited Matthew 23:37 just as we have done, to demonstrate to his contemporaries that God has given man "power of choice."

PART TWO

The History of the Conflict

How War Was Declared—Genesis

We have seen that God's will and plan are not always obeyed in this world; a resistance movement is working against them. How did this resistance movement begin, and in what way was God's plan first violated?

The Bible is God's message to humanity, and it begins at the creation of the world and of its human inhabitants. It would seem that even before this creation Satan had arisen as a spiritual opponent[1] to God, but little is said as to how or why Satan fell. We may, perhaps, surmise that God created spiritual beings to set up love-relationships with himself. Love, by its very nature, seems to require that ability to choose that is part of being a "person." Satan was free to love or to reject God. In choosing the latter path he created his own evil where none had existed before.[2] Capacity to love is also capacity to hate and rebel against the Lord and his anointed. The Bible tells us little about Satan and his fall, but he appears at the outset of human history as the corrupter of mankind. God's message to humanity tells us only such facts about Satan as are relevant to our own history, and with this we must be content. Our question, therefore, must concern the entry of evil into our world rather than into the universe as a whole, and of this God has told us.

However figuratively anyone may take some features of Genesis 2, it is clear that the Lord intended us to understand that a choice was facing the first man. In the idyllic situation in which man was placed, he could eat of any fruit including that of the **tree of life,** but he must not eat of the tree of the **knowledge of good and evil.** Someone would presumably be attracted by the tree of the knowledge of good and evil because of a lust for power through knowledge. He would have a selfish desire to set himself up as a god[3] and so be independent of God. This would lead to a life centered on self and not on God, who is Love. In the day in which Adam chose such a life he (in reality) chose death.[4] It is clear that he could not choose the way of death and also choose to eat of the tree of life. In choosing the one he lost the opportunity to eat of the other. God's command, which was surely also his purpose, was that Adam should eat of the tree of life. Adam disobeyed and rejected God's plan for him. Nevertheless, God's ultimate plan will finally be realized, for we find the **tree of life** and other features of Genesis reappearing in Revelation 22. In Revelation those whose robes have been washed have a part in it.[5] It is for the healing of all, when there shall be no curse any more.[6] We see that finally all will be restored to the harmony with himself which God intended, and his servants will live in adoration of the self-sacrificing "little lamb" and the Father who are their light. Had Adam grasped the nature of this God of the Lamb, he could never have accepted the devil's caricature of God, implicit in the suggestion that a power lust could make anyone resemble him.[7] Ironically, God did intend man to be in his true image, and in becoming sons of God we partake of him and become like him.

Nothing in the Bible hints that Adam's wrong choice might have been the will of God. It is true that God could have prevented Adam's sin by removing his freedom to choose. The trouble with this would have been that a robot or a computer cannot show love; only a free being with an independent will can love. If love was to be a meaningful thing, Adam had to be allowed some form of free choice.[8] God allowed Adam the freedom to choose wrongly, but nothing indicates that he wanted him to do so. If the serpent Satan had been doing God's will, then we might have expected him to receive congratulations and eternal life.[9] Instead his rebellious activities brought a curse and a declaration of war,[10] for God's will was not that Adam should fall. Of course, when Adam did sin, God was not taken by surprise. The divine redemption through the blood of the Lamb was **foreknown indeed before the foundation of the world,**[11] and even in Genesis 3 the declaration of war is followed by a reference to the crushing of the serpent's head. Satan would bruise the heel of the Messiah, but would himself be crushed by the conflict.

BETWEEN ADAM AND ABRAHAM

In the remainder of the period before Abraham, God dealt with righteous and perfect men in their generations like Enoch and Noah,[12] yet there seems to be no sign of any coordinated plan of campaign. We may, however, find some hints of God's intentions. As early as Genesis 4 the acceptable sacrifice of Abel was a lamb—God's battle emblem. In many primitive societies one may find vestiges of this symbol of God's warfare, which is a warfare waged through self-sacrifice. In some places men have misunderstood and perverted its meaning as they have supposed it to be for the placation of the blood-lust of a vindictive tyrant or tyrants. Yet perhaps others between Abel and Abraham grasped a revelation from God of its significance: **God will provide himself the lamb for a burnt offering.**[13] Abraham rejoiced to see the day of the Lamb of God[14]—perhaps it was as he himself raised the knife over his son on Mount Moriah. Years later, in this same area of Mount

Moriah,[15] at a place called Calvary, Abraham's designation "In the Mount of the Lord it shall be provided" became true in a much deeper sense.

NOTES

1. "Satan" means opponent. It can also mean "accuser," for spiritual warfare is conducted with words and ideas. Satan accuses God to man (Genesis 3:5) and man to God (Job 1:11).

2. See also section 14 of our book *That's a Good Question*.

3. Genesis 3:5

4. Genesis 2:17

5. Revelation 22:14

6. Revelation 22:2, 3; see also section 14.

7. Genesis 3:4, 5

8. See also C. S. Lewis *The Problem of Pain,* and our book (above).

9. 1 John 2:17

10. Genesis 3:14, 15

11. 1 Peter 1:20

12. Genesis 5:24; 6:9

13. Genesis 22:8

14. John 8:56

15. There seems no evidence to suggest that the exact position of Abraham's altar was Calvary, but it does seem that the general area coincided. According to the Jewish tradition embodied in 2 Chronicles 3:1, the Temple itself was built on Mt. Moriah. See also the *New Bible Dictionary*.

8

Israel and God's Plan—Abraham

THE BACKGROUND OF PAUL'S ANALYSIS

Most of us realize that Abraham, and with him his descendants, occupy some special place in God's battle strategy in history. But what exactly is it? What was God's appointed role for this special nation with which most of the Old and much of the New Testament is concerned? This question was, of course, a source of much controversy between the early church and the non-Christian Jews. Did the Christian gospel imply that God had broken unconditional promises to the Jews? Many rabbis taught that all Jews (except infamous heretics and other extreme sinners) were to be saved because of the merits of Abraham, the patriarchs, and themselves.[1] The Christian gospel not only said that many Jews would be condemned, but also accepted that some Gentiles would be saved. The common Jewish attitude to such a suggestion is demonstrated by the Jewish audience who listened quietly to the Rabbi Paul's message about Jesus—until he said that God sent him to the Gentiles. At that, a riot arose![2] Even Jewish Christians found it difficult to understand that God was no respecter of persons, but that those in every nation who feared God and did righteously were accepted by him.[3] Paul, therefore, in his systematic treatise to Christians in Rome, finds it necessary to establish right from the start that there are two groups of people:

(a) those who have repented, have faith, and are right with God

(b) those who have not repented and are under his wrath

Both the Old Testament and common experience show that always there have been Gentiles *and* Jews in each group.[4] The Jews do have the special privilege of having the oracles of God—but this means that their condemnation is the greater if they reject him.[5] It is through faith that a man is declared to be right before God, and though the Jews may have had more opportunity, this fact makes the more severe the condemnation of those who reject God's way. Paul first establishes, therefore, the basis upon which an individual may be saved.[6] He then goes on to talk of the special way in which this is shown to Christians.[7] In chapter 8 he describes the destiny of the church. Then in chapter 9 he must return to the big problem at which he has already hinted in Romans 3:1. It is this: If a man's individual salvation is independent of whether he is a Jew or a Gentile, what then is the significance of Israel being the "chosen" nation? In answering this important question the apostle outlines a history of Israel, during which he explains three things about God's choice of them (i.e., about their election). He shows:

(a) *The basis of God's choice.* This was not because of "works" since it predated anything Israel did.

(b) *Its effect on individuals.* God's choice of Israel affected in some way the various individuals (both Jew and Gentile) concerned in the nation's history.

(c) *Its allegorical significance.* God's actions had various symbolical and typological meanings, relevant to the question of who should be saved. (The apostle had already mentioned these in Galatians 4.)

Romans 9 may therefore serve as an admirable framework for our present study of Israel's place in history. It will, however, be necessary at various points to fill in a lot of background information. This information would have been familiar at first hand to Paul's readers in the first-century church at Rome. They had immediate contact with Hebrew thought, whereas we do not.

ISRAEL
STILL CHOSEN

Paul begins Romans 9 by reiterating his own personal attachment to his people. They are Israelites, to them *belong* the adoption, the glory, the covenants, the giving of the law, the service,[8] and the promises. Theirs are the patriarchs and from them came the Messiah as far as earthly descent was concerned. As a nation they received sonship,[9] the glory,[10] the covenants,[11] the Law,[12] and the ceremonies of service.[13] As a nation they paved the way for the Messiah Savior of the world. But if this is so, how is it that so many of the individuals in that nation have rejected their Messiah? This is what the apostle has to explain, and so he introduces the theme for the whole chapter: "The word of God has not come to nothing, his promises have not been broken, for they are not all 'perseverers with God' [Israel] who are descended from the 'Perseverer with God' [Israel]."[14]

In other words, not all Israelites live up to their name and have a personal relationship with God as Jacob did. To explain this, Paul goes back to the start of Israel's history, to the patriarch Abraham. We may best begin our own study in the same way, and so return now to the story of Abraham.

GOD SPEAKS TO ABRAHAM

The story opens with the first recorded words of God to Abraham: **Get you out of your country, and from your kindred, and from your father's house, unto the land that I will show you; and I will make of you a great nation, and I will bless you and make your name great; and be you a blessing; and I will bless them that bless you, and him that curses you I will curse; and in you shall all the families of the earth be blessed.**[15]

What is God's purpose here? What he is certainly *not* doing is choosing Abraham to receive personal redemption and leaving the rest to perish. For one thing it would seem that Abraham already knew God, for the Lord simply begins to speak to him without any introduction. More important, there were at that time other righteous men such as Lot, who were upset by the wickedness of people around them.[16] Some, like that "King of Righteousness" Melchizedek seem even greater than Abraham[17] and were holy enough to be described as **like unto** the one who was truly perfect.[18] The Lord is, in fact, more concerned right from the beginning with the *nation* than with Abraham as such. Abraham is chosen as the head of a **great nation.** Moreover, the purpose of the choice is not simply to give Israel a good time. The Lord makes his purpose clear: **. . . be you a blessing . . . in you shall all the families of the earth be blessed.** God's design is not merely that Israel should be blessed, but that they should be a blessing to others. It is a part of God's strategy in the conflict, which is a battle to bless mankind.

In his first words to Abraham, God is anticipating the time when he will justify the Gentiles through faith, for from Israel came Jesus the Messiah in whom all nations were to receive blessing.[19] How exactly would this blessing be achieved? God had already spoken of this in the garden of Eden, as he looked forward to a Messiah whose heel would be bruised. It would be in the cross of Christ, the focal point of history and the battle. Centuries later, Paul saw that Christ became a curse for us: **that upon the Gentiles might come the blessing of Abraham, in Christ Jesus, that we might receive the promise of the spirit through faith.**[20]

It is vital to our whole understanding of the special place of Israel in God's plan, that we should grasp this point right from the start. The choice of Abraham and Israel was not merely for their own benefit; it was not a guarantee that all Jews would be saved; it was so that God could *through them* do something for the world. Only if we grasp this will we understand Paul's explanation of why, in spite of their "chosenness," many Israelites had been free to reject Jesus and salvation.

ABRAHAM'S RESPONSE

We have seen how God began to deal with Abraham. How did Abraham react? In Genesis 12 Abraham obeyed God's command and **in faith** went out to the land of his inheritance.[21] In Genesis 13, the Lord made the great promise about the numbers of Abraham's descendants. At the beginning of Genesis 15, the promise was repeated. When Abraham pointed out that he still did not have a son, the Lord assured him that he would have one. In verse 6 of this chapter Abraham believed the promise of God and it was counted to him for right standing before the Lord.[22] Then, in Genesis 16 and 17, Abraham listened to the voice of his wife rather than to God. He still had no children, and

God's promise had not come true, so he himself tried to make it come true. It was at that time fairly common practice to take the wife's maid as a concubine and so Abraham did this. This union with Hagar resulted in the birth of Ishmael. It was not, however, a part of God's plan, for he intended Abraham to have a legitimate son as heir. Only later, in Genesis 21, did Abraham's true wife give birth to Isaac. This took place in spite of her great age and apparent loss of capacity to bear children. The birth of Isaac was a divinely wrought miracle. He was the son who fulfilled God's promise to Abraham.

THE DISTINCTION BETWEEN ISHMAEL AND ISAAC

What then, is the distinction between Ishmael and Isaac? We discover that this is in keeping with what we have found about the first call of Abraham: the great and only distinction is that from Isaac would spring the nation whose Messiah would bring worldwide blessing. We remember that although only Abraham was *chosen*, the individuals Lot and Melchizedek were also right with God. Similarly, only Isaac was *chosen*, but there is every reason to believe that, as an individual as distinct from as an heir, Ishmael may also have been acceptable to God. Ishmael was the seed[23] of Abraham, and shared in the duties of a son, such as burial rites.[24] As far as his personal life was concerned, the Scripture clearly tells us that **God was with the lad.**[25] Not only was God present in his life, but his destiny was assured; the angel of the covenant who stayed Abraham's hand and made promises about Abraham's descendants also appeared to Hagar and made similar promises about Ishmael.[26] Hagar even addressed the angel in similar terms to Abraham.[27] The great difference was, of course, that it was only through Isaac that the Messiah would come to bring worldwide blessing. God made this point explicit to Abraham in the words: ". . . **in Isaac shall your seed be called. And also of the son of the bondwoman will I make a** nation because he is your seed."[28] Both Ishmael and Isaac were Abraham's seed, but "in Isaac shall a seed to you be named" (this is the literal meaning of the LXX and Romans 9:7). Paul makes it clear in Galatians 3:14-16 that the "seed named to Abraham" was Jesus Christ, and the blessing which came through Abraham to the nations was in Christ.[29] This is the great difference between Ishmael and Isaac: from Isaac sprang the nation into which Jesus was born. This also explains the climax of Paul's list in Romans 9:4, 5 of the distinctive characteristics of Israel: ". . . of their race, according to the flesh, is the Christ. God who is over all be blessed for ever. Amen" (RSV).

We find, therefore, that God's choice of Isaac rather than Ishmael related to his place in God's battle strategy. There was something that God wanted to do through Israel for the world. Their chosenness did not automatically save them and damn all others.

THE ALLEGORY
OF ISHMAEL
AND ISAAC

Before we return to look explicitly at Romans 9 an important allegorical lesson is to be learned from the story of Isaac and Ishmael. Paul refers to this in Galatians 4:21-31. God had made a great promise to Abraham, which had no apparent likelihood of being fulfilled. Abraham went ahead without God's guidance and tried to fulfill the promise by a device of his own, the result of which was Ishmael. Ishmael, therefore, represented Abraham's "works" in an effort to produce by his own initiative what God had promised. In this sense Ishmael was a "child of the flesh" (Galatians 4:23, 29). When it came to Isaac, Abraham could only consider the womb of Sarah which was then as good as dead, and yet have faith that God would work a miracle.[30] Isaac, therefore, was a "child of the promise," a result sheerly of God's power and Abraham's faith.[31] God has also made a great promise to us, a promise of eternal life. If we go ahead in our own strength and try to earn it or make it come true, then this too would be "works" of a kind comparable with those of Abraham. If we did this, we might (like the Galatians to whom Paul wrote) become enslaved to a series of petty regulations, producing in us a slavish character rather than a holy one. Paul compares this to the son of a slave, the son that Abraham produced in his own strength and "works." If, on the other hand, we have the faith that God will work the miracle of rebirth and continue to bring eternal life to us, we become children of the promise. Paul sees both Abraham's situation and our own as involving a choice between two different pathways to follow.[32] These are:

(a) Promise—works—slavery as a child of the flesh
(b) Promise—faith—God's power brings life as a child of the promise.

This is the allegorical meaning of the story, and it teaches that faith and not works is the method of God. The parallel was not, of course, meant to be taken too far. For one thing the promise concerning Isaac was made to Abraham, whereas the promise concerning us is made to ourselves. Second, the promise to Abraham implied nothing about anyone's individual eternal destination; the promise to us certainly does have such implications. As with his other analogies[33] this allegory of Paul's is helpful only if not pressed to extreme detail. Within the context intended, Paul uses it in a masterly way.

PAUL RELATES THIS TO ISRAEL

With these three trains of thought:
(a) The basis of God's choice of Israel
(b) Its effects on individuals
(c) Its allegorical significance
we are now in a position to return to the text of Romans 9.

We remember how Paul stated that they are not all perseverers with God even though they are descended from the Perseverer with God.[34] He then went back to the start of Israel's history: **Neither, because they are Abraham's seed are they all children; but, In Isaac shall your seed be called.** That is, it is not the children of the flesh that are children of God; but the children of the promise are reckoned for a seed. **For this is a word of promise, According to this season I will come, and Sarah shall have a son.**

He is not at all concerned here, of course, with the individual destinies of Isaac or Ishmael, but he draws out the allegorical meaning very strongly. The line chosen to be the path to the Messiah (v. 7) was that of Isaac, the child of the promise (v. 8). Paul makes it quite clear what promise he is talking about here: it is the promise that Sarah should have a son (v. 9). To us, today, his meaning may seem obscure or difficult, but as a thrust at some of his expert pharisaical Jewish opponents it is masterful. Can they not see that God, even in his original choice of their nation, was implicitly repudiating the "salvation by works" principle which they teach?

This is really ironical. God chose Isaac, and the Pharisees laid claim to a share in this chosenness because they were his descendants. Yet these same Pharisees accepted a principle of works, which was completely contrary to the whole basis of God's choice of Isaac. The birth and choice of Isaac were a result of faith in a promise and in God's power, not of works. The Pharisees thought that God's choice set them for heaven, and Gentiles, with few exceptions, for hell. If they had understood the true reason for God's strategy in choosing Isaac, they might also have understood the allegory it contained, which taught that God's principle was faith.[35]

NOTES
1. See also section 19.
2. Acts 22:22
3. Acts 10:34, 35
4. See also section 19.
5. Romans 3
6. Romans 3:21–4:22
7. Romans 4:22–ch. 8
8. The Greek here means "priestly service" or "Temple worship"
NEB).

9. Exodus 4:22
10. Exodus 40:34; 1 Kings 8:11
11. Exodus 19:5, 6; 2 Samuel 7
12. Deuteronomy 4:8
13. Exodus 40
14. Romans 9:6; Genesis 32:28. It would seem that Paul is making a play on the meaning of "Israel," just as he did on the meaning of "Jew" (praise) in Romans 2:29. There is some doubt over the exact meaning of the word *Israel*, though the AV "prince with God" seems today to have little support. The NEB gives "God strives," the RV and RSV give "God strives" or "he who strives with God." The AV gives "contended with God," and the JB says: "The probable meaning of 'Israel' is 'May God show his strength,' but it is here explained as 'He has been strong against God.'" F. F. Bruce, in the *New Bible Dictionary*, writes: "(*yisrā ēl*, 'God strives') The new name given to Jacob after his night of wrestling at Penuel: 'Your name,' said his supernatural antagonist, 'shall no more be called Jacob, but Israel, for you have striven (*sārîtā*, from *sārâ*, strive) with God and with men and have prevailed' . . . cf. Ho xii. 3f., 'in his manhood he strove (*sārâ*) with God. He strove (*wayyāsar*, from the same verb) with the angel and prevailed.' (RSV)" Derek Kidner, in his Genesis commentary, writes: "*Israel*, is a verbal name . . . In itself it would convey the meaning 'May God strive (for him),' but like other names in Genesis it takes on a new coloring from its occasion, and commemorates Jacob's side of the struggle and his character thus revealed. The key verb, 'strive' (possibly 'persevere'), is found only here and in Hosea 12:4, 5, and its meaning is not certain; but there is no support for deriving it from the noun 'a prince' as in AV (where the whole phrase *as a prince hast thou power* represents this single word)!" An interesting early comment on the meaning of the word occurs in the *Dialogue* of Justin Martyr (c. 114-175 A.D.). He says that *Isra* is a man overcoming and *El* is power, thus *Israel* is a man who overcomes power—which Justin says was truly fulfilled in Christ. Evidently Paul's tendency to an occasional word-play of this type was not lost on the early church.

Whatever the literal meaning of "Israel," it seems clear that to the Hebrews it implied something of Jacob's own perseverance. He had received the name because he himself had striven with and prevailed over God and man—and this is how Hosea looks back at the incident. Yet it was a perseverance that turned into dependence and submission. Kidner writes: "It was defeat and victory in one. Hosea again illuminates it: 'He strove with the angel and prevailed'—this is the language of strength; 'he wept and sought his favor'—the language of weakness. After the maiming, combativeness had turned to a dogged dependence, and Jacob emerged broken, named and blessed . . . The new name would attest his new standing: it was both a mark of grace, wiping out an old reproach (27:36), and an accolade to live up to."

It was just such a personal encounter and experience that Israelites in Paul's day lacked. Though they were "of Israel" (i.e., his descendants), they were not "Israel" (i.e., those who had persevered with God in personal encounter).

(See Kidner's commentary and Edersheim's *Bible History*, vol. i p. 135-137 for further light on the incident in Genesis 32:28).

15. Genesis 12:1-3

16. 2 Peter 2:7

17. Hebrews 7:7

18. Hebrews 7:4

19. Galatians 3:8

20. Galatians 3:14

21. Hebrews 11:8; note that this faith precedes the time in chapter 15—when his belief was "counted to him for right standing."

22. For the interpretation of "righteousness" as "right-standing" see section 16.

23. Genesis 21:12, 13

24. Genesis 25:9

25. Genesis 21:20; and God also heard the voice of the lad as well —see verse 17.

26. Genesis 22:17; 16:10; also 21:18

27. Genesis 16:13; 22:14, lxx "A God of Seeing"

28. Genesis 21:12, 13. We have noted the literal meaning of verse 12 in the text. The av and rv render the Hebrew *zera* (lxx *sperma*) by "seed," both in verse 12 and in verse 13. This is strictly accurate and, although the word is seldom used today, it helps us to understand Paul's interpretation of it. This is that although the lines of Isaac and Ishmael are both true descendants of Abraham, it is only in the Isaacian line that a particular descendent will be "called" (see Romans 9:7; Galatians 3:14-16 and main text). The more modern translations do not seem to make this at all clear. The rsv uses two different words ("descendants" and "offspring") for the same Hebrew word in the two verses, and incidentally conceals the fact (used by Paul) that the word is singular in form. The jb (. . . for it is through Isaac that your name will be carried on) does not really make the meaning clear, and the neb (. . . because you shall have descendants through Isaac) quite obscures it.

29. Galatians 3:14

30. Romans 4:19, 20

31. Galatians 4:23

32. Philippi commented: "Inasmuch as he was born physically, which is here emphasized, 'according to flesh,' he is merely a type of those who are begotten spiritually through the 'promise,' i.e., of the genuine children of God."

33. e.g., in Romans 7:1-14

34. Romans 9:6; see note 14 above.

35. See also section 19.

Israel and God's Plan—
Jacob and Esau

In the next part of Romans 9 the apostle passes on to the next point in the history of Israel: . . . **not only so; but Rebecca also having conceived by one, even by our father Isaac—for[1] being not yet born, neither having done anything good or bad, that the purpose of God according to election might stand, not of works but of him that calls, it was said unto her, The elder shall serve the younger, even as it is written, Jacob I loved, but Esau I hated.[2]**

People often fail to understand that in this whole section the apostle is talking about nations and not about individuals.[3] Turning up the passage quoted by Paul we read: **the Lord said unto her: "Two nations are in your womb . . . And the elder shall serve the younger.[4]** Esau the *individual* never did serve Jacob; in fact it was, if anything, the other way around. Jacob bowed himself down to the ground before Esau,[5] addressing him as "my Lord"[6] and calling himself Esau's servant;[7] Jacob begged Esau to accept his gifts[8] for Esau's face seemed like the face of God to him.[9] Esau the individual certainly did not serve Jacob, it was the *nation* Esau (or Edom) which served the nation Jacob (or Israel). Paul's point is that God's choice of Israel was made when both nations were still in the womb, and neither had done good or evil.[10] The choice of the nation was not a reward for merit, but part of a God-determined strategy.

GOD LOVED JACOB BUT HATED ESAU

Paul's next quotation: **Jacob have I loved but Esau have I hated** comes, as H. C. Moule pointed out, "from the prophet's message a millennium later." F. F. Bruce comments that the quotation is: "from Malachi 1:2f, where again the context indicates it is the nations of Israel and Edom, rather than their individual ancestors Jacob and Esau, that are in view." The Lord has loved the nation of Israel but hated the nation of Edom.

Since God has used these words *love* and *hate* in this way, we must ask whether he anywhere indicates what he means by them. A clue comes first within the history of Jacob itself: **And he went in also unto Rachel, and he loved also Rachel more than Leah, and served with him yet seven other years. And the Lord saw that Leah was hated . . .**[11] The text itself seems to indicate that hated here means "loved less than." Barnes says: "It was common among the Hebrews to use the terms love and hatred in this comparative sense, where the former implied strong positive attachment and the latter, not positive hatred, but merely a less love, or the withholding of expressions of affection";[12] Jesus himself speaks to them using their own language conventions, when he says: **If any man comes unto me, and hates not his own father and mother, and wife and children, yea and his own life also, he cannot be my disciple.**[13] The parallel text in Matthew 10:37 shows us that again the word *hate* is not literal, but implies "love less than."[14]

We may see, therefore, that when the Bible uses the word *hate* as a contrast to *love,* it intends us to understand it to mean "love less than." This is its meaning in all other references, and we must suppose it to be so in Malachi 1:2. The verse does not mean that in a literal hatred of Esau and his descendants God has condemned every one of them to hell. It has reference simply to the higher position of the Hebrew race in the strategy of God. Sanday and Headlam wrote: "The absolute election of Jacob—the 'loving' of Jacob and the 'hating' of Esau—has reference simply to the election of one to higher privileges as head of the chosen race, than the other. It has nothing to do with the eternal salvation. In the original to which St. Paul is referring, Esau is simply a synonym for Edom."[15]

The context of Malachi 1:2 is also important for our understanding of the meaning of Paul's quotation. God said that he had shown special favor to Israel (Malachi 1:2) and when they asked in what way this was so (Malachi 1:2), the prophet pointed out how austerely the Lord dealt with the nation of Edom compared with Israel (Malachi 1:2, 3). Yet the Israelites, the prophet complained, were behaving very sinfully even in spite of this special privilege (Malachi 1:6-14).

Paul may well have had this context in mind when he put the quotation into Romans 9:13. It is, he notes, in the passage where the chosenness of Israel is stated in the strongest terms, that the prophet also berates Israel for their evil deeds. This makes it obvious that God's choice of Israel could not be a result of her merits or works. We must remember[16] that Paul has in mind at this point those of his opponents who believed that "works of the law" were both the reason for God's choice of Israel, and the way to holiness. His introduction of the quotation from Malachi 1:2 is therefore of particular relevance here, and he uses it as he develops his theme that it is God's strategy and not Israel's works which has caused God to choose them.

In summary, then, God's "love of Jacob but hatred of Esau" means this: God has chosen to give to the nation of Israel a special place and privileged position. This is not because of their "works," for the passage that affirms his choice also proclaims their sinfulness. Rather, his choice is a result purely of his own strategy.

NOTES

1. The italicized words in the RV *"the children"* are noticeably omitted by Paul from the Greek text of Romans 9:10; in interpolating them, the translators obscure his argument.

2. Romans 9:11-13

3. The point has, however, been emphatically reiterated by many famous commentaries of undisputed scholarship and authority, such as Barnes, Bruce, Brunner, Doddridge, Dummelow, Ellison, Garvie, Gifford, Gore, Griffith-Thomas, Ironside, and Sanday and Headlam; see especially Sanday and Headlam, and Gore.

4. Genesis 25:23

5. Genesis 33:3

6. Genesis 33:8, 13

7. Genesis 33:5

8. Genesis 33:11

9. Genesis 33:10

10. Romans 9:11 quoting Genesis 25:23

11. Genesis 29:30, 31. The two Hebrew words for love and hate (*aheb* and *sane*) are the same as in Malachi 1:2 and Proverbs 13:24. The Septuagint also used the same Greek words (*agapaō* and *meseō*) in all three of these passages. The New Testament uses the same two Greek words (*agapaō* and *meseō*) in all the verses which contain this form of comparison, (i.e., Matthew 6:24; Luke 14:26; 16:13; and Romans 9:13). There can be little doubt, therefore, that this form of comparison would have been well known to the Jews as an idiom—both in the Hebrew and in the Greek.

12. See also Griffith-Thomas and others. In *Everyday Life in the Holy Land* James Neil remarked on a similar Hebrew figure of speech: "In ever so many places the negative 'not' followed by 'but' does not deny at all; and 'not this but that' stands for 'rather that than this.' Thus God says to Samuel, of the children of Israel, 'They rejected not thee, but they rejected Me,' which must mean, 'They rejected Me rather than thee.' For they *did* very definitely reject Samuel, on the ground that he was old and his sons were not walking in his ways. When Joseph magnanimously said, to comfort his brothers, 'It was not you that sent me here, but God'; his words could only mean, 'It was rather God than you,' etc."

13. Luke 14:26

14. See also Proverbs 13:24; Matthew 6:24 for other uses of love/hate in such comparisons.

15. Sanday and Headlam were, in this instance, quoting Gore in *Studia Biblica* iii p. 44.

16. See section 19.

Israel and God's Plan—Moses

It may be difficult for us in the twentieth century to imagine the type of arguments and opponents Paul had continually to deal with. For this reason we include in section 19 a more detailed outline of early rabbinical and pharisaical teachings. Many of the Pharisees and rabbis were completely bound up in the idea of "works."[1] They thought that Israel was the chosen nation because they had taken on themselves works of the Law, and that they would become holy and achieve salvation through their works. They must have found totally abhorrent the teaching of the ex-Pharisee Paul, that Israel was chosen only because of God's strategy and that individuals in *any* nation could be saved simply by faith. The thought of God giving unmerited privilege as he thought best would provoke in them the immediate reaction: "Is there then unrighteousness with God?" Paul answers "No!" He then goes on in Romans 9:15, 16 to point out that even Moses received God's special favor because God knew best how to allocate it, and not because Moses himself was exceptionally righteous.

The incident to which Paul refers in Romans 9:15, 16 is in Exodus 33:19, and the whole background of it is important.

In Exodus 32:7-10 the Lord tells Moses that the rebellious Israelites have corrupted themselves and that he will destroy them and make of Moses a great nation. We may recall two incidents in the life of Abraham that show similarities to this suggestion made to Moses.

First, we remember that the Lord once commanded Abraham to destroy the chosen line of Isaac. The natural temptation would have been to refuse, and God's command was a test of Abraham rather than any indication of his real intention. Similarly, God's suggestion to Moses that he himself should become head of a new nation may well have seemed tempting to Moses. Perhaps this suggestion, like the command to Abraham, may be regarded as a test of Moses rather than as an indication of God's real intention.

The other incident occurred earlier in the life of Abraham. When God was intending to destroy Sodom he told his servant Abraham about it.[2] In a moving passage, Abraham is shown pleading with the Lord, who finally agreed that for the sake of ten righteous men he would spare the city. Now the Lord knew perfectly well that Lot was the only righteous man in the city, and that Sodom would in any case be destroyed. The point was that in this episode Abraham showed that he was a man after God's own heart, for God also "takes pleasure not in the death of a wicked man, but in the turning back of a wicked man who changes his ways to win life."[3] Abraham did not understand the battle strategy as the Lord did,[4] but his motives were right and God loved him for it.

Moses showed a similar attitude, and showed that he too had a heart like God's own, when he pleaded with God to spare Israel. Then the Lord remembered his promises concerning the descendants of Abraham, Isaac, and Jacob, and so preserved the nation.[5] But notice that it was not because they were righteous or had done good works that he spared them—their sin would still be visited on them,[6] and through unbelief that generation failed even to reach the promised land.[7] They are spared neither because of righteousness, nor because of "merit," but because of God's whole plan which started with Abraham.[8] It was, moreover, no more use for Moses to pray that God would blot him out of the book of life if Israel were condemned, than it was for Paul to wish to be accursed to save them.[9] It is those who sin who are blotted out—and that, notwithstanding that the Lord, as well as Moses, "has no delight in the death of the wicked."[10]

The Lord said that the Israelites were a stubborn people, and he could not go in the midst of them. His purity would consume them.[11] In reply Moses reminded God of his past words of affection and his instructions to lead up this nation.[12] Would the Lord therefore reveal himself so that Moses might receive grace and consider that the (admittedly sinful) Israelites were really chosen?[13] The Lord replied that he would go with Moses and give rest to him.[14] Moses replied that only if the Lord went with them (all) would it be known that both he *and the people*[15] had found grace in his sight. The Lord then agreed to answer Moses' prayer and show him his glory.[16] But he adds: **and I will be gracious to whom I will be gracious, and will show mercy on whom I will show mercy.**

What is the significance of all this? It is impossible to dogmatize, for the replies the Lord gave seem purposely enigmatic throughout this passage. Nevertheless an explanation may be suggested if we notice that the Lord continually replied in the singular (thee) to Moses alone, whereas Moses always tried to involve the whole nation in the blessing.[17] Moses wanted the Lord to go up in the midst of the nation[18] but the Lord could not, lest he consume them. Yet, in a way, the Lord did go up in their midst. To Moses' repeated plea,[19] the Lord made a promise that he would do marvels before Moses' people, etc. When Moses came down the mountain the Lord did indeed go into their midst, for the face of Moses himself shone and the glory of God was in him.[20] This, in its context, suggests the meaning of the words spoken to Moses: **and I will be gracious to whom I will be gracious.** The Lord could not answer Moses' plea in the way Moses wished, for then the people would have been consumed. God knows best how to distribute his special favors. Moses, like Abraham, did not understand his battle strategy. The Lord was shaping the destiny of Israel. They were indeed the chosen descendants of Abraham—but this shaping was to be done through Moses and not in the more direct fashion that the humble Moses would have wished. This can be great encouragement to us. Sometimes we may not understand God's strategy. We may (like Moses or Abraham) be pleading with him to do things that he himself would like to do, but which are impossible because of people's sin. Nevertheless, if our hearts are right with him and if our motives are pure, then we approach closer to his heart and he may be able to use us more.

It was fortunate that God did not merely answer Abraham's prayer (to spare Sodom if ten righteous men could be found there) for then righteous Lot would also have perished. God answered instead the desires of Abraham's heart, and did not "destroy the righteous with the wicked."[21] Thus Lot was saved.

It was fortunate that the Lord did not answer Moses' prayer to go up in the midst of the Israelites, for they would have been consumed. What God did was to answer, as far as was possible, the desires of Moses' heart. God went in their midst by going in Moses—and even then Moses had to wear a veil.

GOD'S STRATEGY NOT DETERMINED BY US

We have arrived at the truth that God is gracious to whom he will be gracious, for only he knows the overall strategy. How does Paul use the allusion he makes to this incident with Moses?

First, we must remember that although individuals are involved, no one's eternal destiny is in question. Moses was "converted" years before this episode, and any attempt to strain Paul's text to make it mean that Moses was eternally predestined to heaven and Pharaoh to hell is totally unwarranted. The question at issue is not the eternal destiny of anyone, but the history of Israel and their significance as the chosen nation. In Romans 9:14-18 Paul holds up the two great figures at the time of Israel's birth as a nation, comparing them and demonstrating the lessons to be learned about Israel. His conclusion will be that the shaping of the destiny of Israel was not decided by what Moses willed (nor by Pharaoh's opposition to the will of God). It is not a result of anyone "willing or running,"[22] but of God breaking into history to shape his plan as he knows is best.[23]

We may remember that in these verses Paul is repudiating the suggestion that there is unrighteousness with God, a suggestion he had put into the mouth of an opponent in Romans 9:14. Some commentators on Romans seem to suggest that Paul is rather awkwardly trying to say: "God can do anything he feels like—saving or damning—since everyone deserves hell anyway." What Paul actually says bears no resemblance to such a thought; his is a deeper and more consistent outlook. With the Hebrew background in mind the implications of his words become more clear. He is saying to opponents at that time: "Of course there is no unrighteousness with God! Moses found it difficult to see why the Lord was acting as he was, and the Lord had to explain that he knew best the way to distribute his favor. It is not a matter of what *you* would like—for even Moses didn't get his wishes—it is a matter of God-determined strategy. If you object to the way in which God is dealing with Israel this only shows your misunderstanding of the principles on which God works. God's dealings with Israel at the time of Moses were certainly not decided by Israel's supposed merits and works, for they were very sinful. Even the merits of righteous Moses did not enable him to direct God's dealings. God acted according to his whole strategy for his plan in history. This plan, however, does not compromise his justice in any way, for God says that the principle of individual choice and responsibility never alters: **Whosoever has sinned against me, him will I blot out of my book.**"[24]

It would be foolish to suppose that God's strategy would

be determined by man's will and exertion, but this is no reason to doubt that there are reasons for God's actions when he does something we did not expect. Such actions never compromise his justice and love.

When today, we partake in the battle through prayer, we may perhaps **know not how to pray as we ought** because of our **infirmity** or our lack of understanding of God's strategy. Yet if we, like Abraham and Moses, lay open our hearts before the Spirit of God, then he will answer the groanings of our hearts which cannot be uttered, rather than the mistaken petitions of our minds. The Spirit knows the plan of God and his strategy in the battle. Thus he can transform our prayers (in spite of our mistaken ideas) as long as our hearts are pure before him.[25]

NOTES

1. It is important for us to understand exactly what and against whom Paul is arguing here. He was not denying that God had reasons for his decisions, nor that these reasons were somehow connected with the characters of those involved. What Paul is attacking is the rabbinic idea that man might obtain "merits" for the works of the Law, which would enable him or his descendants to have some control over God.

2. Genesis 18:20, 21

3. Ezekiel 33:11 JB; see also 18:23.

4. See also section 18 of our book *That's a Good Question* for some suggestions about the strategy involved.

5. Exodus 32:12-14

6. Exodus 32:34

7. Hebrews 3:19

8. Exodus 32:13

9. Exodus 32:32; Romans 9:3

10. Exodus 32:33; Ezekiel 3:1

11. Exodus 33:5; note that in verses 7-11 it is specified that the tent and pillar of cloud were "without the camp." Only Moses and Joshua went to it.

12. Exodus 33:12

13. Exodus 33:13

14. Exodus 33:14; The word rendered "thee" (RV, AV) in this verse, is singular in the Hebrew—though this fact is unfortunately lost in the modern versions which render "you."

15. Exodus 33:16

16. Exodus 33:17-19

17. Exodus 33:13, 14, 15, 16, 17; 34:9, etc.

18. Exodus 34:9

19. Exodus 34:9, 10

20. Exodus 34:29-35
21. Genesis 18:23
22. The metaphor of running is a favorite one with Paul; see 1 Corinthians 9:24-26; Philippians 2:16; Galatians 2:2; 5:7, and cf. Sanday and Headlam or Philippi
23. We may note the total difference between this view and the rabbinic concept. Davies, in *Paul and Rabbinic Judaism*, writes: "According to one rabbi the division of the sea at the Exodus was the result of the merit of Joseph; according to R. Nehemiah (A.D. 140-165) the redemption from Egypt was for the merit of Moses and Aaron; and a later rabbi, R. Nahman, the son of R. Samuel B. Nahamani, explained the redemption from Egypt as the result of the merit of Abraham, Isaac, Jacob, Moses, and Aaron." (p. 270) The Apostle Paul was totally opposed to any suggestion like this (even if less extreme in form) that man could, by his merits, control God's strategy. He does not, however, say that God has no reasons for what he does, nor even that we cannot see something of what they are. He is not saying that God is arbitrary or secretive, but that he is in no way bound by man's supposed "merits."
24. Exodus 32:33
25. Romans 8:26-28

11

Israel and God's Plan—Pharaoh

At the time of the birth of Israel as a nation there were two great figures: Moses and Pharaoh. Paul continues his outline of key points in Israel's history by taking a brief look at the story of Pharaoh. Moses' heart was in tune with the heart of his God, and God used this beyond Moses' understanding. Pharaoh made his heart resistant to God's purpose and God used this also, beyond the feeble understanding of that "might is right" monarch: **For the Scripture says unto Pharaoh, For this very purpose did I raise you** up, that I might show in you my power, and that my name might be published abroad in all the earth.[1]

Sensitive hearts have often been distressed by misunderstandings of this passage, which arise from failure to study in detail what the Scripture teaches about the "hardening" of Pharaoh's heart. To grasp what Paul intended to convey to the recipients of his epistle, we must understand the Hebrew and scriptural background of his words—common to himself, his readers, and his opponents.[2] We hope, therefore, that the reader will bear with us in examining some of the background behind Paul's terse and brilliant outline.

HEBREW WORDS FOR "HARDEN"

Three distinct Hebrew words are used in Exodus in connection with the "hardening" of Pharaoh's heart:

(a) *qashah*: From this verb (or root) are derived words indicating stubbornness. The root is used only twice (Exodus 7:3 and 13:15); in one case the agent is God and in the other it is Pharaoh. In both cases it refers to the whole general process during which Pharaoh became progressively more set in his evil way. In neither case is the word used to refer to any particular time or incident.

(b) *kabed*: The basic meaning of this root is "heavy" (as RV margin) and from it come the terms applied to Pharaoh's heart meaning "heavy" or "insensitive" or "immovable." Ironically, God sent during the plagues a *kabed* swarm of flies, a *kabed* cattle plague, a *kabed* hailstorm and a *kabed* swarm of locusts. The RV renders words from this root as "stubborn" or "harden" when they refer to Pharaoh's heart.

(c) *chazaq*: The basic meaning of this root is one of "strength" or "strengthen," but it is also used in contexts where we would use words like "encourage" or even "repair." The Hebrew word does not carry any of the sinister connotations conveyed by the English word *harden;* it is therefore unfortunate that the AV, RV, and RSV render it thus when it refers to Pharaoh. Elsewhere the most common rendering is one such as "strengthen" (see the word study in section 17, and in references to Pharaoh; therefore, we have used the RV marginal renderings, i.e., "strengthen" or "make strong," since this seems less likely to mislead the English reader).

PHARAOH HARDENS HIS HEART

Right at the commencement of Moses' mission, the Lord predicted that Pharaoh would let the people go only if compelled by a strong hand.[3] Even before the Lord began to deal with Pharaoh the latter adopted a very defiant attitude toward him.[4] After the incident of the serpents, **Pharaoh's heart was strong** (*chazaq*), **and he hearkened not unto them; as the Lord had spoken. And the Lord said unto Moses, Pharaoh's heart is stubborn** (*kabed*), **he refuses to let the people go.**[5] Symbolically, Egypt's great serpent emblem had already been defeated. Next the Nile itself was turned to blood; yet Pharaoh did not lay even this to heart, for **Pharaoh's heart was strong.** During the plague of frogs he became a little more concerned, and for the first time promised to release the Israelites; but later **Pharaoh saw that there was respite, he hardened** (*kabed*) **his heart and hearkened not unto them** as the Lord had predicted. After the plague of lice, Pharaoh's magicians had to admit that it was God at work, but **Pharaoh's heart was strong** (*chazaq*). During the plague of flies Pharaoh agreed to let the people go a little way into the wilderness; but when the plague was lifted **Pharaoh hardened** (*kabed*) **his heart this time also, and he did not let the people go.** After this broken pledge came a cattle plague during which none of the Israelites' cattle were affected, but **the heart of Pharaoh was stubborn** (*kabed*). The next plague was an outbreak of boils, and after this, Pharaoh's magicians could not continue the contest! It was then, for the first time, that **the Lord strengthened** (*chazaq*) **the heart of Pharaoh, and he**

hearkened not unto them; as the Lord had spoken unto Moses. (Exodus 9:12) God had already prophesied in Exodus 7:3 that the strategic way in which he would act would make Pharaoh ever more stubborn, as gradually the hand of God in the signs and wonders became ever more apparent. Finally, through this strategy, no one would be in any doubt that the true and living God had taken Israel to be his special people. But this was a general reference to God's whole (future) course of action. There had been an even earlier prophecy in Exodus 4:21 that God would strengthen Pharaoh not to be cowed by the signs that Moses would do. The fact remains that the first instance of any act of God on Pharaoh's heart does not come until Exodus 9:12, after Pharaoh himself has repeatedly rejected God's request.

GOD STRENGTHENS PHARAOH'S HEART— BUT WARNS HIM

The Lord's act of strengthening is followed by a solemn warning to Pharaoh. God explains that he could have easily destroyed the Egyptians if his sole purpose had been to release Israel. But God has other purposes too and has not only let Pharaoh live but has even given him the strength to continue in his rebellious resolve. God's purpose in making Pharaoh stand even in the face of the miraculous signs is primarily that many people (including the Egyptians and even Pharaoh himself) should be able to recognize that the God of Israel is the true and living God.

Therefore, although Pharaoh is making his own moral decision, God is going to give him the strength to carry it out. Pharaoh must, therefore, be sure that in spite of the eventual consequences, this is really the course he is set upon. The words of God's admonition to him are: **For now I had put forth my hand, and smitten you and your people with pestilence, and you had been cut off from the earth: but in very deed for this cause have I made you to stand, for** to show you my power, and that my name may be declared throughout all the earth. As yet do you exalt yourself against my people, that you will not let them go? Behold, tomorrow at this time I will cause it to rain a very grievous hail . . .[6] Pharaoh might have given way, but it would not have been from repentance but because he was faint-hearted and afraid. It was in this situation that the Lord strengthened his heart. The wicked desire was already in Pharaoh; the Lord's action simply gave him courage to carry it out.

Yet in the mercy of God, after this first "strengthening" God warned him that it was he himself who had made him stand. It seems that Pharaoh was then given a last chance to turn from the path of defiance he had chosen. During the supernatural fiery hail that followed, Pharaoh recognized for the first time that he was indeed in the wrong, and promised to release them.[7] Moses replied, however, that (although some Egyptians did believe[8]), Pharaoh still had not repented of the sin which even he himself now admitted to; Pharaoh still did not really "fear God."[9] Moses' words proved true, and when Pharaoh saw that the **rain and the hail and the thunders had ceased, he sinned yet more, and hardened** (*kabed*) **his heart, he and his servants. And the heart of Pharaoh was strong,** (*chazaq*) **and he did not let the children of Israel go; as the Lord had spoken by Moses.**[10] In spite of God's warning, Pharaoh had chosen his path; he had decided to carry on along his way of broken pledges and sinful rebellion.

The Lord, therefore, seems to say: "Very well, if he is determined to be hard and unrepentant then I will make his heart hard, just as he wishes." Exodus 10:1 records: **the Lord said unto Moses, Go in unto Pharaoh: for I have hardened** (*kabed*) **his heart, and the heart of his servants, that I might show these my signs in the midst of them.**[11] From this point onward we read again and again that the Lord "strengthened Pharaoh's heart" to carry out his own wicked desires—even though his guilt became increasingly apparent.[12] When any normal person would have given in because of fear, Pharaoh received supernatural strength to continue with his evil path of rebellion.

PHARAOH'S GUILT AND GOD'S PURPOSE

Was God's intention to increase the guilt of Pharaoh? It is sometimes suggested that God's strengthening of Pharaoh's heart was a "judicial hardening" and that he condemned him to have a progressively more evil nature and greater guilt. Is this true?

In considering this question we must take into account certain of the words of Jesus in the sermon on the mount. He seems to imply that if a man wants to commit adultery and is deterred only by fear or lack of opportunity, then he has committed adultery in his heart.[13] Does this mean that the desire itself makes a man as guilty as the act? We might, perhaps, distinguish two areas of a man's guilt: the effects on himself and the effects on others. In both of these areas the relative guilts of desire and action are difficult to assess meaningfully. A desire repressed through fear may have worse effects on the man concerned than the act. On the other hand the act (in a sense) "commits" him, and it may make it easier for him to go further into sin. In many cases only God himself could tell which would be worse. The possible effects on others are no less difficult to assess. If a man seduces a woman he desires, then this would be leading her into sin. But this could, in some cases, lead her to remorse and reassessment of her spiritual condition—thus leading to blessing. Who can say whether the net effect of a sin on others is good or bad? Moreover a person who has (through fear) repressed a sinful desire may vent his frustration in other ways, again with unassessable effects on others. It is, in short, almost impossible for us to determine whether or not a sinful act is worse than the suppression, through fear, of a sinful desire. The Lord's words in Matthew certainly seem to indicate that both are serious affairs.

The above difficulties will arise as we consider the instance of Pharaoh. God did not give Pharaoh the wicked desire to rebel against him. What God did was to give him the stubborn courage to carry out that desire. Thus God's action merely made the difference between a wicked act and the suppression of an evil desire through fear. The fact that Pharaoh actually *did* refuse to liberate God's people may have made it easier for him to refuse again, even when his guilt became more obvious. In this sense God's action may have indirectly encouraged Pharaoh along a path that led to more guilt. This is certainly a possibility—though the phrase "judicial hardening" does not seem an altogether suitable way of describing it. But even if God's actions did lead in some way to an increase in Pharaoh's guilt, there is no evidence at all to indicate that God's *motives* included such an increase. He himself tells us what his motives were in his dealings with Pharaoh. They were:

(a) That Israel should clearly understand who had delivered them (Exodus 6:6, 7; 10:2; 13:14, 15).

(b) That they should carry possessions with them away from Egypt (Exodus 3:21, 22).

(c) That God might multiply his signs and bring them forth in great acts, so that the Egyptians should know that he was the true God (Exodus 7:3, 4; 11:9; 14:4, 17, 18).

(d) That his name might be declared not only in Egypt but in the whole earth (Exodus 9:14-18; Joshua 2:10, 11; 1 Samuel 8:8; Exodus 15:13-18).

ISRAEL'S PLACE AND GOD'S EMBLEMS

The Apostle Paul brings together in Romans 9:14-18 God's dealings with Pharaoh and special favor shown to Moses. Neither of these acts of God concerns the destinies of the individuals as such, and Paul is not concerned with such questions here. Neither Moses' nor Pharaoh's eternal destiny is in question. It is the bearing of Moses and Pharaoh on the earthly function and destiny of the nation of Israel that is at issue. God's actions do, of course, affect the two individuals concerned, but do not alter their eternal and personal destinies. The latter are not the concern of this passage.

Paul is interested in the way in which God is intervening in history to shape the course of the chosen nation of Israel. Here he shows special mercy to their leader, and through him to the nation; there he causes someone to have the courage to stand and carry out rebellious designs; and God's plan for Israel is being worked out.

It seems to have been God's intention that Israel should go straight into the promised land.[14] The episode with Pharaoh had so frightened the Canaanites[15] that Israel could have easily conquered them. This should, moreover, have enabled the nations around about to recognize that the true God was with Israel. Then, when the Temple was built, they could indeed have been ready to look toward it for the true God[16] and to admit that "to Israel belonged the services."

The Lord moves in history, strengthening resolve or showing special favor,[17] and the purpose of it all is the strategy of development of the nation of Israel. This is in turn the preparation for that Seed of Abraham who was to come to redeem the world.

The question of Paul's critic: "Is there then unrighteousness with God?"[18] is thus shown to be senseless. It would be foolish to expect that man could by his own efforts direct God's strategy in history. Righteousness and unrighteousness simply do not enter the question, for it could only conceivably be "unfair" if through study and "works" a man could become as well able to direct God's actions as God himself! But it is obvious that God alone knows the best way for him to intervene in the affairs of men as he seeks to extend his plan of salvation. The origin of Israel, God's election of them in Jacob, and the events surrounding their emergence as a nation: these all demonstrate this principle of God-determined strategy—there is no trace of a principle of "works."

From the point of view of this book we might also notice the emblems of God's warfare that appear again at the time of Israel's birth as a nation. In the final and conclusive plague, any house that marked itself with the blood of God's symbol of the slain lamb escaped the wrath. At this, the emergence of the nation, the Lord was looking forward to that greater victory and the method of its achievement in Christ the Paschal lamb.

Pharaoh and his hosts were overcome by the Red Sea. The nation of Israel was "baptized into Moses" as they passed *through* the same Red Sea.[19] Here God was showing that the way of escape from the forces of evil is through "baptism"—which we know represents the path of suffering, death, and resurrection.[20] The suffering and atoning death of Christ, and the suffering and death of the martyrs, will finally be too much for the forces of evil. The horse and his rider will be thrown into this "sea." God's strategy today is similar to then. In the church he is teaching us (like Moses) to stand, that we may see the salvation of our God.[21] The church is moving toward the "evil day" in the battle of the Lord. In this day we must withstand, and having done all must stand . . .[22]—as though trapped between Pharaoh and the Red Sea. Through this will come the final overthrow and exhaustion of Satan and his power, in which the knowledge of God will fill the universe as the waters cover the sea.[23]

NOTES

1. Romans 9:17

2. It seems to us quite wrong to suggest, as some have, that Paul is merely stringing together "proof texts" with no thought of their original context and which fail to answer the question anyway. Paul was not some mere quibbling rabbi, but the mouthpiece of the Holy Spirit and the authorized messenger (apostle) of Christ.

3. Exodus 3:19

4. Exodus 5:2

5. Exodus 7:13, 14

6. Exodus 9:15-18; the Hebrew "made to stand" could also mean "allowed to stand," and the Septuagint (LXX) takes this line. Sanday and Headlam point out, however, that Paul purposely changed the LXX word to another which is sometimes used for God raising up men and nations on the stage of history (as LXX Habakkuk 1:6; Jeremiah 27:41; compare Judges 3:12 where *chazāq* is used in similar sense.) We accept, therefore, the RV rendering as given. Gifford points out

that Paul made another change in the LXX to emphasize that God's purpose in showing his power is secondary.

7. Exodus 9:27

8. Exodus 9:20

9. Exodus 9:30

10. Exodus 9:34, 35

11. This is, incidentally, the sole reference in Exodus to a specific act of God in hardening. It comes after Pharaoh has clearly made his own choice. This may, perhaps, be one of the reasons why Young in his literal translation rendered it: "I have declared hard . . ."—though see also section 17.

12. Exodus 10:20; 10:27; 11:10; 14:4; 14:8; 14:17; we have, incidentally, adopted the traditional view making God the active agent in strengthening Pharaoh's heart. There is, however, an ambivalence in the Hebrew piel conjugation (see the Hebrew Grammars of Gesenius ed. Kautzsch, trans. Cowley, p. 141; and Davidson, 24th edn 1956, p. 92) and it could mean something like God allowed or encouraged Pharaoh to be strong. Although this is linguistically possible it would be an unusual rendering of the Hebrew phrase, and since it seems unsuited to the context we have not adopted it.

13. Matthew 5:28

14. Numbers 13—14

15. Exodus 15:15; Rahab remembered it fearfully over forty years later (Joshua 2:9, 10).

16. As Solomon hinted in 1 Kings 8

17. Romans 9:18

18. Romans 9:14

19. 1 Corinthians 10:1, 2

20. Romans 6. The emblems Christ left for his church were the Lord's supper (i.e., the communion service) and Christian baptism. These are reminders for us, just as there were reminders for Israel, of the methods by which God works.

21. Exodus 14:13

22. Ephesians 6:13

23. Isaiah 11:9; Habakkuk 2:14

12

Objectors and Vessels

We remember how Paul had been dealing with the subject of God's choice of Abraham, Isaac, and Jacob, and with the patriarchal age. He imagines the question being thrown up at him: "Is there then unrighteousness with God?" He answers No, for God explained to Moses that he knew best the way in which his special favor should be distributed. If he had answered Moses' request in the way he expected, the nation would have been consumed. Similarly the story of Pharaoh shows that it is not man's will but God's strategy that ultimately shapes history, and in this instance the Scripture even clarifies for us the Lord's motives and purposes in his actions.

Paul's allusions here, however, although full of meaning, would hardly silence the critic who was casuistic enough to suggest that Paul's message was: **let us do evil, that good may come.**[1] The same sort of critic could be relied upon here to throw up the objection: **why does he still find fault, for who withstands his will?**[2]

It is important for us to realize the nature of the question and questioner at this point. The sincere questionings of God's ways that come from a man like Habakkuk[3] do not provoke a command from God to keep quiet. The Lord gives a reply to Habakkuk,[4] who breaks into a hymn of praise[5] as he realizes God's strategy. Similarly the Lord commends what Job has said in his sincere bewilderment at what he thought were God's actions. It is never the Lord's way to condemn or knock down the questions or objections of a sincere man wanting to be real with him. The Apostle Paul is always reasonable in his replies to honest questioners. He becomes angry only with quibblers who willfully or carelessly misrepresent his view. Such is his critic in Romans 9.

One may further note that the objector here is obviously Hebrew. For this reason Paul's angry reply makes use of Scripture as an authority. Had the question come from someone who doubted God's existence or Scripture's authority, we may be sure that Paul would have followed his usual practice of beginning his discussion from what the person did believe.[6]

Paul's critic had willfully misunderstood the gospel of grace in Romans 3. Likewise he makes out in Romans 9 that Paul is saying that God's will for an individual is irresistible.[7] Paul has pictured God as moving in history: **He has mercy on whom he will, and whom he will he hardens.**[8] Yet Paul does not say here (nor anywhere else) that God's plan or will for an individual is irresistible—and Luke in his inspired text plainly says they are not.[9] We have seen that the Exodus story to which Paul alludes is far from implying any "irresistible will." It is true that God will ultimately achieve his plan for the world in spite of those who resist it, but the individual still has his own moral choice of whether or not to reject God's plan for him. The question of Paul's critic in Romans 9:19—"Why does he still find fault? For who can resist his will?" (RSV) is based on a flagrant misrepresentation of Paul's teaching. How does Paul react?

We may remember an earlier question (Romans 3:8) also based on a misrepresentation: "Why not do evil that good may come?" (RSV) Paul was angry at this, but did not bother to take time to destroy it in detail.[10] Instead he simply said: "Their condemnation is just," and passed on.

Here, in Romans 9:19, the equally untrue misrepresentation of what he has said is likewise passed over without detailed refutation. Yet Paul's angry reply: **Nay, but O man, who are you that replies against God?** itself demonstrates the stupidity of such a misrepresentation. How could the man reply against God if, as he supposed, he could not resist God's will? Therefore Paul says "Nay rather,[11] you yourself are resisting it now!"[12]

Why was Paul's Pharisee critic resisting God's revelation of his ways? It may have been because he disliked the way in which God was using his nation of Israel without any reference to the merits he supposed it to have. This sentiment was not new, and Paul goes back to a previous instance. The prophet Isaiah had a similar vision of God using some specially chosen figure in the shaping of Israel's history. Cyrus, a heathen king, was anointed as God's shepherd[13] for the sake of God's chosen servant Israel.[14] At that time, just as in the time of Paul, someone objected to God controlling such temporal features of his creation and using his anointed Cyrus and servant Jacob in these ways.[15] Isaiah attacked such people who thought themselves wiser than God: **Woe unto him that strives with his maker . . . shall the clay say to him that fashions it, what are you making? or, your work, he has no hands?** (handles).[16] Just as a potter decides on the special privileges of a pot (having handles) so special privileges like the election of a nation are decided by God alone, for he knows the best strategy. It would be ridiculous for a mere creature to set itself up as knowing better.

THE POTTER
AND THE CLAY

God is using his chosen nation Israel to demonstrate his truths to the world. He has now fully revealed his will to show two things in particular through them. One part of the nation he will shape into a **vessel unto honor** and the other part into a **vessel unto dishonor.**

It is unfortunate that the fatalistic image brought to our western minds by this metaphor of the potter is almost the reverse of what would occur to a Hebrew mind knowing the background of the Old Testament. Paul's words are colored by the parable of the potter in Jeremiah 18. Through Jeremiah the Lord says: **O house of Israel, cannot I do with you as this potter?**[17] Israel is in his hands like a potter's clay. If the Lord promises to "pluck up, break down, and destroy" a kingdom, and if after this they repent, then he will repent of the evil he would have done to them. If he promises to build up a nation and then they turn away from him, he will destroy them. The basic lump that forms a nation will either be built up or broken down by the Lord, *depending on their own moral response*. If a nation does repent and God builds them up, then it is for him alone to decide how the finished vessel will fit into his plan—and whether or not it will have handles! God alone determines the special privileges of a nation. Nevertheless it is the actions of the nation itself that determine whether it shall be built up into some type of "vessel unto honor," or broken down and destroyed.

Paul's adversary in Romans 9:19 is, as we have observed, a Hebrew. As such he would accept the prophet's picture of God building up or breaking down the lump of clay forming a nation. Paul, therefore, further asks: **has not the potter a right over the clay, from the same lump to make one part a vessel unto honor, and another unto dishonor?** God obviously has the right to make from the nation of Israel two vessels rather than one, just as a potter can divide one lump and make two pots. This is, in fact, what God has done. The unrepentant portion of Israel has become a **vessel unto dishonor**, and the faithful part[18] a **vessel unto honor**.

VESSELS UNTO HONOR AND NO-HONOR

We must pause briefly here to explain why we believe it correct to accept Ellison's translation[19] of "no-honor" rather than the more common one of "dishonor." First, Paul uses exactly the same phrase in 2 Timothy 2:20, 21, and is surely not exhorting Timothy to purge himself with a selfish motive of increasing his own honor. In those days gold and silver vessels did not bring honor to themselves, but rather to the master of the house. We are to purge ourselves in order to become vessels bringing honor to our master, ready for him to use us as a great man would utilize his expensive vessels. For the purpose of bringing honor, vessels of wood and earth are of no use whatever; this is the meaning of Paul's imagery here. The individual faces a choice, and Paul urges Timothy to "purge himself" and become a vessel bringing glory to God. The use of the same phrases "vessels unto honor" and "vessels unto no-honor" in Romans 9:21 would seem to indicate a similar meaning. The two vessels made from Israel bring honor or no-honor primarily to God rather than to themselves.

In addition to the evidence from 2 Timothy, we notice Paul's deliberate use of the different prepositions.[20] Someone to whom God has shown mercy is called a "vessel *of* mercy" and someone to whom God has shown wrath is called a "vessel *of* wrath." If God were to give honor *to* someone, it woud seem natural to call him a "vessel of honor," but, in fact, Paul deliberately uses a different preposition and says: "vessel *unto* honor" and "vessel *unto* no-honor."

It seems fairly certain, therefore, that the honor or no-honor is brought *by* the vessel *unto* God. Israel is known to be God's special people entrusted with his oracles, etc.[21] When people see the repentant section of Israel, living in harmony with God's will and exhibiting the fruits of his Spirit[22] it will be just like looking at a beautiful gold vase. Glory and honor will then be brought to the master of the house. When, however, anyone looks at that section of God's people who are in rebellion against him, then no-honor is likely to be given to God. Perhaps even the name of God may be blasphemed among the Gentiles because of them.[23]

VESSELS
OF WRATH
AND VESSELS
OF MERCY

The vessel unto honor is made up of **vessels of mercy,** that is, of individuals to whom God has shown mercy. Upon them God wishes to **make known the riches of his glory.**[24] As we have already seen, the glory of God as revealed by Jesus is in his giving of himself to his creatures. How better to make known such a glory than himself to pay the price of showing mercy to undeserving though repentant sinners? God's continual love and mercy to his unworthy servants is a tremendous revelation of his glory.

The vessel unto no-honor is made up of **vessels of wrath.** Those Israelites who rejected God's plan for them and refused to repent, had the wrath **come upon them to the uttermost.**[25] Soon after this time the physical Temple was destroyed. Those of the nation who had rejected Jesus, who was the true Temple, were scattered among the Gentiles. If they would not hearken unto God, he would scatter them among the nations.[26] If they did evil in the sight of God to provoke him to anger, he would scatter them among the peoples.[27] Yet if from thence anyone should seek God with all his heart, he would find him.[28] Any individual Israelite who (like Paul himself) repented and sought the Lord, would become a **vessel of mercy.** He would then become part of the vessel unto honor, and God's glory would be made known upon him. We must not imagine that God ever drew hard and unchangeable lines between the vessel of honor and that of no-honor. Many Jews who were under the wrath of God did, in fact, repent.[29] Others missed the obvious teachings about Jesus in their own scriptures because "a veil lay over their hearts."[30] Yet, if their heart **shall turn to the Lord,** if in their hearts they truly seek him, **the veil is taken away.**[31] As the light of God began to shine in their hearts he would make known his glory on them as they were transformed into the image of Jesus.[32] A vessel of wrath could turn to the Lord and thus become a vessel of mercy, upon whom God would show his glory.

Why does God endure with much longsuffering the vessels of wrath which are fit only for destruction?[33] He himself gives as his reasons:

(a) to show his wrath

(b) to make his power known

(c) and that (i.e., "in order that") he might make known the riches of his glory upon vessels of mercy.

One may see in the situation of Israel in Paul's time some similarity to the situation of Pharaoh which we have considered. One might regard Pharaoh as a (a) vessel of wrath, for God certainly showed his wrath on Pharaoh. Further, God could have easily destroyed the Egyptians with a plague[34] but instead[35] he endured them with much longsuffering in their rebellion against him. His purpose at that time was (b) to make his power known on Pharaoh, just as he would make it known on the vessels of wrath in Paul's day. But God's purpose never seems to be merely to exhibit power. In the case of Pharaoh God wanted to show the Hebrews, the Egyptians, and the surrounding nations that he was the true God and that Israel was his people.[36] Later, according to Romans, God endured the Hebrew vessels of wrath, showing his power on them (c) in order that he might make known his riches on the vessels of mercy. Those of God's special people who rebel against him are allowed to live, but he shows his power and wrath in the dispersion of the nation. He intends that some should be led by this to repent. Paul might ask them: despise you the riches of his goodness and forbearance and longsuffering, not knowing that the goodness of God leads you to repentance? but after your hardness and impenitent heart treasure up for yourself wrath in the day of wrath . . . These words (he says) apply even more to the Jew than to anyone else.[37] The wrath of God *is* revealed from heaven against those who in unrighteousness ignore the truth,[38] yet his longsuffering in not destroying them immediately is meant to lead them to repentance.

God's strategy is perfect. It is for him to choose the shape of a vessel unto honor or the shape of a vessel unto no-honor. Pharaoh chose to rebel, and God decided to use him as a special demonstration of his wrath. In this way someone like Rahab could be stimulated to repent and through faith become right with God.[39] In this way God "got him honor on Pharaoh," though Pharaoh in himself was bringing him no honor.[40] Similarly God could use even that part of Israel which rebelled against him. He used them to demonstrate his wrath, and so their disobedience led indirectly to the extension of the gospel among the Gentiles.[41]

GENTILES
MAY ALSO
BECOME VESSELS
OF MERCY

In Romans 9:1-23 Paul has been dealing with the Jewish question. At this juncture he breaks off to point out that Gentiles can also have a place. The vessels of mercy whom God has called[42] include people **not from the Jews only, but also from the Gentiles.** The prophet Hosea had many years previously outlined the principle involved here. At the time of Hosea, God had called Israel "Not-my-people" because of their sin. Yet he promised that when they repented he would rename them as his people. One must realize the great significance of names to the Hebrew mind; to rename a person or a group had great significance.[43] The principle in Hosea, therefore, is this. God might, should he consider it necessary, remove or bestow a privileged name and position as he thought fit. Paul considered the same principle to be involved in God's actions in his own age. Those who have been "named"[44] include some who—as Gentiles—formerly did not have a name as people of God. What (through Hosea) God said he could do for rejected Israel, so in the time of Paul he has done for repentant Gentiles.

Gentiles, then, as well as Jews, are called sons of the living God. He has shown them mercy. They are known to be his and are part of the vessel unto his honor.

NOTES

1. Romans 3:8
2. Romans 9:19
3. Habakkuk 1:2; 2:1
4. Habakkuk 2:2
5. Habakkuk 3
6. See, e.g., Acts 14:15-17; 17:22-31; and see also our book *That's a Good Question*, section 12.
7. Ellison says of the critics: "Like most controversialists, he distorted his opponent's arguments—Paul is not inventing him; he must have met him often enough." *Mystery of Israel*, p. 52.
8. Romans 9:18
9. Luke 7:30; even on a human level Luke was Paul's friend and traveling companion and would surely have used similar terminology.
10. There are, in fact, striking similarities between Romans 3:3-8 and Romans 9:14, 19. Compare the following:

A. (i) Romans 3:5—Is God unrighteous who visits with wrath? . . . God forbid; for how then shall he judge the world?
   (ii) Romans 9:14—Is there unrighteousness with God? God forbid. For he says to Moses . . .
B. (i) Romans 3:7—Why am I also still judged as a sinner? and why not . . .
   (ii) Romans 9:19—Why does he still find fault? For who withstands his will?
C. (i) Romans 3:5—I speak after the manner of men.
   Romans 3:8—As some affirm that we say.
   (ii) Romans 9:19—You will say to me then . . .

It seems clears that it is the same critic (or bearing Acts 13:45 in mind we might say "heckler") who appears in both Romans 3 and Romans 9. The idea that no one can resist God's will is no more a part of Paul's teaching than is the idea that we should do evil that good may come. The latter is a quite unjustifiable deduction from Paul's teaching that God's faithfulness is shown all the more by man's lack of it. The former is a quite unjustifiable deduction from Paul's teaching that God's strategy is not under man's control. To the critic in Romans 3 Paul simply gives a crushing retort—not bothering to answer the charge in detail. This was not, of course, because Paul had no answer; his whole theology shows the foolishness of the suggestion. It was because the apostle did not wish to break the flow of his argument to answer a misrepresentation which was either foolish or willful. Paul's treatment of the critic in Romans 9 is similar. Paul does not stop to give a cool detailed demonstration that his teaching does not imply that no one can resist God's will. This is not because Paul can't, but because it would break the flow of his argument. Instead he makes a crushing allusion to the irony of the objection: "Nay rather, who are you who are yourself resisting God's will?" The critic is a living demonstration that his criticism is nonsense! But Paul is not content merely to couch his remark as a statement. He throws it in as a question, thus also forcing the critic to see where he is putting himself. (Compare similar ironical questions in Romans 2:17, etc.) Then the apostle proceeds to the point at issue, the reason behind the critic's emotional resistance to God's revelation: "Shall the thing formed say to him that formed it, Why did you make me thus? Or has not the potter a right [authority] over the clay . . ." The real question at issue, underlying the accusations and misrepresentations, was whether man had the right or authority to control God's strategy.

11. Abbot Smith and Sanday and Headlam render it thus; Bagster gives "Yea rather . . ."

12. It is interesting that Luke 7:30 refers to the Pharisees and lawyers (or rabbis) who rejected for themselves the will of God. In Romans 9 it might be just such a one who demands of Luke's friend Paul: "Why does God still find fault, for who can withstand his will?" (and the same Greek root for "will" is used). Paul's response implies: "You can, for one, for you are doing so now!" Paul here applies to a specific case what Luke said of the group generally.

13. Isaiah 44:28; 45:1

14. Isaiah 54:4

15. God's strategy did not, of course, predetermine the eternal destiny of either Cyrus or the Israelites. Isaiah in chapters 44-45, like Paul in Romans 9, was concerned with God's movements in history and not with the final destiny of individuals involved.

16. Isaiah 54:9

17. Jeremiah 18:6

18. This faithful section of Israel are like the natural branches of an olive tree and the Christian Gentiles like wild branches that have been grafted into it. Paul alludes to this teaching when he adds in verse 24 that the "vessel unto honor" is made up not only of some Jews but of some Gentiles as well.

19. *The Mystery of Israel*, p. 53

20. The Greek text indicates this by using *eis* with the accusative in the case of the vessels of honor and no-honor, and the genitive in the case of the vessels of wrath and of mercy.

21. Romans 3:2; 9:4, 5

22. Galatians 5:22, 23

23. Romans 2:24

24. Romans 9:23

25. 1 Thessalonians 2:16

26. Leviticus 26:27-33

27. Deuteronomy 4:25-27

28. Deuteronomy 4:29

29. See section 20.

30. 2 Corinthians 3:15

31. 2 Corinthians 3:16

32. 2 Corinthians 3:14—4:6

33. Romans 9:22, 23

34. Exodus 9:15

35. to use the language of Romans 9:22

36. see above, section 11, p. 75.

37. Romans 2:4-10

38. Romans 1:18

39. Joshua 2:9, 10; Hebrews 11:31; James 2:25

40. Exodus 14:4

41. Romans 11:30

42. The Greek word can mean either "called" or "named"; the latter sense is obviously the one intended here because of the reference to "renaming" from Hosea.

43. e.g., Abraham, Sarah, Israel, and Peter. In *Rabbinic Theology* R. A. Stewart says: "Knowledge of a proper name was supposed to give a certain measure of power over its bearer . . ." (p. 43). To have authority to rename a person would be even more significant. In addition to Stewart see: *Everyday Life in the Holy Land* by James Neil, pp. 126-134; *The People of the Book and Their Land* by W. N. Carter, pp. 28-32.

44. Romans 9:26; the name being "sons of the living God."

The Present Conflict

THE ELECTION OF GRACE

Paul spends much of the remaining part of Romans 9-11 demonstrating that the principles upon which God is working are not new. Paul points out that on various previous occasions he had to judge his people Israel when they were rebellious. Yet there was always a section of them who were the chosen of God on a basis of faith and grace.[1] There is, we must realize, more than one context and meaning for the word *chosen* in Paul's writing.[2] In one sense the whole nation of Israel was undoubtedly chosen by God. In another sense only those who had individually accepted God's grace were really his "choice" people. Some Israelites, although in the chosen nation, had rejected God's grace and were therefore not in the "election of grace."

Why was this? Paul explains at least part of the answer. A number of Israelites, such as the Pharisees, were almost obsessed with the idea of being acquitted by God according to his Law.[3] What they did not grasp was that the way to "righteousness"[4] was through faith and not through meritorious acts and strict conformity to ceremonial law.[5] Moses had, in fact, made it clear from the beginning that simple trust in what God had done was more necessary than any deed of great prowess.[6] How ironical that some Gentiles, who had never been so obsessed with being right before God's bar of judgment, had obtained just such an acquittal because they understood and applied the more readily the principle of faith and grace.[7] Paul is careful to point out that the idea of Gentiles being right before God is not a new one. The Old Testament says that *whoever* shall call on the name of the Lord shall be saved—which includes Gentiles as well as Jews.[8]

THE CHURCH
AND ISRAEL

Paul has progressed from discussing the historical position of Israel into discussing the first-century position. Many of the Israelites had rejected God and were under God's wrath, but some had accepted Christ and (together with believing Gentiles) became the church. Paul nevertheless made it clear that the believing Gentiles should not exult over those Israelites who did not believe.[9] The believing Gentiles had received great benefit from God's messianic program involving Israel. It is as though the Gentiles were wild olive branches grafted into the olive tree of the messianic program, and some of its natural branches have been cut out.[10] Gentiles must not, therefore, exult. Moreover, if any of the unbelieving Israel repent they can the more easily be grafted back by God into his plan and program. The Gentile believers must themselves be careful, for it is only by their faith that they have become part of God's messianic plan. If they cease to exercise daily faith they will no longer be of use in it.

Paul further explains the position of unbelieving Israel by picturing the two different feelings of God toward them in a typically Hebrew exaggerated contrast.[11] They are the chosen nation and their descent and heritage from the patriarchs give them a special place before God, i.e., they are **beloved for the father's sake.** Yet, as far as their opposition to the gospel is concerned, they are "enemies" of God.[12] The actual words of Paul are that **they are enemies for your sake;** God has used the disobedience of some Israelites to show his wrath and thus to lead some Gentiles along the path of repentance to receive mercy.[13] God's wrath is not for its own sake. He does not want Gentiles to exult over Israel because of the wrath. His intention is that Christians should be vessels on which he may so pour out his mercy that those Jews who disbelieve are provoked to repentance.

How utterly contrary to God's will it is that some calling themselves Christians have persecuted the Jews. God's wrath did come upon the bulk of the nation at the time of Paul, but his intention was that the grace shown in the church would provoke them to repentance. God's wrath was not for its own sake. God's aim in drawing out the lessons of obedience and disobedience was to have mercy on all,[14] and eventually the whole of Israel would come in.

PAST PRINCIPLES GUIDE PRESENT UNDERSTANDING

Certain principles emerge from God's treatment of Israel; these may help our understanding of God's methods in the present. The same God is at work today, in the church phase of the conflict. We may draw out these principles as follows:

God's Sovereignty. God's choice of Abraham rather than of Lot or Melchizedek was not because of his deeds, nor even, necessarily, because of his faith. It was because God knew the best strategy. God alone decides what part he will assign to us in his great plan for mankind. He used his sovereign choice again in deciding that Isaac rather than Ishmael should be in the line of descent to the Messiah.

Paul shows us[15] that his choice was not made without reason—but none the less he alone made the choice. We are not explicitly told the reasons for God's choice of Jacob rather than Esau, but perhaps hints are given in the later history of the individuals and their descendants.

Today also, God assigns his servants to different positions and functions. It is not our business to question this, but to seek to fulfill to his glory the role with which he has privileged us.[16] Failure to accept gladly the position that God has assigned to us in the body of Christ is one great source of spiritual sterility and failure.

God's Foreknowledge. God's sovereign and strategic assignment of positions is made in the full light of his foreknowledge. For one thing, God knows the hearts of men and how they will react to what he says. Before Moses ever began his task, God knew that the Israelites would hearken to his voice.[17] In the same passage he also told Moses: **I know that the king of Egypt will not give you leave to go.**[18] The Lord assigns positions in the full knowledge of the man, for **the Lord looks on the heart.**[19]

God also foreknows the distant future. This is seen in his prophecy to Abraham that all nations shall be blessed by the latter's messianic seed. Another example is seen in the prophecy at the time of the birth of Jacob and Esau that one nation would serve the other. God may today send us somewhere or inspire us to do something for reasons we do not understand. Yet when he does this we may be sure that he knows what the repercussions of our actions will be —even far into the future.

God Maneuvers Good and Evil. God was able to use the faith and obedience of his servants Abraham and Moses, but he was also able to encompass even the hard heart of Pharaoh into his plan. Moses chose to follow God's way and was used beyond his intellectual understanding of God's strategy. Pharaoh chose the path of rebellion and God maneuvered him into a position where the consequences of an evil heart were made clear to all, and it was shown that Jehovah was the true and living God. Such a demonstration could be used by God to bring repentance and life to many. Similarly, when part of Israel rejected the Messiah and rebelled against God they were used as vessels to demonstrate his wrath. This again he utilized to stimulate repentance and to bring life.

Thus we see that God can use even the evil in the world to bring in blessing. This is not to say that he wills evil himself, or even that he willingly allows it, but such is his greatness that he can use it for good. When the enemy brings some disaster or failure into our lives we must remember this.[20] It may not be God's will that it should happen—any more than it was God's will that Pharaoh should rebel against him—yet nevertheless God is able to overcome and utilize it for his own ends. **We know that in everything God works for good with those who love him.**[21] Whenever disaster or failure strikes, we know that God will be there, wanting us to cooperate with him to bring good from it. What seemed to be the greatest disaster ever, Christ's crucifixion, was in fact used by God to bring untold blessing to mankind.

O the depth of the riches both of the wisdom and the knowledge of God! How unsearchable are his judgments and his ways past tracing out (Romans 11:33).

THE CROSS
IN HISTORY
AND ETERNITY

We have been looking at God's strategy in his choice of Israel. We have seen how this, and all his actions in human history, were part of a plan to prepare for Jesus' coming and death. Now we must pause to consider more explicitly the implications of the cross for our theme. How does it fit into the pattern of God's dealings with his creatures?

We may discern two main fields of operation in which the cross is effectual. First, it enabled sinful man to be put into a right relationship with God, and so enter the spiritual battle. Second, it had direct effect on the spiritual forces themselves. These two aspects are brought out well in Colossians 2:14, 15: **Having blotted out the bond written in ordinances that was against us, which was contrary to us; and he has taken it out of the way, nailing it to the cross; having put off from himself the principalities and the powers, he made a show of them openly, triumphing over them in it.**[22]

We see, therefore, that there are two aspects of the work of the cross: the atonement for man and the victory over Satan. Both should be borne in mind as we look now at the setting of the cross in time and in eternity.

In eternity dwells God who is timeless. It seems, moreover, that the atonement which Christ brought between this God and the human race operated in eternity rather than in time. In other words, believers in Old Testament times, no less than those in New, were redeemed through the life given up by Jesus on the cross.[23] Thus the atoning effects of the cross reach backward as well as forward from the date of the crucifixion. The atonement operates in eternity rather than in time.

But, although this is true, we must beware of treating the cross as a wholly isolated or self-contained event. It is also God's key move in his activity throughout a whole chain of events in human history. Right from the beginning God looked onward to the coming One through whom the serpent's head would be crushed.[24] His action in choosing Abraham and the Jews was, as we have seen, with the purpose of preparing the way for Jesus the Messiah.[25] Throughout history God's actions prepare for the cross, and at key times his symbol of the slain lamb appears. It comes in the story of Abel at the beginning of history.[26] It appears at the start of Hebrew history, in the words of Abraham.[27] And it appears in the passover ceremony at the time of Israel's birth as a nation.[28] God always points onward to the cross.

After the crucifixion had occurred, what then? God continued his action in human affairs as the power and message of the cross began to be applied in human lives. Christ's chosen apostles were intended to carry this message to the ends of the earth.[29] There is, then, a sense in which throughout the period before the crucifixion God is preparing for it, and in the period after the crucifixion is working to apply its power in human lives.

We may therefore compare the eternal and temporal aspects of the cross for humanity. On the one hand the death of Christ was effective in eternity in bringing atonement to anyone at any time who has faith in God. On the other hand, the cross has a place as one link, albeit the vital one, in a whole coordinated plan of God as he intervenes in human history according to his own strategy.

We may consider further the effects of the cross on Satan's forces. The cross has, of course, enabled men to be used as God's agents. This is important since the revelation of those believers conformed to the image of Christ will contribute to the destruction of Satan's power. The cross is obviously basic to this part of God's plan.

But there is also, as we have said, a direct effect of the cross on Satan's forces. The historical date of the crucifixion did not, of course, mark the time of Satan's final overthrow and destruction—for we know that he is still very active today.[30] What it did was to provide Christ and his followers with powerful weapons against Satan, and also insure his eventual overthrow. It is like the key move in a game of chess, the move that finally seals the fate of an opponent. Scripture teaches that a new increase in Christ's power was marked by his death and resurrection.[31] Christ's servants also, who fight in his armor, know the power of the blood and name of Jesus in their lives.[32] When Satan's forces make war in heaven[33] they are overcome by the blood of the Lamb and the revealing power of truth spoken by martyrs. It is as the Lamb that Christ himself is pictured as fighting the satanic forces in Revelation—it is because he was slain as an innocent sacrifice that the sight of him is so terrible to the evil forces. It is, in other words, through the cross that eventually the final overthrow of Satan will be made.

This completes, then, this brief outline of the setting of

the cross in God's strategy, both in time and eternity. These ideas may be borne in mind as we continue to look both at the present conflict and at its final future culmination and completion.

GOD'S
INSTRUMENT
TODAY—THE CHURCH
IN CHRIST

Whatever the church is or possesses is "in Christ." The battles of the "saints of the most high" are, as we have already noted,[34] the battles of Jesus the Messiah. We are his body and wear his armor, the armor of God. We fight in the strength of his might. Our whole life and battle are in him.

This incorporation in Christ is brought out vividly in Ephesians. The grace of God was bestowed on us *in Christ* and it is Christ "in whom we have redemption by his blood."[35] It is because we are *in him* that we have boldness and confidence to approach God.[36] Further, since Christ has been raised from the dead and made to sit in the heavenly places at God's right hand, God has also **raised us up with him, and made us to sit with him in the heavenly places in Christ Jesus.**[37] We have, therefore, been blessed with **every spiritual blessing in the heavenly places in Christ.**[38] This, then, is the Lord's chosen position for the church in Christ: to be in the heavenly places at God's right hand. God **has blessed us with every spiritual blessing in the heavenly places in Christ: even as he chose us in him before the foundation of the world, that we should be holy and without blemish before him.**[39] We share in both the *position* of Christ beside God and the *chosenness* of Christ by God. God said of Christ: **this is my son, my chosen, hear you him.**[40] Elsewhere Christ is said to be the servant whom God has chosen.[41] The chosenness of Christ has, of course, nothing to do with going to heaven or to hell. He is not chosen to go to heaven but to be God's servant, God's "suffering servant", for the redemption of the peoples. The fact that he is chosen affects his function in God's plan, but does not mean that he is given an easy time while others suffer. Rather, he himself is in the thick of the battle.

There were not, moreover, a great number of others whom God could equally well have chosen to fulfill the office of suffering servant. Jesus was unique, and was also the chosen or choice one of God in the sense of being closest to the heart of the Father.[42]

We are chosen in Christ. This does not mean that we were chosen *to be put into* Christ. It does not mean that God chose to make us repent but left others unrepentant! It means that as we repented and were born again into the body of Christ, we partake of his chosenness. He is chosen, and we are chosen in him. This was, of course, planned by God in his foreknowledge even before the world began.[43] God decided that the church in Christ should be holy and blameless before him and should (also in Christ) be seated in the heavenly places. Yet these heavenly places are not, as might be imagined, a haven of rest. Rather, we must wrestle there against the **spiritual hosts of wickedness in the heavenly places.**[44] Our chosenness in Christ is not merely a privilege but also a call to a task. In God's workings, privilege inevitably implies responsibility. It was, for example, a great privilege to be an Israelite, for the whole nation was chosen by God. Yet only some Israelites were faithful in fulfilling the purpose that God intended for them. There were, as we have seen, the "elect according to grace" —those who had the inner experience for which the nation had so many outward symbols. Other Israelites were also part of the chosen nation, but tried to claim the privileges without accepting the responsibilities. This would not, and could not, work.

For us today it is an even greater privilege to be chosen in Christ, to be seated in him before God's throne in the heavenly places. Yet this also gives us the responsibility of (in Christ) fighting the spiritual hosts of wickedness. Thus Peter calls on us to fulfill God's purpose for us, i.e., to "make our calling and election sure."[45] This is our calling or vocation and it is what we were chosen in Christ to do.

Peter is not telling us to make sure that we don't go to hell, for the calling and election are not primarily concerned with this. He is concerned that our personal characteristics be such that we are neither barren nor unfruitful in our knowledge of Jesus, that we are fully prepared to enter richly into the Lord Jesus' eternal reign which is to come. Thus we find that the present runs on into the future, for there is to be an end to the present warfare in the heavenly places. One day Satan's power in the universe will be destroyed, and the church is destined to play a part in this. The final purpose of God, and the role in this of the church in Christ, are the subjects of the next section.

NOTES
1. Romans 11:5
2. See also section 15
3. Romans 9:31, compare 10:20
4. See also Section 16
5. Romans 9:30-33
6. Romans 10:5-8
7. Romans 9:30-33
8. Romans 10:12
9. Romans 11:13-24
10. Commentators on this text have interpreted the "root" in verse 16 in different ways. Some regard it as Abraham, others as Christ, and others as the first Christians. Whichever of these we accept, Paul's meaning is obviously that Gentile Christians benefit from the heritage of God's messianic program in Israel.
11. See the comments above in section 9.
12. Romans 11:28
13. Romans 11:30
14. Romans 11:32
15. See above in section 8, pp. 54, 55.
16. To put this strikingly: When God puts a particular task before us, it is our responsibility to run well and finish the course. (1 Corinthians 9:24; Hebrews 12:1; 2 Timothy 4:7). But as to what course God shall set us, that is not a matter of us willing or running (Romans 9:16) but of God's strategy and mercy.
17. Exodus 3:18
18. Exodus 3:19
19. 1 Samuel 16:7
20. At first Moses seemed only to have made matters worse with Pharaoh (Exodus 5:21, 22). He was disheartened, but he took his disappointment to the Lord who directed him how he should continue in order to obtain eventual blessing.
21. Romans 8:28 RSV. The RSV or NEB translations seem the more likely ones. See above, note 25 to section 2.

22. The blood of Christ, symbolizing his life given up, similarly has a dual function—see, e.g., Hebrews 9:14; Revelation 12:11.

23. John 14:6

24. Genesis 3:15

25. Genesis 12:3; and see above pp. 51, 52.

26. Genesis 4:4

27. Genesis 22:8

28. Exodus 12:4

29. Matthew 28:19, 20; Acts 1:8

30. Thus the injunction to resist him, etc.—James 4:7; Ephesians 6:11, 12

31. Luke 12:50; Romans 1:4

32. This is especially true of Christians who have dealt with evil spirits.

33. Revelation 12:7—presumably this war arose after the cross, showing just how active Satan still is!

34. See section 4.

35. Ephesians 1:7

36. Ephesians 3:12

37. Ephesians 1:20; 2:6

38. Ephesians 1:3

39. Ephesians 1:3, 4

40. Luke 9:35

41. See section 15 for further details of this concept.

42. See section 15 for the connection between "belovedness" and "election."

43. See, e.g., 1 Peter 1:2. Dr. J. A. Beet gives some interesting discussion on God's motives and timing in election and predestination of the believer in his commentary on Romans Div iii sec 26 and Div iv sec 28.

44. Ephesians 6:12

45. 2 Peter 1:10

God's Great Project and the Final Battle

GOD'S PURPOSE FOR CHRIST

God has seen fit to reveal to us his eternal purpose to **sum up all things in Christ, the things in the heavens and the things upon the earth.**[1] God will, through Christ, finally reconcile to himself all things in heaven and on the earth—and all the works of evil will be destroyed.[2] Christ will have preeminence in all things, and to him every knee shall bow.[3] Christ has been appointed as heir over all things.[4] It is against this appointment that Satan is in rebellion. Isaiah seems to refer to Satan as the "Day Star" and "Son of Morning" who sought to exalt himself above God and was cast down.[5] We know, moreover, that he offered to give Christ all earthly kingdoms if only he might receive the preeminence for which he lusted.[6] Satan hates it that Christ, and not himself, should have preeminence. He hates God for determining that it should be so. He hates the church because it will both share in Christ's reign and be used by God to establish that reign. He hates the church because of the great destiny that God intends for it. What, we might ask, is the greatest possible destiny that God could have conceived for those who believe in him? Surely it is that they should become like him, for nothing is greater than

God. This is, in fact, what God has ordained. This is the great project of God for man, against which Satan will fight to the end. Yet Satan will finally fail, for even before time began God foresaw the achievement of his chosen destiny for man.

PREDESTINATION

Perhaps the most important point to grasp about predestination[7] is that it concerns man's future destiny. It does not concern who should, or should not, *become* Christians, but rather their destiny *as* Christians. The word is used only four times with reference to the church,[8] twice in Romans 8 and twice in Ephesians 1. Both of these passages are concerned with the future destiny and tasks of the church. They are not concerned with how anyone came to be a Christian. Let us consider these passages in detail:

The Origin of Predestination. Predestination was not a result of some arbitrary fiat. Its origin is in the essentially personal being of God. Way back before the foundation of the earth, before time began, God could look ahead. He foreknew[9] all about those who would repent in response to his Holy Spirit and would put their hope for the future in Christ.[10] God had to decide what their fate should be. They earned nothing by repenting and could have been condemned. Yet the essential being of God is Light[11] and Love.[12] His decision, therefore, reflected his essential nature. His decision was made "in love."[13]

Scripture reflects this pattern of God's decision: First, God foreknew what we should do: **For whom he foreknew, he also foreordained . . .**[14] His decision concerned us: **we who had before hoped in Christ.**[15] And **he destined us in love to be his sons.**[16]

The subjects of God's decision and his motives for it are thus made clear. It is those who are bound up in Christ who, because God is Love, were given a glorious future destiny.

Predestined to Sonship. Predestination does not concern who should be converted; it concerns our future destiny. It is not that we are predestined *to be* Christians, it is rather that *as* Christians we receive a glorious future destiny. Scripture puts it thus: **For whom he foreknew, he also fore-ordained to be conformed to the image of his Son.**[17] God **foreordained us unto adoption as sons through Jesus Christ unto himself.**[18] Paul adds that this foreordination will be **to the praise of his glory.**[19] It is, however, always viewed as a predestination concerning our future, not as an explanation of how we came to be as we are.

Our Predestined Task. Christ is the heir of all things[20] and in becoming conformed to his image we become **joint heirs with Christ.**[21] When all things are summed up in Christ it will be seen that we also have an inheritance in him.[22] It is as sons of God that we enter into the cosmic inheritance, and it will be our task to deliver it from its present bondage of corruption.[23] The creation waits in earnest expectation for the day when the sons of God will be revealed and it will share the freedom of their glory.[24] This day of the revelation of the sons of God is also termed their "adoption." This word which our versions render "adoption" means literally "son-placing" or "placing-as-sons." It does not refer to our entry into God's family, for we were "born" into that. According to the New Testament our adoption is still in the future: **we ourselves groan within ourselves waiting for our adoption, to wit, the redemption of our body.**[25] The time of our placing-as-sons will be at the resurrection, when God will reveal us in our redeemed bodies. The Lord Jesus was the **firstborn from the dead,** and by his resurrection was "declared" or "designated" to be the Son of God in power.[26] God intends that Christ should be the **firstborn among many brethren**[27] and so our resurrection will also be the time when we are designated sons of God, i.e., when we are placed-as-sons.

The universe will be delivered from its bondage and corruption through the revealing of men conformed to the image of Christ, who is the firstborn from the dead. What was the nature of this Christ to whom we shall be conformed? Above all things Christ was a servant—and a suffering servant at that. He came not to be served but to serve and to give his life.[28] He said that the greatest in his kingdom would be the one who was the servant of all, and he demonstrated this by washing their feet.[29] This was (as seen in section 5) the "glory" of Christ. The "liberty of the glory"[30] of those conformed to his image must be similar. We are to deliver the universe by becoming servant-like. Only a self-sacrificing attitude like that of Christ will meet the needs of the universe.

The Glory of Predestination. We were, as we have seen: **foreordained . . . to the end that we should be unto the praise of his glory.**[31] We have been **sealed . . . until the redemption of the purchased possession, unto the praise of his glory.**[32] Our predestination to be revealed and placed-as-sons in our redeemed bodies is for the praise of God's glory. What could be more glorifying to God than to have many sons who reflect his glorious nature? Christ will bring many sons to glory[33] and Paul considers that **the sufferings of this present time are not worthy to be compared with the glory that shall be revealed to us-ward.**[34] Yet this glory is glory as taught to us by Christ.[35] It is the type of glory that enhances both giver and receiver. It is to God's glory that we become glorified, for then we shall become Christ-like and self-sacrificing in love.

Paul places the whole process right outside of time in Romans 8:30. God conceived his great project for man before time began. He then "called" or "named" us—that is he gave us a position before him. As he named us, so he justified us (that is, declared that we were right with him). Finally he will glorify us—and Paul regards this as so certain as to be placed in the past tense. (There can, of course, be little meaning to tenses in this process, for the plan was conceived in the mind of God outside of time.) **For whom he foreknew he also foreordained . . . and whom he foreordained them he also called; and whom he called, them he also justified; and whom he justified, them he also glorified.**[36]

A FORETASTE
AND A TRAINING
PROGRAM

God has given us a foretaste of our inheritance. He has given us a kind of down-payment or deposit to indicate that there is more to follow. The phrase used in the RV is "the earnest": **You were sealed with the Holy Spirit of promise, which is the earnest of our inheritance, unto the redemption . . .**[37] The Holy Spirit is he in whom **you were sealed unto the day of redemption.**[38] The Spirit is also termed the "firstfruits" —a foretaste of the great harvest to come: **ourselves also, which have the firstfruits of the Spirit, even we ourselves groan within ourselves, waiting for our adoption, to wit, the redemption of our body.**[39] The Holy Spirit is the "earnest" or "firstfruits" of our inheritance. Having received this pledge, we await the time when we shall come into that inheritance, i.e., the day of redemption when we shall be placed-as-sons (adopted). The Holy Spirit, therefore, is also called the "Spirit of son-placing." Paul says: **but you received the spirit of adoption whereby we cry, Abba, Father. The Spirit himself bears witness with our spirit, that we are children of God: and if children then heirs; heirs of God and joint heirs with Christ; if so be that we suffer with him, that we may also be glorified with him.**[40] Our adoption is not past but future, and the Holy Spirit is called the "Spirit of adoption" because he is the earnest of it.

Paul explains this elsewhere, comparing it to the development of a son in everyday life of those times. First, a baby boy is born into a family. For the first few months he is not conscious at all, either of being a son or having any relationship with the family. Gradually he learns to say Dad (in Hebrew *Abba*) and becomes conscious of his position as a son in the family. He is taken to school by a special slave, called a "child-conductor" (*paidagōgos*). At school he begins to learn more fully of his position in the household, the duties he has and the roles he must play. He is now conscious of his inheritance as the son of his father, but he has not yet come into that inheritance. He is no longer a baby, and he can fulfill some of the functions of a son. Nevertheless, until he comes of age he does not have any real authority over his inheritance; he is not treated as an adult. Although he is already living in and enjoying his father's house, his "coming of age," as we would call it, is the time when he really comes into his inheritance.

It has sometimes been a puzzle to people that the Old Testament says little about the afterlife and kindred subjects. Paul's metaphor of family and sonship goes at least some way toward explaining this. Before Christ came, the Jews were "children" in God's family but not yet fully conscious "sons."[41] They knew God and they were his children, but they did not fully understand what sonship meant. They knew little about their inheritance as fellow-heirs with Christ, and little of the future day of coming of age or son-placing when they would enter into that inheritance. A baby in God's family is an heir, but is under guardians and stewards and is not conscious of his position as a son.[42]

The Law was just like the child-conductor who took children to school.[43] The Law was intended to conduct God's children to Christ.[44] But when they fully understood faith in Christ they were past the stage of being little children.[45] Now, Paul says to them, **You are all sons of God, through faith, in Christ Jesus.**[46] Now that they are in Christ they realize their inheritance and have become fully conscious sons. Part of Christ's mission was to enable them to be put in line for this inheritance. Christ was sent so that they might receive the placing-as-sons, i.e., the redemption of their bodies.[47] If Christ had not come, there could never have been a day when the sons of God should be revealed. Those who believe in Christ are sons. Moreover, because we are sons: **God sent forth the Spirit of his Son into our hearts, crying, Abba, Father. So that you are no longer a bondservant, but a son; and if a son then an heir through God.**[48]

Paul tells his Jewish readers that they have left the baby stage. The Law has conducted them to Christ. A new era in mankind's education has arrived. Christ will be their teacher while, as sons, they are training for the time when they will be placed-as-sons. We too are sons, and should be training for what we might call our coming of age as sons. Such training is partly the purpose of this present age. God intends that we should begin to reflect the glory of the Lord and be **transformed into the same image from glory to glory, even as from the Lord the Spirit.**[49] Our transformation into the image of Christ has already begun, by the indwelling Spirit of adoption. The day of the revealing of the sons of God will be the culmination of a process of training. God leads and trains in different ways each one of the many sons who shall be brought to glory. Yet we have as the captain of our salvation one who was made complete and perfect through sufferings.[50] We who are being conformed to his image and may therefore undergo a training with some resemblance to his. Paul says he longs: **that I may know him, and the power of his resurrection, and the fellowship of his sufferings, becoming conformed unto his death; if by any means I may attain unto the resurrection from the dead. Not that I have already obtained, or am already made perfect; but I press on, if so be that I may apprehend that for which also I was apprehended by Christ Jesus. Brethren, I count not myself yet to have apprehended: but one thing I do, forgetting the things which are behind, and stretching forward to the things which are before, I press on toward the goal unto the prize of the high calling of God in Christ Jesus.**[51] Paul is glad of his experiences because they are part of his training for that day when at last he will attain the high calling given him in Christ. He hopes to attain the resurrection in the day of glory, the day of the revealing of the sons of God. His sufferings do, of course, serve some purpose in the present, and he says: **Now I rejoice in my sufferings for your sake, and fill up on my part that which is lacking of the afflictions of Christ in my flesh for his body's sake, which is the church.**[52] But part of Paul's consolation, something that helps him to rejoice even despite his sufferings, is the knowledge that he is being inwardly built up for the coming glory: **Wherefore we faint not; but though our outward** man is decaying, yet our inward man is renewed day by day. For our light affliction, which is for the moment, works for us more and more exceedingly an eternal weight of glory; while we look not at the things which are seen, but at the things which are not seen: for the things which are seen are temporal; but the things which are not seen are eternal.[53]

We may find difficulties and trials in doing the will of God in this life. Yet our day by day problems are part of the larger battle between God and Satan. They are helping to build our characters for the day when we shall be placed as sons, and in this we may rejoice; we rejoice in our sufferings, knowing that suffering produces endurance, and endurance produces character, and character produces hope . . .[54] We also know that neither death, nor life, nor angels, nor principalities, nor things present, nor things to come, nor powers, nor height, nor depth, nor any other creature, shall be able to separate us from the love of God, which is in Christ Jesus our Lord.[55]

THE LAST BATTLE

We may see, therefore, how the future destiny of man—predestination—is vitally connected with the subject of God's strategy in history. The final overthrow of evil and release of the universe will come when God's sons are revealed and they fulfill their destiny. God's strategy now, and his training of us through suffering, look forward to that great day of release.

How does Satan react to this project of God? We have already mentioned that Satan hates the church because of what it is becoming. The nearer the great project comes to fulfillment, the more furious he becomes.[56] Before that day of adoption he will throw all his forces into a last desperate battle. This will be a final showdown between God and Satan, good and evil, love and hate, self-sacrifice and power-lust. Satan's hatred of God and his Son is heightened by the thought of the universe being overrun by the divine image in man.

Throughout the book of the Revelation we see the battle raging. Again and again there is "war in the heavenly places" (e.g., 12:7). The battle intensifies. Satan gives all his authority to dehumanized masculinity personified in the Beast, and the Beast makes war on the saints. Perverted femininity is personified in the Harlot, who rides the Beast. Insatiable in her lust for pleasure, the Harlot drinks the blood of the martyrs of Jesus, thus administering her own intoxicating destruction. Associated with the concept of the Harlot is that great city of commerce called Babylon. This seeks to exploit and eliminate the church through economic pressures. The Beast, the Harlot, and the city are symbols of the forces of Satan. They represent lust for power, lust for pleasure, and greed. They are, in a sense, Satan's perverted counterfeit for Christ the Lamb, God's people the Bride, and the heavenly city of the New Jerusalem. We might, similarly, think of Satan, the Beast, and the false prophet as a diabolical counterfeit of the Father, Son, and Holy Spirit. Yet God's way is self-sacrifice. The forces of good give glory to one another and build each other up.[57] The forces of evil carry the seeds of their own destruction, and so the Beast consumes the Harlot which is the city.[58] Finally, Christ and the Bride are attacked by the Beast and the false prophet with their army.

What weapons does the Lord use in this conflict? We can only suppose that they are the weapons mentioned above in section 4, which destroy evil by revealing its nature. The sword coming from Christ's mouth[59] represents his word of truth which reveals evil in all its horror. The light and brightness of his presence illuminate it. His blood witnesses to the depths of its ugliness. In the face of such revelation, evil can only shrivel into itself and die. The Lord is not simply meeting force with greater force. The weapon he wields is different in kind from the brutal and depraved weapons of evil. It is as though God finally allowed the tremendous beauty and love of the Lamb of God to stand forth in all its glory.[60] It is as though this light spread through all the universe, and the evil simply shriveled and died.[61] The assault on Christ and the Bride is defeated by the revelation of what he is. Satan's forces are overthrown. Satan's final assault on the saints and the beloved city is overthrown by the fire[62] from God himself. Evil is destroyed and a new heaven and a new earth appear.[63] God's final purpose is accomplished.

NEW HEAVEN AND NEW EARTH

So, God's plan is finally achieved; his great project is accomplished. God has three things in the glorified church. He has a bride to reciprocate his love.[64] He has a "tabernacle" or "city" in which to dwell.[65] And he has many sons with whom he can share his life and character.[66]

We find that things are restored to something like the situation in the garden of Eden.[67] There is a river, but now it proceeds out of the throne of God and contains water of life.[68] The tree of life is there, but now its leaves may be used for the healing of the nations.[69] The precious things which were raw materials in Eden have been built up into something beautiful and everlasting.[70] They have been built into a dwelling place for God, so that the intermittent communion he had with man in the garden of Eden is exchanged for continuous and clear communion.[71] There is no mention of the tree of the knowledge of good and evil, for those who dwell in the new world have the Lamb of God to enlighten them.[72] No one needs to lust to "become like gods" for they see what the God of the Lamb is really like—and they themselves are already in his image.[73] There is no serpent there, for nothing unclean may enter[74] and so there is no curse.[75] Those who overcame in the battle have inherited these things,[76] and shall reign with the Lamb for ever and ever.[77] Hallelujah the Lord Omnipotent reigns, and the throne of God and of the Lamb shall be for evermore!

NOTES

1. Ephesians 1:10
2. Colossians 1:20
3. Colossians 1:18; Philippians 2:10
4. Hebrews 1:2
5. Isaiah 14:12, 13; Isaiah's words ostensibly refer to the evil king of Babylon, but ultimately may be applied to the latter's satanic master himself.
6. Matthew 4:9, etc.
7. *Predestination* is the word used in the AV; other versions (e.g., the RV) use *foreordained.*
8. The word is used altogether six times in the New Testament. Four times it refers to the church, once it concerns God delivering up Christ to die (Acts 4:28; see also Acts 2:23), and once it is used generally of God's eternal plan for us (1 Corinthians 2:7).
9. Romans 8:29; see also section 18, pp. 196, 205.
10. Ephesians 1:12
11. 1 John 1:5
12. 1 John 4:8, 16, John Blanchard makes this point well in a recent Banner of Truth book, *Right With God*: "It is not just that God possesses love as one of His qualities, or that love is one of the things God exercises, but rather His very essence is love. God *is* love, and love governs His every activity" (p. 47).
13. Ephesians 1:5
14. Romans 8:29
15. Ephesians 1:12
16. Ephesians 1:5, RSV; the RSV translation is certainly better here since it links the words "in love" to the predestination. The idea of being presented without spot or blemish is complete in itself (see also Ephesians 5:27 and Colossians 1:22) and the words "in love" do not belong with it. For this point see also the *New Bible Commentary Revised.*
17. Romans 8:29
18. Ephesians 1:5
19. Ephesians 1:12
20. Hebrews 1:2
21. Romans 8:17
22. Ephesians 1:11
23. Romans 8:21
24. Romans 8:19-21
25. Romans 8:23. The word *predestination* seems to be used little by early Christian writers—though they did, of course, use other means of reference to our future destiny. One of the few mentions comes in Clement's anti-gnostic work *Stromata*. Bruce explains the background of this work: "The influence of Gnosticism on the Church was partly good and partly bad. It was good in so far as it stimulated intellectual activity in the Church and made the orthodox leaders, like the writers already mentioned (Ireneus and Clement), present reasoned statements of their faith. Clement of Alexandria went so far as to present what he called the true Christian *gnosis* by contrast with the false; one might be an orthodox Gnostic, he held, by contrast with the heretical Gnostics . . ." (*The Spreading Flame*, p. 250).

Smith adds: "To his mind, the Christian was the only person with the right to be called 'Gnostic' (the Knowing One), because only the orthodox Christian had access to the true knowledge of God" (*From Christ to Constantine*, p. 112).

Stromata, Bk. vi, ch. 9 may be strictly rendered:

"For it were no longer seemly that the friend of God, whom 'God has foreordained before the foundation of the world' to be enrolled in the highest 'adoption,' should fall into pleasures or fears, and be occupied in the repression of the passions. For I venture to assert that as he is predestinated through what he shall do and what he shall obtain, so also he has predestinated himself by reason of whom he knew and whom he loved. Not having the future indistinct, as the multitude live conjecturing it, but having grasped by [true Christian] knowing faith what is hidden from others."

Let us note:

(a) Predestination is linked with "adoption" which concerns "what he shall do and what he shall obtain." Clement is arguing that with this future destiny in store it would be strange for a man to be occupied in repressing passions.

(b) Clement is making a play on the Greek word *dia,* which is first used with the genitive (rendered "through") and second used with the accusative (rendered "by reason of"). The first gives the immediate cause of a man's predestiny as that he has a God-given task to do and a God-given heritage. When the Sons of God are revealed in the day of their adoption then there is something they will do (liberate the creation) and something which they will obtain (their heritage as co-heirs with Christ). But, on the other hand, Clement "ventures to assert" that in one sense the Christian has received this predestiny *by reason of* WHOM HE KNOWS AND WHOM HE LOVES. Clement himself gives a further clue to his meaning here when (earlier in the section) he refers to the Christian: "now that he associates through love with the Beloved One, to whom he is allied by free choice." Clement would not, of course, have suggested that a man could receive this destiny through what he had *done*—for that would be "works." His view is rather that man's link in a love relationship with Christ is the basis on which he has received this destiny. This, perhaps, echoes Romans 8:28, 29 which links predestination to "them that love God."

This Clementine passage is interesting in that it shows that the earliest Christian teaching on predestination certainly did not regard it as an unalterable decree as to who should be converted. It was seen, quite biblically, to concern the future "adoption" and task of Christians, not how they came *to be* Christians. The passage also shows that (although not necessarily standard teaching) it was the view of at least one important early Christian that a man came to have this destiny through his love for Christ.

26. Colossians 1:18; Romans 1:4
27. Romans 8:29
28. Matthew 20:28; Mark 10:45
29. Luke 22:25, 26; John 13
30. Romans 8:21
31. Ephesians 1:11, 12; also 1:5, 6

32. Ephesians 1:13, 14; AV
33. Hebrews 2:10
34. Romans 8:18
35. See above, section 5.
36. Romans 8:29
37. Ephesians 1:13, 14; see also 2 Corinthians 1:22; 5:5
38. Ephesians 4:30
39. Romans 8:23
40. Romans 8:15-17
41. Galatians 4:3
42. Galatians 4:3
43. Galatians 3:24; the words *tutor* (RV, NEB) and *school-master* (AV) are misleading for they do not convey the meaning of the Greek. RSV translates it better as *custodian* and Young gives its real meaning: *child-conductor*.
44. Galatians 3:24
45. Galatians 3:25
46. Galatians 3:26
47. Galatians 4:5; Romans 8:23
48. Galatians 4:6, 7; cf. the language of Romans 8:15-17 above.
49. 2 Corinthians 3:18
50. Hebrews 2:10
51. Philippians 3:10-14
52. Colossians 1:24
53. 2 Corinthians 4:16-18
54. Romans 5:3-5 RSV
55. Romans 8:38, 39
56. Revelation 12:12
57. e.g., John 7:18; 8:50; 17:22; 13:32; 14:13; 16:14; 17:1
58. Revelation 17:16
59. Revelation 1:16; 2:12; 19:15-21
60. The "sons of God" who are conformed to Christ's image are also to be "revealed," and their brightness will add to his. (Romans 8:19, 29)
61. Isaiah 11:1-9 is a passage bringing many of these ideas together. In verse 4 there is reference to the weapon of truthful words coming from Christ's mouth. Verses 6-9 describe the idyllic peace which is to come, and verse 9 explains more how this will be achieved. "They shall not hurt nor destroy," because the earth will be filled with the knowledge of God as the waters cover the sea. The knowledge of the beauty of Christ will spread out through the universe, revealing evil and thus destroying it.
62. To the ancient world a light would have been a flame, and so fire and light are associated. One might therefore consider such verses as: 1 Corinthians 3:10-15; 2 Thessalonians 2:8; 1 John 1:5; Revelation 20:9-10; 21:23; to be associated. As the light of what God is, spreads throughout the universe, it destroys evil and purges believers. Then God's sons may live in the light of him.
63. Revelation 21:1
64. Revelation 21:2
65. Revelation 21:3, 10
66. Revelation 21:7

67. See above section 7, p. 46.
68. Revelation 22:1; Genesis 2:10
69. Revelation 22:2; Genesis 2:9; 3:22
70. Genesis 2:11, 12; Revelation 21:18-21
71. Genesis 3:8
72. Revelation 21:23
73. Revelation 22:4
74. Revelation 21:27
75. Revelation 22:2
76. Revelation 21:7
77. Revelation 22:5

PART THREE

Key Concepts in the Conflict

15

Word Study—Chosen and Elect

The subject of this study is the Greek word *eklektos*, which is translated in our versions either as "chosen" or "elect." This is used in six different contexts:[1]

(1) *Of Christ*: Luke 9:35; 23:35; 1 Peter 2:4; 2:6; (Isaiah 42:1)

(2) *Of the church in Christ*: Romans 8:33; Ephesians 1:4; Colossians 3:12; 1 Thessalonians 1:4; 2 Timothy 2:10; Titus 1:1; 1 Peter 1:2; 2:9; 5:13; 2 Peter 1:10; Revelation 17:14. (Matthew 24:22-31; Mark 13:20-27; Luke 18:7?)

(3) *Of the nation of Israel*: Acts 13:17; Romans 9:11; 11:28 (Isaiah 45:4; Deuteronomy 7:7)

(4) *Of believers within the nation of Israel*: Romans 11:5, 7.

(5) *Of the twelve disciples*: Luke 6:13; John 6:70; 13:18; 15:16, 19; Acts 1:2, 24, 25.

(6) *Of Paul*: Paul occupied a special position as an "apostle of Christ" with the others, and is thus called a "chosen vessel" in Acts 9:15. See also Acts 22:14; 1 Corinthians 9:1, 15; etc.

What did the New Testament writers mean to convey by the word *eklektos?* The primary idea in the above cases seems to be that God has bestowed an *office*. Today we often tend to think of "election" as implying unmerited privilege.[2] This may, of course, have been implied—for it is a privilege to hold an office. Nevertheless, the main idea in the New Testament seems to be one of responsibility and a task to perform. In this sense it seems to be close to the concept of a "calling" or vocation. God bestows an office, and with it he also gives a "name" or "calling" to the agent concerned. This being so, it is possible to refuse to live up to that calling, i.e., to fail in the task that one has been chosen to do. One cannot, of course, "un-call" one's self! If God has chosen us for an office then it is not possible for us to cancel his choice. We can, however, refuse to perform the task concerned.

It may be difficult for us today to grasp these aspects of the meaning attached by the Hebrews to the word *chosen*. It will therefore be useful to illustrate them by looking at some of the "elections" mentioned above.

THE ELECTION
OF THE
TWELVE DISCIPLES

Some of the aspects of this may be set out as follows:

(a) Jesus chose twelve from all his followers. . . . **he went out into the mountain to pray; and he continued all night in prayer to God. And when it was day, he called his disciples: and he chose from them twelve, whom also he named apostles.** (Luke 6:12, 13; the word *apostle* means "messenger")

And he goes up into the mountain, and calls unto him whom he himself would: and they went unto him. And he appointed twelve, that they might be with him, and that he might send them forth to preach, . . . (Mark 3:13, 14)

(b) All twelve were chosen—Judas too. **Jesus answered them, Did I not choose you the twelve, and one of you is a devil? Now he spake of Judas the son of Simon Iscariot,** for he it was that should betray him, being one of the twelve. (John 6:70, 71)

(c) Jesus foreknew their reactions. . . . you also ought to wash one another's feet. For I have given you an example, that you also should do as I have done to you. Verily, verily, I say unto you, A servant is not greater than his lord; neither one that is sent greater than he that sent him. If you know these things, blessed are you if you do them. I speak not of you all: I know whom I have chosen: but that the scripture may be fulfilled. He that eats my bread lifted up his heel against me. (John 13:14-18)

(d) The apostolic task was to witness to Jesus' life and resurrection. You did not choose me, but I chose you, and appointed you, that you should go and bear fruit . . . you also bear witness, because you have been with me from the beginning. (John 15:16, 27)

. . . of the men therefore which have companied with us all the time that the Lord Jesus went in and went out among us, beginning from the baptism of John, unto the day that he was received up from us, of these must one become a witness with us of his resurrection. (Acts 1:21, 22; see also Acts 1:2, 3; 3:15)

Him God raised up the third day, and gave him to be made manifest, not to all the people, but unto witnesses that were chosen before of God, even to us . . . And he charged us to preach unto the people. (Acts 10:40-42)

(e) Judas fell from God's chosen office for him. For he (Judas) was numbered among us, and received his portion in this ministry . . . His office let another take. Of the men therefore which have companied with us . . . of these must one become a witness with us of his resurrection . . . And they prayed, and said, You, Lord, which know the hearts of all men, show of these two the one whom you have chosen, to take the place in this ministry and apostleship, from which Judas fell away, that he might go to his own place. (Acts 1:17-25)

All too often "election" has been viewed as an irresistible ticket to blessing, rather than as the bestowal of an office.

Thus, for example, the words "You have not chosen me but I have chosen you" have been made into the assertion about God selecting who should be saved.[3] This is unjustifiable, for the whole passage is addressed specifically to the apostles.[4] The choice Jesus mentions is linked specifically to their "appointment," i.e., to apostolic office. Moreover, Judas himself was chosen with the other eleven, but "fell from his office." This is very important. Jesus says: "Did I not choose you the twelve, and one of you is a devil?" John goes on to emphasize that Judas was "one of the twelve." Jesus does not say: "I have chosen eleven of you but the other is a devil." The election of Judas was no different from that of the others. Peter does not say that Judas was never really an apostle; he says that he "fell away" from the apostolic ministry. The point is that this election had nothing to do with whether a person went to heaven or to hell; it was the bestowal of an office and a task.

There are two aspects of such a bestowal; over one a man's will has control and over the other it does not. The disciples' own wishes could not determine Jesus' choice of apostles, nor could they appoint themselves to the office. Jesus says: "You have not chosen me but I have chosen you." They did not choose to have the calling (or naming) applied to them; that choice was made in God's free strategy. It was based on his foreknowledge, but was not directed by any human will. The office, calling, and task to fulfill, were ordained by God alone.

What God did not ordain was how they would match up to the task he had allotted them. Eleven of them chose to fulfill their calling through the power of the Spirit. Not, of course, that they could do anything in their own strength. "Without me," said Christ, "you can do nothing."[5] It is only possible to wage Christ's warfare if one is fighting in him and in the strength of his might. We cannot achieve the task God gives us without his aid. (He does not expect us to.) There is, however, something on which his aid is conditional. Let us note carefully Paul's words in Romans 7: "in me, that is, in my flesh, dwells no good thing": Man is bound to sin, sold under sin, carnal, hopeless, impotent.

But, after this most complete statement of human depravity, Paul goes on: "I can will what is right but I cannot do it." (verse 18; RSV) God wants us to have a *willingness* to perform the task; he supplies the means. In the eleven faithful apostles, athough the "flesh was weak," the "spirit was willing."[6] This was what God wanted of them, willingness, and he would not force it on them. But although the eleven were willing to perform their task through God's power, Judas was not. He had received the same calling, he had been chosen and appointed to the same office, he had shared in the ministry of that office, but he fell away from it. Peter does not say that God made Judas fall away, he simply says that he did fall away. It was his own choice. It was not that he could somehow un-choose or un-call himself, for both calling and election were Jesus' decision. What Judas could (and did) do was to fall away from the ministry he had been given, and so forfeit the blessing he could have brought and enjoyed.

The election of the apostles was unmerited. It was an office none of them had earned, and none had taken for himself. It was an unmerited privilege, but (as always in God's dealings) it involved responsibility of like proportion. Being named as an apostle brought the great opportunity to be built by God into the foundations of the church of Christ.[7] But to that one who fell from this ministry, his privilege turned to great condemnation and crushing guilt at the enormity of his sin. Privilege from God is an opportunity for blessing, but also for condemnation. The same principle applies (below) to the election of Israel. Not only salvation but also condemnation came "first to the Jew and also to the Gentile."[8] Election is an office, a responsibility, a privilege. It is never an irresistible selection for final blessing.

God, of course, assigns callings according to his foreknowledge. But although Jesus may have known the hearts and reactions of those he chose, nevertheless his choice of Judas was no different from his choice of John. He said that he knew a disciple would betray him, but he did not *cause* Judas to fall.

THE ELECTION
OF THE NATION
OF ISRAEL

The election of Israel shows many similarities to the election of the apostles. Some of these may be summarized into sections similar to those used for the apostles:

(a) God chose them alone from all the nations.

(b) The whole nation was chosen.

(c) God knew in advance what their reactions would be.

(d) Their task was to prepare the way for the Messiah to bless the world, and then "arise and shine" with him.

(e) Some fell away from God's purpose for them.

Other similarities also exist: The choice of the nation of Israel, like that of the apostles, did not determine their final destiny as individuals; it had nothing to do with whether they went to heaven or to hell.[9] Paul, in fact, strongly attacks in Romans 2 and 9 the idea that national election was a pledge of national salvation. Their election concerned the office and function to which the nation was called in this earthly life. Its only connection with the issue of heaven and hell was that the greater responsibility it brought would give greater opportunity for blessing if they repented and greater condemnation if they rejected God's plan for themselves. Both salvation and condemnation came to the Jew first and also to the Gentile.

Like the election of the apostles, the election of Israel was unmerited and unearned. Jesus said: "You have not chosen me but I have chosen you"; Paul said of the choice of Israel: "It is not of him that wills, nor of him that runs, but of God that has mercy." God's choice of Israel was declared while Israel and Edom were both still in the same womb. It was not earned, either by works or by foreseen works. Their election was not something they took for themselves. It was a choice made in God's free strategy. This is not to say that it was arbitrary, for God doubtless foreknew, when he made it, what Jacob's (and Israel's) reaction would be. It may even be that we can discern something in the attitudes of

Jacob and Esau that explains the choice (though it certainly is not "works," for Jacob's behavior was far from exemplary).

Though Israel's election by God was free, unmerited, and unearned, the privilege it brought was accompanied by great responsibility. God had put his name upon the sons of Israel[10] and they had to live up to this calling (or naming). Some of them were reprobate and failed in this. Therefore the name of God was blasphemed among the Gentiles because of it.[11] Jews who did not live up to the task that was implied by their chosenness lost the blessing God intended. In Paul's day this was true of those who failed to arise and shine as God intended when the great light of Jesus came to them.[12] If they refused to repent and become part of a golden vessel to shine forth bringing honor to God, they would be under his wrath and be used instead as a vessel to no-honor (see section 12). The great thing about God is that he is able, in his foreknowledge, to make use even of those who rebel against him. Thus, although Judas rejected him, God used this rejection to set in motion the events leading to Christ's atoning death. Similarly, although some Israelites fell away, God used them to stimulate others to repentance.[13]

There is one important difference between the election of the twelve disciples and that of Israel: the latter, unlike the former, had a strong corporate aspect. It was the *nation* which was the elect rather than the individuals in it who were elect. God obviously did not choose to make certain people into Jacob's descendants. Rather, it was because they were such descendants that they were elect. Being born into the nation, they were born into its election. But this was not the only way for a person to enter the election of the nation. Ruth is an example of someone who did not enter this election by birth but by choice. To Naomi she said: **your people shall be my people, and your God my God.**[14] It was clearly her own choice to become a proselyte to the Jewish nation and faith. In entering the nation she entered also its election. We see this clearly from the fact that she was the great grandmother of King David, and so was an ancestor of Jesus himself.[15] We must remember that the whole election of the nation, as announced to Abraham, was with the object of preparing for a seed (Christ) through whom all nations would be blessed. Ruth, although she entered the election of the nation by choice and not by birth, partook of that election so completely as to become part of the line of descent to that seed. Ruth was not chosen to become part of the nation of Israel; rather, in becoming part of that nation she entered its chosenness.

THE ELECTION
OF BELIEVERS
WITHIN ISRAEL

We must now also consider a slightly different use Paul makes of the word *elect*. Not only does he regard the whole nation of Israel as elect, but he also speaks of a remnant within the nation who are "elect according to grace."[16] What does he mean?

We should bear in mind certain features of the epistle to the Romans. The first is its repeated contention that within Israel, no less than in other nations, there has always been a believing and an unbelieving section.[17] The second is that, in Romans, Paul contrasts "works" with "faith" and "works" with "grace," but never "faith" with "grace." To him, faith-grace were inseparable. Romans 4:2-6 reads: **For if Abraham was justified by works, he has whereof to glory; but not toward God. For what says the Scripture? And Abraham had faith in God and it was reckoned unto him for righteousness. Now to him that works, the reward is not reckoned as of grace, but as of debt. But to him that works not, but has faith in him that justifies the ungodly, his faith is reckoned for righteousness. Even as David also pronounces blessing upon the man, unto whom God reckons righteousness apart from works . . .**[18] Paul is here contrasting the concept of God (in his grace reckoning faith as right-standing) with the Jewish rabbinical concept (right-standing *earned* through works of the Law—see section 20). He does not, of course, mean that God gave Abraham no choice but to have faith. What he says is that *in itself* Abraham's faith earned him nothing, but it was *reckoned* as right-standing. Faith brings right-standing only because God, in his grace, reckons it as such on the basis of Christ's finished work. Thus faith and grace are inseparable, and faith-grace is contrasted with works-debt, for both grace and faith are unnecessary to a principle of works of the Law.

This pattern is well reflected in Romans 9-11. Paul notes that the Jews are "following after"[19] or "seeking"[20] a right-standing before God. They are, in fact, so obsessed with it that, in comparison, the Gentile interest is as nothing: **What shall we say then? That the Gentiles, which followed not after righteousness, attained to righteousness, even the righteousness which is of faith: but Israel, following after a law of righteousness, did not arrive at that law. Wherefore? Because they sought it not by faith, but as it were by works . . . For being ignorant of God's righteousness, and seeking to establish their own, they did not subject themselves to the righteousness of God. For Christ is the end of the law unto righteousness to everyone that has faith.**[21] Romans 10 continues to explain that all the "work" necessary has been done by Christ. Confession and faith in him are all that is needed. Then, in chapter 11, Paul returns to the contrast between faith-grace and works-law: **Even so then at this present time also there is a remnant according to the election of grace. But if it is by grace, it is no more of works: otherwise grace is no more grace. What then? That which Israel seeks for, that he obtained not; but the election obtained it . . .**[22] What Israel sought was obtained only by those who had sought it in God's way and so had obtained his grace. The rabbis believed that if a man entered into the election of the nation of Israel (either by birth or by choice) he was assured of a right standing before God.[23] Paul denies this, for to enter the "election" of the nation is insufficient; a man must also enter the "grace-election" or "election of grace." How may a man do this? Paul does not reiterate it in Romans 11:7, but he has already given us the answer: it is by confession and faith. God did not issue some arbitrary fiat as to who should partake of the election of grace. Grace is given to those who seek it in God's way of faith.[24]

This may be seen in Paul's development in these chapters of the "remnant" idea in the Old Testament. In chapter 9 he uses various allegories to show that not all of Israel are living up to what their name, heritage, and election signify. In Romans 9:21 he affirms that although, in Jeremiah's parable of the potter, God treats nations as units, he has now divided the lump of Israel to make *two* vessels. Paul then makes a digression dealing with Gentiles, and returns to deal with Israel in Romans 9:27-29: **And Isaiah cries concerning Israel, If the number of the children of Israel be as the sand of the sea, it is the remnant that shall be saved: for the Lord will execute his word on the earth, finishing it and cutting it short. And, as Isaiah has said before, Except the Lord of Sabaoth had left us a seed, We had become as Sodom, and had been made like unto Gomorrah.** This quotation is from the very first chapter of Isaiah, where the Lord adds: **If you are willing and obedient you shall eat the good of the land; but if you refuse and rebel, you shall be devoured by the sword; . . . Zion shall be redeemed by justice, and those in her who repent, by righteousness. But rebels and sinners shall be destroyed together, and those who forsake the Lord shall be consumed.** (Isaiah 1:19, 20, 27, 28 RSV) Only those who repent and are faithful will form a remnant to rebuild the nation. Thus he later says: **And it shall come to pass in that day, that the remnant of Israel, and they that are escaped of the house of Jacob, shall no more again stay upon him that smote them; but shall stay upon the Lord, the Holy One of Israel, in truth. A remnant shall return, even the remnant of Jacob, unto the mighty God. For though your people Israel be as the sand of the sea, only a remnant of them shall return.**[25] If the Lord had not let the faithful remnant live, then the nation would have ceased to exist—just as did Sodom. These passages of Isaiah certainly vindicate Paul's assertion that there has always been a believing and an unbelieving part within Israel.

Turning to Paul's other reference we find in 1 Kings 19:

17, 18: **him that escapes from the sword of Hazael shall Jehu slay: and him that escapes from the sword of Jehu shall Elisha slay. Yet will I leave me seven thousand in Israel, all the knees which have not bowed unto Baal.** Strictly literally, the Hebrew in both these verses is in the past tense, but both verses clearly refer to future events.[26] The meaning is that in the coming civil war, amid all the carnage, God will preserve seven thousand men who have stayed faithful to him. As is common in Hebrew, the coming events promised by God are regarded as so certain as to be put in the past tense. Paul himself recognized this practice[27] and must surely have understood its usage in Kings; although in Romans 11:4 he translates the Hebrew literally: **I have left for myself seven thousand men who have not bowed the knee to Baal.**

Paul's citation of this particular incident may reflect some of the personal anguish he felt for Israel. Although so many of the Israelites have rejected his gospel, his heart yearns for his people. As a true Hebrew his whole being revolts at the idea that God has cast off his people.[28] So he turns to consider the time when, as far as Elijah was concerned, things looked even blacker. Elijah thought that he alone was left; God must now have given them up. Yet God could say that seven thousand men were still faithful to him and would be spared in the coming judgment meted out by his two anointed kings and his prophet. The story, then, illustrates two things. It shows that there has always been a faithful and an unfaithful section in Israel. It shows that even in the blackest periods many have remained faithful.

What decided whether or not a man was part of this remnant? Isaiah had testified that much of the Law was kept even by those whom God condemned.[29] Elijah says that the altars and methods of fulfilling the Law have been destroyed, and since the seven thousand lived in the northern kingdom they did not even have the Temple. Yet God accepted them—so it could not have been "works of the Law" that made them right with him. Paul does not draw out these points in Romans 11, but simply says: **Even so** then at this present time also there is a remnant according to the election of grace. But if it is by grace, it is no more of works: otherwise grace is no more grace. When then? That which Israel seeks for that he obtained not; but the election obtained it, and the rest were hardened:[30] This shows some resemblance to Romans 4:14-16: For if they which are of the Law be heirs, faith is made void, . . . For this cause it is of faith, that it may be according to grace; to the end that the promise may be sure to all the seed.

The phrase "according to" (Gk: *Kata*, with accusative) is rather imprecise. But, clearly, to Paul a blessing that has to be received by faith is still "according to grace," in contrast with one that depends on works of the Law. Works "makes void" both grace and faith, for grace and faith are complementary. Thus from God's point of view what distinguished the remnant was that they had received grace; while from their own point of view the path to receiving grace was through repentance and faith. Has God cast off his elect nation of Israel? No, for there is also within the nation a remnant who are elect as far as grace is concerned, an election of grace. It is not enough to enter into the elect nation, one must enter also into the election of grace. Israel, apart from the remnant, did not achieve the right-standing they sought, because they sought it through works and not through faith. Only the remnant who sought it in God's way achieved it. The rest were blinded to the clear indications of the messiahship of Jesus. Because they sought right-standing through works, they "stumbled at the stone of stumbling."[31]

THE ELECTION
OF CHRIST

The election of Christ shows differences as well as similarities to the other "elections" already dealt with. In the book of Isaiah God speaks of the coming Messiah in similar terms to those used of Israel; thus we find a similarity. To Israel he says: But you, Israel, my servant, Jacob whom I have chosen . . . You are my servant, I have chosen you

and not cast you away.[32] Then of the Messiah he says:
**Behold my servant, whom I uphold; my chosen, in whom
my soul delights; I have put my spirit upon him; he shall
bring forth judgment to the Gentiles.**[33] The Messiah, like
the nation, was chosen to do a task. He was chosen to be
the suffering servant who would be a light to the Gentiles.
The same idea recurs in Isaiah 49. In verse 3 God says:
You are my servant; Israel, in whom I will be glorified. He
seems, however, to be giving this task to Israel's Messiah,
for *he* is the One who fulfilled Israel's task of bringing God
glory. The first of the tasks assigned to him is to "bring
back Jacob and gather Israel unto God" (verse 5). The second
task is: **I will also give you for a light to the Gentiles, that
you may be my salvation unto the end of the earth.**[34] The
next verse again introduces the idea of the chosenness of
the Messiah to whom God speaks—though the LXX introduced it even earlier in the passage by translating verse 2:
"He has made me a choice (*eklekton*) arrow." We also,
incidentally, see a reference in verse 2 to the type of
weapon the Messiah will use: **he has made my mouth like
a sharp sword.**[35]

But, although the Messiah has been chosen for a task, we
should not think that the idea of selection is strong here. It
would be strange if not blasphemous were we to think of
God as passing by other "possible candidates" for the Messiahship.[36] Jesus was *the* eternal Son. No one else was
good enough to pay the price of sin. It is not selection but
function that we must understand from "chosen."

We may understand this better if we realize the close
connection between the words *eklektos* (chosen) and
agapētos (beloved) in reference to Christ. This is shown
most clearly in the way in which the Gospel writers translate into Greek the words which God spoke (presumably in
the Aramaic language) during the transfiguration of Christ.
Matthew renders it: **This is my beloved (*agapētos*) Son,
in whom I am well pleased; hear you him.**[37] Mark is
similar: **This is my beloved (*agapētos*) Son: hear you
him.**[38] Luke, however, renders the same words using the
Greek word for chosen: **This is my Son, my chosen (*ekle-***

legmenos): **hear you him.**[39] We thus see that when the word *elect* or *chosen* is applied to Christ, its primary meaning is not one of selection, but one of belovedness. The point may also be illustrated from Matthew's rendering of Isaiah 42:1. The Hebrew of Isaiah reads: **Behold my servant, whom I uphold; my chosen, in whom my soul delights.** The LXX quite naturally renders the word *chosen* by the Greek *eklektos*, but Matthew does not follow the LXX in this instance. Instead he renders the Hebrew using the Greek word *agapētos* (beloved), thus: **Behold my servant whom I have chosen; My beloved** (*agapētos*) **in whom my soul is well pleased.**[40] Matthew, therefore, uses the word *beloved* as a substitute for the word *chosen* in this context. This type of interpretation of the word *chosen* is not unlike that of the LXX itself when it speaks of choice silver[41] or describes a beautiful girl as "choice as the sun."[42] The emphasis is not on selection, but on the value set on the object described.

Only three other verses in the New Testament refer directly to Christ's chosenness. In two of them the connection with belovedness is marked.[43] Thus in 1 Peter 2:4 we find that he is: "a living stone . . . with God elect, precious" and in 1 Peter 2:6 that he is "a chief cornerstone, elect, precious." The double linking of the election of Christ to his preciousness to God shows us the connotation of the term.

We must, therefore, bear this link in mind when we consider the election of Christ. Since also the church is elect *in Christ* we will find that the same link is important to the next section.

THE ELECTION OF THE CHURCH

The central idea in the election of the church may be seen from Ephesians 1:4: it is that we are chosen *in Christ.* The church is elect because it is in Christ and he is elect. There is, moreover, a task involved in the election. The previous verse of Ephesians states that we have been "blessed with every spiritual blessing in the heavenlies in Christ." This is, indeed, a blessing, but it is also a call to battle. It is in the heavenlies that the battle against powers of wickedness is raging.[44] Being chosen in Christ implies that we are to fight in the armor which he wore as Messiah, the armor of God.[45] This is our calling, our vocation, and God's chosen task for us in Christ. We have already seen how the words of Isaiah 49 apply to the Messiah, describing his task as to "bring back Israel," and to act as "a light to the Gentiles." We know that the church also has to act as the "light of the world" just as Christ is the "light of the world."[46] We will not, therefore, be surprised to find Paul and Barnabas applying the words of Isaiah 49 (about being a light of the Gentiles) to their own task as part of Christ's body the church.[47] They have taken up the task of the chosen One of God, for they are part of his body and share in his chosenness.[48] We also find that God's discription of the Messiah in Isaiah 49:3 as One "in whom I will be glorified" may be extended to the church in Christ. Thus in Ephesians 3: 21: **unto him be the glory in the church and in Christ Jesus unto all generations** . . .

Later in the church's history rather different ideas arose concerning the election of the believers, perhaps because the New Testament mentions it only a few times. Since the early fifth century a most common idea concerning election is that it determines who should become Christians, i.e., who should repent.[49] Thus God was pictured as selecting some to be made to repent, and passing over others whom he could equally well have selected had he so wished. This idea, surely, has no Scriptural foundation.[50] The Bible does not say that we are chosen *to be put into* Christ, but that we were chosen *in Christ*. Our election is not separate from his election. The meaning of Christ's election was certainly not that he should repent, and since it is this same election that we share *in Christ*, how can it be anything to do with why we repented? We may well believe that God, in his grace, placed us in Christ (to share his election) *because* we repented; but it is an in-

131

verse logic that ascribes the repentance itself to the election. Christ's election implied two things for him: (a) a task and (b) a belovedness. This is what it also implies for us when we share in that election.

This comes out strongly in Ephesians 1:3-14: **Blessed be the God and Father of our Lord Jesus Christ, who has blessed us with every spiritual blessing in the heavenly places in Christ: even as he chose us in him before the foundation of the world, that we should be holy and without blemish before him in love: having foreordained us unto adoption as sons through Jesus Christ unto himself, according to the good pleasure of his will, to the praise of the glory of his grace, which he freely bestowed on us in the Beloved: in whom we have our redemption through his blood, the forgiveness of our trespasses, according to the riches of his grace, which he made to abound toward us in all wisdom and prudence, having made known unto us the mystery of his will, according to his good pleasure which he purposed in him unto a dispensation of the fullness of the times, to sum up all things in Christ, the things in the heavens, and the things upon the earth; in him, I say, in whom also we were made a heritage, having been foreordained according to the purpose of him who works[51] all things after the counsel of his will; to the end that we should be unto the praise of his glory, we who had before hoped in Christ: in whom you also, having heard the word of the truth, the gospel of your salvation,—in whom, having also believed, you were sealed with the Holy Spirit of promise, which is an earnest of our inheritance, unto the redemption of God's own possession, unto the praise of his glory.**

This passage shows us how we must be careful never to belittle the work of Christ for us. Christ is belittled if we think that God first forgave and redeemed us and *then* put us in Christ; we should rather believe that it is only *in Christ* that we have received redemption and forgiveness. Christ is also belittled if we think that God first chose us and then put us in Christ; it is rather that those in Christ share in his election, and so are chosen in him. There are, in fact, many wonderful things that the church has *in Christ*:

(a) 1:3; 2:6—we have been blessed with all spiritual blessing and made to sit in the heavenlies *in Christ*

(b) 1:4—we have been chosen *in Christ*

(c) 1:6—we have been favored with God's grace *in Christ*

(d) 1:7—we have received redemption and forgiveness *in Christ*

(e) 1:11; 1:13—we have received an inheritance and a guarantee of that inheritance *in Christ*

(f) 2:13—the Jews and Gentiles have received a unity of reconciliation *in Christ*

(g) 3:12—we now have boldness and access to God with confidence *in Christ*

A second major point from the passage is the association of our position and heritage in Christ with a task. In 1:3 and 2:6 we find that we are seated in Christ in the heavenlies, which is where the battle is at present raging (6:12). In 1:5 we find that it is in and through Christ that we have received our destiny of "adoption." As we saw in section 14, this adoption refers to our future revelation as sons of God who have been conformed to the image of his Son, which revelation is to release the creation from its present bondage. In 1:11 this predestiny is quite naturally linked with the inheritance we have received in Christ: that as co-heirs with him we shall have the task of reigning with him.[52] We have also (1:14) received a guarantee or seal of this inheritance in the form of the Holy Spirit or Spirit of adoption.[53] Neither chosenness nor predestination concern how we came to be Christians. Chosenness concerns our present position and task in Christ. Predestination concerns our future task and inheritance with and through him.

We note one last point from this passage, a hint rather than an explicit teaching. We have seen how the chosenness of Christ emphasized belovedness rather than selection. The present passage shows the connection incidentally in 1:6: **his grace, which he freely bestowed upon us in the Beloved:** The grace received in the Beloved is thus placed in close juxtaposition with our sharing in his chosenness or belovedness.

The connection is much stronger in other passages. Thus we read: **Put on therefore, as God's elect, holy and beloved, a heart of . . .** We also read: **knowing brethren, beloved of God, your election, how that . . .**[54] The link is even found when Paul uses another word for chosenness: **we are bound to give thanks to God alway for you, brethren beloved of the Lord, for that God chose you from the . . .**[55] This is a rather different context, but shows how strong was the association of ideas between belovedness and any concept of chosenness. The connection is even seen in other uses of *eklektos*.[56] Certainly we must at least conclude that when *eklektos* is used of the church, no less than when it is used of Christ, the implication of belovedness rather than of selection suggests itself.

The emphasis on our chosenness being *in Christ* is deeply embedded in most of the eleven New Testament references to the election of the church. In 2 Timothy 2:10-12 we read: **Therefore I endure all things for the elect's sakes, that they also may obtain the salvation which is in Christ Jesus, with eternal glory. Faithful is the saying: For if we died with him we shall also live with him: If we endure, we shall also reign with him:** These verses are paralleled in Romans 8:17, 18. Their meaning is that the elect are those who in Christ will achieve the future salvation, the liberation of creation with eternal glory, and the reigning over it with Christ. The Christ-centeredness of election is apparent.

Paul also mentions election in Romans 8:32-34: **He that spared not his own son, but delivered him up for us all, how shall he not also with him freely give us all things? Who shall lay anything to the charge of God's elect? It is God that justifies. Who is he that shall condemn? It is Christ Jesus that died, yea rather, that was raised from the dead, who is at the right hand of God.** It is important to remember that the issue of "no condemnation" was first raised in Romans 8:1—**There is therefore now no condemnation to them that are in Christ Jesus.** There is no condemnation "to the ones in Christ," and when Paul returns to this theme in Romans 8:33, 34 he naturally refers to "the chosen ones of God." They are chosen *in Christ,* and so are free from condemnation. The link may become even clearer to us if we consider Isaiah 50:6-9: *I gave my back to the smiters and my cheeks to them that plucked off the hair. I hid not my face from shame and spitting. For the Lord God will help me; therefore have I not been confounded: therefore have I set my face like a flint, and I know that I shall not be ashamed. He is near that justifies me; who shall contend with me? Let us stand up together; who is mine adversary? let him come near to me. Behold the Lord God will help me; who is he that shall condemn me?* In this passage Isaiah is speaking of the Messiah, the elect One of Isaiah 49:7. Paul, however, in Romans 8:31, 33, 34, applies these words to the church, the "elect ones of God." Surely the thinking behind this is that the "elect ones" are able to say "Who shall condemn?" because they are in Christ, the elect servant of God, who alone could say such a thing in his own right. We are elect and free from condemnation only because we are in the elect One of God.

The implications of being chosen in Christ may be made clearer by analogy, and it might be best to begin with an analogy implied in Scripture itself. This is the analogy of God's choice of Jacob. The descendants of Jacob were not chosen *to be put into* Jacob; rather, they were chosen *in* Jacob. Their chosenness was not distinct from his chosenness. Individuals were chosen only because they were part of the chosen nation; the election was a corporate one. This is even clearer if we consider Gentiles who became proselytized into the Jewish nation and faith.

We have already looked at a good example of this in the person of Ruth the Moabitess. In becoming an Israelite she became part of the chosen nation. She was now chosen *in* the nation of Israel. This did not mean that she was chosen *to be put into* Israel, for that was her own decision. Rather, she was chosen *in* Israel, and Israel's election had now become her election. Likewise all other proselytes entered into Israel and so shared Israel's election.

An obvious parallel exists between this and the Christian's election in Christ. When people enter into Christ then not only does his death become theirs, but his election becomes their election. They are chosen in him, and this chosenness was established even before the foundation of the world. But to be chosen in him is not the same as being chosen to be put into him. The validity of this analogy with the election of Israel as a nation seems to be implied by the Apostle Peter. He first mentions election in 1 Peter 1:1, 2, calling his readers "elect according to the foreknowledge of God." He returns to the subject in chapter 2, noting first Christ's election and then their own.[57] He also draws a close analogy between their position as Christians, and that of Israel. They are an elect race, a royal priesthood, a holy nation, and a people of God (1 Peter 2:9, 10), descriptions first applied to Israel in Exodus 19:5, 6. Peter makes more mention of the election of the church than any other New Testament writer, and it is significant that he chooses deliberately to maintain its close analogy with the election of Israel as a nation.

The prime point is that the election of the church is a corporate rather than an individual thing. It is not that individuals are in the church because they are elect, it is rather that they are elect because they are in the church, which is the body of the elect One. Ruth was not chosen to become an Israelite but in becoming an Israelite she partook of Israel's election. A Christian is not chosen to become part of Christ's body, but in becoming part of that body he partakes of Christ's election. Although God, in his foreknowledge, doubtless knew which individuals would repent and so be joined by him[58] to Christ's body, this is not at all the same thing as picking them out to make them repent. God's choice is not an individual one of who should repent; it is a corporate choice of the church in Christ. Peter recognizes its corporate nature, and again seems to treat it as such in his last mention in 1 Peter 5:13: **She that is in Babylon, elect together with you** (or "co-elect") **salutes you.**

Another analogy may be drawn from the time of the flood. Noah was the only righteous man and so he alone found grace in the eyes of the Lord.[59] God chose Noah to start a new world when the existing one had been destroyed: **And the Lord said to Noah, Come you and all your**

house into the ark; for you have I seen righteous before me in this generation.[60] In a sense, therefore, Noah's family were "chosen in him." It was not that God selected seven people to be made into Noah's family. Rather, because they were his family they shared in his election. Similarly we might metaphorically be said to share in the election of Christ because we are joined with him as his family. We are chosen in Christ.

Those in the early church seem to have grasped much more readily than ourselves the concept of being chosen in Christ. Ignatius, for example, wrote soon after the apostolic age. At the beginning of his letter to Ephesus, the corporate nature of our election and predestination comes out strongly. He writes: "Ignatius to the church at Ephesus . . . being blessed through the greatness and fullness of God the Father, and predestined before the world began, that it should be always unto an enduring and unchangeable glory; being united and chosen through his true passion, according to the will of the Father . . ." We see here Ignatius' vision of the corporate nature of our destiny and election. It is not that selected individuals have been destined to join the church, but rather that the church as a whole, as a unit, has received a future destiny. Similarly we notice that he does not say "chosen to be united" or even "chosen and united." He says: "united and chosen through (Jesus') true passion." The unity is put, logically, before the election, and the election is attributed to Christ's achievement as the elect One.

The teachings of the apostles are even more clearly represented in the first epistle of Clement. This epistle is one of the earliest noncanonical Christian writings in existence. It was never regarded as inspired Scripture, but was held in great respect by the early church and even appears in one of the three main early codices of the Bible. It is, in fact, a letter from the church at Rome to the church at Corinth, though Clement is universally accepted as one of the leaders in Rome who may have compiled it. The writer is accepted as being one of the immediate successors of the apostles, and he shows good understanding of salvation by faith.[61] He grasps clearly the apostolic teaching that our election is "in Christ," like other privileges, though he slightly changes the emphasis. This change of emphasis is in that instead of saying in (*en*) Christ, Clement says through or by (*dia*) Christ. Since we are elect in Christ it is only because of, or through him, that we are elect. Election in Christ implies election "through" him. Thus Clement says: "God . . . who has chosen our Lord Jesus Christ, and us through him to be his special people . . . the grace of our Lord Jesus Christ be with you, and with all that are anywhere named by God through him."[62] Here Clement directly links the election of Christ with the election of those who are "chosen through him." We note also the reference to Christians as God's "special People," making this passage reminiscent of 1 Peter 2. Christ's election comes to us through him because we enter into him. Clement repeats this idea elsewhere,[63] and it is not ignored by other Christian writers such as Clement of Alexandria.[64]

In summary, we see that the consistent apostolic and early church teaching was that Christians are chosen only in and through Christ. There is never any hint that they were chosen to be put into Christ. Rather, as members of his body they share in his election.

POSTSCRIPT

Words from the Greek word group *klētos, kaleō, kaleomai,* and *klēsis* are usually translated "called" or "calling." The word, as in English, can mean either "invited" or "named." In the New Testament the latter meaning seems to be the more usual: e.g., **he should be called a Nazarene.**[65] With the special significance of names in Hebrew thought, there was great meaning in the Lord's words to Peter: **You shall be called Cephas.** This was the "calling" of Peter, almost equivalent to setting a vocation. In similar vein are the words: **Every male that opens the womb shall be called holy to the Lord.**[66] Likewise we read that Paul was "named an apostle"[67] and that we are "named saints" and "named children of God."[68] We are told, therefore, to live up to our

"calling" or "vocation."[69] We should make our calling and
election sure,[70] for those who overcome with Christ are
called and chosen and faithful.[71] There seems, then, to be
little difference between being "chosen in Christ" and
"called children of God," other than that of emphasis.[72]
This is what we have assumed in the above section.

For this reason one can only take Jesus' words: "Many
are called but few are chosen" to be intended as a cryptic
paradox similar to his words "seeing they see not."[73] He
seems to be playing on the double meaning of *klētos*, intending to convey: "Many are invited [called] but few are
named [called]." Instead of using *klētos* for the second adjective, the Lord substitutes the equivalent term "chosen,"
to show better his meaning.

A further point of interest is that the wedding guest,
whose invitation had been quite genuine, was cast out for
not wearing a wedding garment. This garment surely represents the work of Christ in us and is therefore the mark
of those who are "chosen in him." Perhaps Jesus means
that many receive the name but few are really abiding and
chosen in Christ. There may even be a connection with
John 15:6, which pictures the "casting out" of branches that
do not abide in Christ. In any event this particular saying
of Jesus does seem to be rather cryptic, and one should
hesitate before attempting to be dogmatic about its meaning. The lesson for us, however, seems to be the same as
that in 2 Peter 1:10—give the more diligence to make your
calling and election sure.

NOTES

1. The list given includes verses containing the adjectival or
verbal forms of the word, as well as the noun (*eklektos*). The verses
"Many are called but few are chosen" are not listed, but are dealt
with at the end of the section. The only other uses of the word
choice or *election* are in Luke 10:42; 14:7; Acts 6:5; 15:7; 15:22; 15:
25; Romans 16:13; 1 Corinthians 1:27, 28; 1 Timothy 5:21; James 2:5;
2 John 1, 13. None of these is important to our study.

2. We are referring here, of course, to "election" in the religious
sense, not to its political usage to describe a democratic process. In
the religious sense "election" is a *choice* made by God, though further
aspects of the word will be seen from the study.

3. It is interesting to see the difficulties into which Augustine placed himself in this respect. His attitude to "election" is reflected in the following passage: "He, therefore, works the beginning of our faith who works all things; because faith itself does not precede that calling of which it is said . . . 'Not of works but of Him that calls.' (although he might have said 'of him that believes'); and the election which the Lord signified when He said: 'You have not chosen me but I have chosen you.' For He chose us, not because we believed but that we might believe, lest we should be said first to have chosen Him, and so His word be false" (*Predestination of the Saints*, sec 38).

Here he takes Romans 9:11 (which is speaking of the election of *Israel*) and John 15:16 (which is speaking of the election of the *apostles*) and applies both comments as though they referred to the election of *believers in Christ*. Augustine quotes John 15:16 seven times in the space of a few paragraphs, and although he recognizes that the words are addressed "to the disciples" he clearly equates this election with the election of believers. Now Augustine also believed that such election brought irresistible blessing, thus: "Those then, are elected, as has often been said, who are called according to the purpose, who are also predestinated and foreknown. If any one of them perishes God is mistaken; but none of them perishes, because God is not mistaken" (*Rebuke and Grace*, section 14). This immediately leads him to a difficulty, for if Judas was chosen, and such chosenness brings irresistible blessing, then how could he fall away? Augustine, therefore, goes on: "Moreover they are elected to reign with Christ, not as Judas was elected to a work for which he was fitted . . . When, therefore, we hear 'Have I not chosen you twelve, and one of you is a devil?' we ought to understand that the rest were elected through mercy, but he through judgment; those to obtain His kingdom, he to shed His blood!"

Augustine is not simply saying here that Judas received a similar election to the others but that it had a different *effect* on him. This would be true enough, but it would not be consistent with his assertion that "none of them perishes, because God is not mistaken." Augustine, therefore, has to suppose that the election of Judas was somehow different from theirs, i.e., it was an election to a different task. Given his theology it is difficult to see what other conclusion he could have reached, but the distinction he tries to make is simply not supported in the Scripture. The Scripture says that Jesus chose *twelve* and named (or "called") them apostles. It in no way implies that the election or calling of Judas was in any way different. Moreover, Peter says that Judas "fell away" from the ministry for which he had been chosen; he does not say that Judas was chosen for a different purpose.

We must try in our thinking to maintain distinctions between "elections" where the Bible makes such distinctions—and not make distinctions where it does not.

4. In John 13:5 we read that Jesus began to wash the disciples' feet. In John 13:12 we read that when he had washed their feet he sat down and began to talk to them. Verse 16 refers to their task as "servants" who are to be "sent." In verse 18 he says that not all will

follow his words. He "knows" or "understands fully" those whom he has chosen, and realizes that the Scriptures will be fulfilled that one of them will betray him. This verse is markedly similar to John 6:70—Did I not choose you the twelve, and one of you is a devil? The word *chosen* refers to his choice of them as apostles, not to the election of believers. Verse 18 finishes with a reference to "him that eats bread with me," and verse 21 reemphasizes that it is one of them, the apostles, who shall betray him. The whole discourse is addressed to the twelve apostles, and, after Judas leaves, to the remaining eleven. In John 14:26 Jesus promises them that the Holy Spirit will teach them all things and remind them of what he has told them. This verse is surely a key verse concerning their special authority *as apostles*, to set out Christ's teachings; it applies to them in a way it has not applied to anyone else. John 15:3 continues the pattern with a reference back to 13:10, again concerning the eleven. John 15:27 refers specifically to their apostolic function as witnesses —reminding us, among other verses, of the Acts 10:40 reference to "witnesses that were chosen before of God."

The whole of the last supper discourse, then, even up to 18:1 where Jesus rose *with his disciples*, is addressed to the apostles as his chosen witnesses. Some of his words, to be sure, we may apply to other Christians as well, but we must be careful which of his words we use in this way. Verses like John 14:26 and 15:27 refer specifically to aspects of their ministry as apostles, and no direct application may be made to others.

With this in mind, what are we to understand from the words in John 15:16? They are: "You have not *chosen* me, but I *chose* you and *appointed* you." Both of these words *chosen* and *appointed*, are words the Gospels use in definite reference to their apostleship. In Luke 6:13 we see how Jesus *chose* twelve, and he says in John 6:70— "Did I not choose you the twelve . . ." In Mark 3:14 we read how he *appointed* twelve to preach and receive authority. It is, therefore, very difficult indeed to see how John 15:16 could be referring to anything other than Jesus' choice and appointment of them *to be apostles*. There is no thought whatsoever that this "choice" might concern whether they went to heaven or to hell.

5. John 15:5
6. Matthew 26:41
7. Revelation 21:14
8. Romans 2:9, 10
9. In note 3 above, we have seen how Augustine applied Romans 9:11 to eternal salvation. In *Enchiridion*, chapter 25, he made it clear that he took this whole passage of Romans to imply that Esau was damned and Jacob was saved. This is, however, a strange interpretation. Since the context is speaking of the two *nations* Israel and Edom it would imply that all Edomites were damned and all Israelites were saved. This is, ironically, exactly the view that Paul is attacking in Romans 9!

The words of Romans 9:11 do not refer to anyone's eternal destiny, but to the office to which the nation of Israel was elected by God in this life.

10. Numbers 6:27

11. Ezekiel 36:20; Romans 2:24

12. Isaiah 60:1

13. See section 12, pp. 85, 86.

14. Ruth 1:16

15. Ruth 4:22; Luke 3:23-32

16. More precisely "an election of grace" or "grace-election"; Romans 11:5-7

17. The first such comparison of the believing with the unbelieving is in Romans 1:16-18: "for (the gospel) is the power of God unto salvation for everyone that believes . . . for therein is the righteousness of God revealed from faithfulness to faith: as it is written: the just shall live by faith. But the wrath of God is revealed from heaven against men who suppress the truth in unrighteousness . . ." The comparison is even clearer in Romans 2:6-11. In Romans 3:9ff. Paul points out that the Jewish authority—the Old Testament—had accused both Jewish and Gentile groups of being "under sin" and of oppressing God's true people. Paul establishes that there are two sections in Israel as well as among Gentiles. He establishes that the only basis for real righteousness is Christ's work and faith in God—not works. Then he leaves the theme of the "two sections" in order to deal with the mechanics of justification and salvation (Romans 4-8) finishing with thoughts on the future of the church. He then returns to deal with the Jewish question in more depth, and so returns again to the theme (repeated throughout 9-11) that there are two sections in Israel, and God now has made the one lump of Israel into two separate vessels, etc.

18. The verses Romans 4:2-6 are quoted from the RV except that the word *believed* has been replaced by the phrase "had faith in." This has been done because the RV, as it stands, does not make it clear to the English reader that "believe in" and "have faith in" are alternative translations of the same Greek verb for which the noun is "faith."

19. Romans 9:31

20. Romans 11:7

21. Romans 9:30-32; 10:3, 4; the words "that believes" have again been replaced by "that has faith" for greater clarity.

22. Romans 11:5-7

23. See section 20. The rabbis thought that in order for an Israelite to be excluded from "the world to come" he had to be an exceptional sinner.

24. The phrase "to partake of His election" seems first to have been used by Clement of Rome in his famous first-century epistle.

25. Isaiah 10:20-22

26. The LXX reads: *"you shall* leave in Israel seven thousand men . . ."

27. Cf. Romans 8:30 and see p. 103.

28. Romans 11:1; 10:1

29. Isaiah 1; cf., e.g., Isaiah 1:10-17 and Matthew 23:23, 24

30. Romans 11:5-7

31. Romans 9:33; 11:11

32. Isaiah 41:8, 9. The chosenness of Israel is linked with their task of servanthood in a high percentage of times that it is men-

tioned, e.g., 1 Chronicles 16:13; Psalms 89:3; 89:19; 105:6; 105:42, 43; Isaiah 65:15

33. Isaiah 42:1

34. Isaiah 49:6; see also Luke 2:32

35. See also section 4.

36. The nearest that the Bible seems to come to such an idea is in Isaiah, where the Lord says that he "looked but there was none to help" and so his own right arm brought him victory. But this is far from a passing by of other "candidates"—it is a total lack of them!

37. Matthew 17:5

38. Mark 9:7

39. Luke 9:35

40. Matthew 12:18; English readers may find it strange that Matthew has apparently rendered a Hebrew word meaning "uphold" by a Greek word meaning "chosen." It may help us to understand this if we note that the Greek word which Matthew uses is not the normal word for "chosen," but a rarely used word *hairetizō*, which is from the same root as *haireō*. The meaning of the latter is to "take" or to "take up," and so we can see that there is at least some connection even if Matthew's rendering is a free one.

41. Proverbs 8:19

42. Song of Solomon 6:10; the LXX uses *eklektos* in a free rendering of a Hebrew word meaning "pure" or "clear."

43. The other reference is Luke 23:35, where Luke renders the Aramaic words of the crowd as: let him save himself, if this is the Christ of God, his chosen.

44. Ephesians 6:12; see also section 3.

45. Ephesians 6:11; Isaiah 59:17

46. Cf. Matthew 5:14 with John 8:12

47. Acts 13:47 quotes the LXX of Isaiah 49:6

48. It may also be because the very word *chosen* has come to have implications for us which it did not have for early Greek writers. In note 24 above, we noted the phrase "to partake of His election." Also of interest is a sentence in the *Shepherd of Hermas*. This is a rather strange second-century book, but one held in high esteem by the early church. In Vision 2:14 we read: "For the Lord has sworn by His glory concerning the elect, having determined this very time, that if any one shall even now sin, he shall not be saved." We may not agree that salvation could be lost, but the fact that Hermas could so write demonstrates that to the early church the word *election* carried no overtones of the negation of effective responsibility.

49. The spread of this new system, introduced by Augustine, is dealt with in our appendix. Augustine wrote: "Therefore God elected believers; but He chose them that they might be so, not because they were already so" (*Predestination of the Saints,* chapter 34). See also note 3 above.)

Several features of his analysis are unfortunate. The most important of these is that he tends to speak as though the only alternative to his own view was that which he ascribes to the Pelagians. The latter he states thus: "For they themselves think that 'having received God's commands we are made holy and immaculate of ourselves by the choice of our free-will in His sight in love; and since God foreknew that this would be the case,' they say, 'He therefore chose and predestined us in Christ before the foundation of the world.'" (*Pred. Saints,* chapter 38). But, in spite of his assumption, there is a third possibility. The three views might be summarized thus:

(a) Because of our works and merits we have earned the right to share the election of Christ (the Pelagian view).

(b) God chose us individually before the world began, and because of that choice he gave us faith as an irresistible gift and put us into Christ (Augustine).

(c) God placed us in Christ not because we earned it or deserved it, but because in his free grace he counted our faith as right-standing. Since we are in Christ, and he is the chosen One, we are chosen *in him* and share his election.

Augustine was right to condemn view (a), but there are serious problems in his own view—in spite of its triumph in western Christianity. What, in his view, is the significance of the phrase "in him"? In Ephesians the phrase "in Christ" occurs 14 times, "in whom" occurs 6 times and "in him" 4 times—always in reference to Christ. Ephesians 1:3 speaks of the blessings we have *in Christ,* and verse 4 is a direct continuation to add that we were also chosen *in him.* If Augustine were right then Paul surely needed only to say: "even as he chose us before the foundation of the world . . ." But Paul in fact says: "even as he chose us *in him* before the foundation of the world . . ." Why should Paul have added the phrase "in him" if it had no function? As it is, its addition seems directly to contradict Augustine's view. Surely to be a "believer" in this context means nothing else than to be "in Christ." Thus Augustine's words could be rendered as: "He chose them that they might be 'in Christ,' not because they were already so." But Paul does not say that we were chosen *to be put into* Christ, but that we were chosen *in Christ.* If we were chosen (in Christ), then surely we were chosen *because* we were in him (and he has been chosen)—which is exactly what Augustine denied.

We have already seen (in note 3 above) the confusion caused by Augustine's application to the election of the believers, of Christ's words to the apostles in John 15:16. Yet it is this verse which Augustine used as the main support for his view! Thus we find him repeating three or four times an argument like this: "I ask, who can hear the Lord saying, 'You have not chosen me, but I have chosen you,' and can dare to say that men believe in order to be elected, when they are rather elected to believe . . ." This is the mainstay of his argument, on the basis of which he effectively ignores the phrase "in him" in Ephesians 1:4.

These then, are the very serious problems in Augustine's view of election. But his view became so influential in western Christianity that it has profoundly affected our thinking today—and that even though we may have read not one word of Augustine's own works! Because of his influence, we also tend to think of the issue as a choice between views (a) and (b) above, which it certainly is not. Any true Christian must rule out view (a), as did Augustine, but whether Augustine's own view or view (c) is the correct one needs to be given full consideration.

Even a work of the stature of the *New Bible Dictionary* seems to be influenced by Augustine's confusion. It says:

"It has been argued that God's foreknowledge is not foreordination and that personal election in the New Testament is grounded upon God's foresight that the persons chosen will respond to the gospel of themselves. The difficulties in this view seem to be: (1) this asserts in effect election according to works and desert, whereas Scripture asserts election to be of grace (Rom. ix.11; 2 Tim. i.9), and grace excludes all regard to what a man does for himself (Rom. iv.9; xi.6; Eph. ii8f.; Tit. iii5, RV); (2) if election is *unto* faith (2 Thess. ii.13) and good works (Eph. ii.10) it cannot rest upon foresight of these things; (3) on this view Paul ought to be pointing, not to God's election, but to the Christian's own faith as the ground of his assurance of final salvation; (4) Scripture does appear to equate foreknowledge with foreordination (cf. Acts ii.23)."

Let us note that:

(a) There is no such thing in the New Testament as personal (individual) election of believers. Christ is *the* chosen One, and believers are elect because they are *in him*.

(b) It is God's free gift that we are *in Christ*, but he himself makes that gift conditional on our response of acceptance (e.g., John 1:12). In this sense our sharing in Christ's election depends on our response, but it is quite untrue to conclude that this "in effect" means election according to "works and desert." Acceptance of a free gift does not mean that one has either earned or deserved it. Of the two verses cited: Romans 9:11 refers to the national election of Israel, not to believers' election; 2 Timothy 1:9 does indeed rule out "works" but makes it clear that the calling, etc., was given us corporately *in Christ*.

(c) Grace does not exclude *all* regard to what man does; it excludes "works." Paul makes it clear that receiving a free gift is *not* works, for works *earn* whatever is received. The four verses cited do rule out "works," but Romans 4:4 makes it clear that receiving a free gift is not a work.

(d) 2 Thessalonians 2:13 does not say election is *unto faith* (see note 50). It does, indeed, not rest on foresight of good works, but on being *in Christ* (and Ephesians 2:10 itself speaks of this); this is not conditional on works, but on acceptance of a free offer.

(e) Our assurance is not based on our faith, but on the fact that we know that, having repented, God has put us *in Christ*, and we are elect in him.

(f) Scripture never equates foreknowledge with foreordination, either in Acts 2:23 or anywhere else.

50. As may be seen from the list given, the application of *eklektos* to believers is not frequent. There is no indication in any of the verses that election involves a divine decision about who should believe. 2 Thessalonians 2:13 is sometimes cited as having such an implication, so it may be useful to consider this verse in some detail.

It is, in fact, difficult to base very much on this verse for there are two different renderings of it, both of which are well supported.

One of these is *ap archēs* (from the beginning) and the other is *aparchen* (firstfruits). Both are well attested and the context would allow either meaning, so a final decision seems impossible. We have, therefore, tried to consider the implication of each of the two renderings in turn.

(1) Ap archēs (from the beginning)

The verse under consideration reads: **And then shall be revealed the lawless one, whom the Lord Jesus shall slay with the breath of his mouth, and bring to nought by the manifestation of his coming, even he, whose coming is according to the working** (energizing) **of Satan with all power and signs and lying wonders, and with all deceit of unrighteousness for them that are perishing, because they received not the love of the truth, that they might be saved. And for this cause God sends them a working of error, that they should believe a lie: that they all might be judged who believed not the truth, but had pleasure in unrighteousness. But we are bound to give thanks to God alway for you, brethren beloved of the Lord, for that God chose you from the beginning unto salvation in sanctification of the Spirit and belief of the truth: whereunto he called you through our gospel, to the obtaining of the glory of our Lord Jesus Christ. So then, brethren, stand fast, and hold the traditions which you were taught . . .** (2 Thessalonians 2:8-15)

The phrase *ap archēs* is used in two main contexts in the New Testament:

(a) to mean "from the beginning of creation"; e.g., Matthew 19:4; 2 Peter 3:4; 1 John 3:8

(b) to mean from the beginning of something more recent; e.g., Luke 1:2; 1 John 2:7

In which of these senses should we understand 2 Thessalonians 2:13? It is sometimes suggested that Paul's thought is similar to that in Ephesians 1:4 ("He chose us, in him, before the foundation of the world"), and that by "from the beginning" he means the beginning of creation. There are three main reasons why this seems to us to be unlikely: First, it is difficult to see why Paul should have said "before the creation" in Ephesians and "since the creation" in Thessalonians. Second, he does not use the word for "chosen" used in Ephesians (*eklektos*), but a different word (*haireomai*). Third, he uses the word *archē* to imply a time in only two other places—and neither of them means "since the beginning of creation." The first of these places is in Acts 26:4, where he means "since his youth up." The second, the only use in the epistles, is in Philippians 4:15, 16: **And you yourselves also know, you Philippians, that in the beginning of the gospel, when I departed from Macedonia, no church had fellowship with me in the matter of giving and receiving, but you only; for even in Thessalonica you sent once and again unto my need.** This is very significant since Paul's first journey to Thessalonica is specifically mentioned as the "beginning of the gospel." Thus when he tells the Thessalonians: "God chose you from the beginning" it would seem obvious that he means the beginning of the gospel.

We must also consider the meaning of the various other terms Paul uses: "salvation," "sanctification," "belief of the truth," and "chosen."

The word *salvation* must be seen in the light of the great interest in the Thessalonian epistles in the second coming of our Lord Jesus Christ. It is used only in 2 Thessalonians 2:10, 13, 1 Thessalonians 2:16, and 1 Thessalonians 5:8, 9. The last reads: **for a helmet, the hope of salvation. For God appointed us not unto wrath, but unto the obtaining of salvation through our Lord.** This shows that the "salvation" is a future event, like also 2 Timothy 2:10—**Therefore I endure everything for the elect's sake, that they also may obtain the salvation which is in Christ Jesus with eternal glory.** This shows the link between election and the future "salvation" of those in Christ, when the sons of God shall be revealed for the liberation of the creation and the glory of the children of God (cf. Romans 8). It is this future event Paul has in mind as 2 Thessalonians 2:8 also indicates.

The word *sanctification* is used here, and also in 1 Thessalonians 4:3, 7 where he told them: "this is the will of God even your sanctification . . . For God has not called us for unrighteousness, but in sanctification." Sanctification, like calling (see 2 Thessalonians 1:11), is something which (as God's will for him) a man may accept and live up to, or reject. Thus Paul urges them to walk in the way of acceptance.

The phrase "belief of the truth" emphasizes the comparison between the true Christians and the false. The false **received not the love of the truth, that they might be saved for they believed not the truth but had pleasure in unrighteousness.** The true Christians will be saved by **belief of the truth,** for they received the word of the truth which works in them (cf. 1 Thessalonians 1:6; 2:13). The false Christians will not obtain salvation, but this is not because God does not want them to, for God "wills that all men should be saved and come to the knowledge of the truth." It is rather because they themselves preferred unrighteousness to truth—and so God has allowed them to become deceived by the pretended wonders of the false prophets who work according to the energizing of Satan.

The word for "chosen" is not the usual *eklektos* but *haireomai*. This is used in only two other places in the New Testament—Hebrews 11:25 and Philippians 1:22. Both of these indicate a person taking one of two paths to follow or groups to align with, and do not seem immediately helpful to our understanding of the passage we are considering. There is, however, a derivative *hairesis* which is used more often. This is the word for "sect"—a group which is divided off from others. Paul says that there must be such "divisions" in order that the genuine Christians may be recognized (1 Corinthians 11:19). The true Christians in Thessalonica, then, have been "divided off" by God from those who follow the energizing of Satan and his pretended signs and wonders. They are, in a sense, a "sect"—but they are the one true sect who will obtain salvation through sanctification of spirit and belief of the truth. God divided them off in this way right from the beginning—also showing that they were the true chosen group by the power of the Holy Spirit working in them and the true assurance he brought (1 Thessalonians 1:4, 5). As a group they had received the true marks of God's approval. Another word associated with the same word group is *haireō* (to take). Perhaps there is a hint of God "taking them" or "separating them" as a group, to achieve his purpose through separation (sanctification) of spirit and belief of truth.

In summary, we take its meaning to be that from the beginning God divided off those who were willing to repent and believe in the truth, from those who preferred unrighteousness. The true believers have God's word working powerfully among them; the false follow the pretended signs and wonders that Satan energizes. Eventually there will be a final confrontation of God and Satan, good and evil, when those who follow God will obtain the salvation of themselves and the creation, and the glory of Christ, while those who follow Satan will receive damnation.

(2) *Aparchen* (firstfruits)

Paul does not use the phrase "from the beginning" (*ap archēs*) anywhere in the epistles, but uses "firstfruits" (*aparchen*) six times. This (and see especially Romans 16:5; 1 Corinthians 16:15) indicates that it may well be the correct rendering in this context also (compare also James 1:18). If this *is* the correct rendering then we might read (as RSV margin): "God chose you as the first converts." However, the meaning would in this case be little different from that already outlined under the other rendering. It would simply increase the emphasis that they were "chosen" or "separated off" as those who were willing to accept the truth, i.e., as the first converts.

51. In section six we have seen that this word *work* is really "energize," and has a definite usage in Pauline writings (see pp. 22, 23).

52. See also section 14.

53. See also section 14.

54. Colossians 3:12; 1 Thessalonians 1:4

55. 2 Thessalonians 2:13; see also the note 50 (above) on this verse.

56. Thus Acts 15:25 refers to sending: "Chosen men, with our beloved Barnabas." Romans 11:28 says: "as touching the election they are beloved for the fathers' sake."

57. We note that the Christians are "living stones" just as Christ is (1 Peter 2:4, 5), and they are elect just as he is (v. 4, 6, 9). This is logical, for as living stones they are being built into the "Temple" of his body the church of which he is the foundation and cornerstone, so as part of that building they share its election. Just as the corporate nature of election is often underemphasized, so the corporate nature of our "Templehood" is often underemphasized. In 1 Corinthians 3, Paul also calls us "God's building" (v. 9), and says "you are the Temple of God" (v. 16). The word *you* here is plural, but "Temple" is singular. The church *collectively* is God's Temple, built on the foundation of Christ. The church as a whole is an organism with Christ as head—an organism built of *living* stones. To become part of that building, through God's grace, is to share in its election.

58. What God demands of man is not that he should earn salvation by good works; it is not even primarily that he should have faith; what God demands of man is *repentance* (Acts 17:30). When we tell a man to "Repent and believe . . ." then the priorities are right. If a man is prepared to repent, God will help him to believe. Even then, faith cannot be said to *cause* a man's regeneration. God gives the gift of regeneration and rebirth to those who repent; it is a di-

vinely wrought miracle in their lives. Having given them rebirth God joins them to Christ—again it is his action and not directly their repentance that does this. God demands repentance before he will do this. A man is free to reject his plan for him and refuse to repent, but if he does repent, his rebirth and entry into Christ are wrought by God alone.

There may be something of this reflected in a verse for which the Authorized Version gives a rather unfortunate rendering: Acts 2:47. The RV rendering is certainly more correct in giving: **the Lord added to them day by day those that were being saved.** It is God who adds a man, as he is being saved, to the body of the church.

59. Genesis 6:8, 9
60. Genesis 7:1
61. See also the appendix, pp. 249, 250
62. 1 Clement 24:1-4
63. Clement 1:1 reads: "to the church of God which is at Corinth, elect, sanctified by the will of God through Jesus Christ . . ." 1 Clement 21:15 refers to: "those who are chosen by God through Jesus Christ . . ." In similar vein we read: "Wherefore, we, being a part of the Holy One, let us do all those things which pertain to holiness" (1 Clement 14:1). In Clement 13:6 he uses the interesting phrase: "Merciful Father, who has made us to partake of His election." Lastly, we might mention 1 Clement 20:13, 14: "And again in another place he says: With the pure you shall be pure, (and with the elect you shall be elect), but with the perverse man you shall be perverse. Let us therefore join ourselves to the innocent and righteous, for such are the elect of God." This again surely shows a highly developed sense of the corporateness of our election.
64. Clement of Alexandria uses a similar mode of expression to Clement of Rome: "This blessedness came on those who had been chosen by God through Jesus Christ our Lord" (*Stromata*, Bk 2).
65. Matthew 2:23
66. Luke 2:23
67. Romans 1:1; 1 Corinthians 1:1
68. 1 Corinthians 1:2; 1 John 3:1
69. Ephesians 4:1 AV
70. 2 Peter 1:10
71. Revelation 17:14
72. Sanday and Headlam say that the terms *called* and *chosen* in Paul's writings "are not to be opposed to each other (as they are in Matthew xxii.14) but are rather to be identified. By reading into *klētos* the implication that the call is accepted, Saint Paul shows that the persons of whom this is true are also objects of God's choice. By both terms Saint Paul designates not those who are destined for final salvation, but those who are 'summoned' or 'selected' for the privilege of serving God and carrying out His will. If their career runs its normal course it must issue in salvation, the 'glory' reserved for them; this lies as it were at the end of the avenue; *eklektos* only shows that they are in the right way to reach it. At least no external power can bar them from it; if they lose it, they will do so by their own fault."
73. Cf. Matthew 22:14 with Matthew 13:13

149

16

Word Study—Righteousness[1]

This is a study of the words *justify* and *righteous* which are from the same Greek root. The material is drawn from that very worthwhile study book by Dr. Leon Morris, *The Apostolic Preaching of the Cross*. Our aim here is not to restate Morris's arguments, but simply to outline some of his conclusions. To help those who wish to study further, page numbers are given with the quotations from his book.[2]

Justify. On the meaning of the word *justify* Morris concludes: "When we turn to these passages where the verb 'to justify' occurs, there can be no doubt that the meaning is to declare righteous rather than to make righteous" (p. 259).

Righteous. Of this word Morris writes: "In the Scriptures 'righteousness' does not have exactly the same meaning as it has come to have in western civilization of the twentieth century" (p. 269). He goes on to explain how today we mean by a "righteous" man someone who lives up to a certain code of conduct. To us, a perfectly righteous man would be one who lived completely according to certain moral laws. This means that we view the word *righteous* as an ethical term, i.e., one that concerns living up to a code of ethics. In this the ancient Greeks were similar to us, for they viewed a man as "righteous" if, for example, he exhibited the four cardinal virtues. When, on the other hand, a Hebrew used the word *righteous* his primary emphasis in meaning was not the same as ours. Morris writes: "The Hebrew concept is not grasped by making a facile equation with the Greek . . . or the English 'righteousness'; it is not an ethical term but a religious" (p. 260).

It is a religious term because to the Hebrews the word *righteous* meant primarily that a man was right with God and only secondarily that he would behave in a way befitting this position. Morris writes: "The righteous are those acquitted at the bar of God's justice, and righteousness is the standing of those so acquitted" (p. 260). He adds: "This sort of thinking was developed and elaborated by the rabbis. They pictured a great assize where all men would be tried before God. Some would be accepted as righteous, while others would be condemned as wicked. It is from minds accustomed to this way of regarding righteousness that the New Testament terminology is derived. Basically the righteous man is the one who is accepted before God, the one who conforms to His way" (p. 269).

This certainly did not mean that the Hebrews believed that God was uninterested in ethics and morality. It did not imply that one's standing before God was unconnected with one's ethics and moral standards. Someone who was in a right relationship with God would be expected to have some kind of exacting ethical standards. The point, however, is this: In our western tradition we tend to put it that if a man kept the moral law perfectly then he would, by definition, be "righteous," and God would accept him *because* he was righteous. To the Hebrew, however, being righteous meant, by primary definition, being "right with God"—and a man's ethical behavior was expected to be a result and reflection of this. Although moral overtones may have been implied by the word *righteous* they did not constitute its basic meaning. Morris puts it: "It is, of course, true that 'righteous' comes to have an ethical meaning and in many places this is to be stressed. But this meaning develops naturally out of the forensic idea and we need not doubt that the legal idea is the basic one" (p. 261).

GOD'S RIGHTEOUSNESS

To some people it may be a puzzle how God himself can be righteous if the word means "right with God." The word does, however, mean slightly more than this, as Morris explains: "The adjective . . . is applied to God in five passages (Jn. 17:25; Rom. 3:26; 2 Tim. 4:8; 1 Jn. 1:9; Rev. 16:5). In the first of these the reference is quite general, 'O righteous Father, the world knew thee not'; but in the last of them the meaning clearly has to do with the process of judging, 'Righteous art thou, which art and which wast, thou Holy One, because thou didst thus judge.' Here there can be no doubt but that God is shown to be righteous by the process of just judgment, and this accords with the expression 'the Lord, the righteous judge' (2 Tim. 4:8). In 1 John God is spoken of as 'faithful and righteous to forgive us our sins,' which we may well understand as indicating that God's forgiveness is in accordance with the laws of His holy nature. The remaining passage is that in which Saint Paul says that the propitiatory death of Jesus was 'for the showing of [God's] righteousness at this present season: that he might himself be just, and the justifier of him that hath faith in Jesus . . .'" (p. 272).

JOB AND RIGHTEOUSNESS

We may understand the book of Job much better if we grasp the Hebrew meaning of righteous. As Christians we have seen the moral perfection of Christ, and so our standards of ethics are very high. If the word *righteous* were taken in our western sense we should be surprised at the Bible calling any mere man righteous, for the only ethically perfect one was Christ himself. If the word meant "ethically irreproachable" then men like Noah and Lot were manifestly not righteous (Genesis 7:1; 2 Peter 2:8; compare Genesis 9:21; 19:30-38). Since, however, the word implies mainly that a man is in a right standing before God, we may see why the word is applied to them. The same is also true of Job. The Lord himself declared Job to be blameless and upright. This did not mean that Job had no faults, but that he was in a fundamentally right standing before God.

To our western minds, the word *righteous* not only implies ethical perfection; it tends also to have connotations of *self*-righteous. These two associations of ideas might easily have led us to condemn Job for continually protesting his innocence and righteousness. When we see what his claim really was—to be in a fundamentally right standing with God—we may understand why God condoned what he said. Job is indeed righteous before God and is right to say so. Morris explains for us some of the implications of a correct understanding of "righteous" in the book of Job. He writes: "The forensic use of words from this root is often found in the book of Job, as when the patriarch says: 'Behold now I have ordered my cause; I know that I shall be justified' (Job 13:18). Here he can mean only that he will be declared righteous, as by a judge giving sentence in a lawsuit. So also, when the Lord says to Job, 'Wilt thou also dissanul my judgment? wilt thou condemn me, that thou mayest be righteous?' (Job 40:8), the forensic note of the passage and the opposition of condemning to being righteous show that 'righteous' here means something very like 'declared righteous legally.' It is this which gives us the background against which we must understand the question thrice repeated with slight changes: 'How should a man be just with God?' (Job 9:2, and see 15:14; 25:4). In each case it is standing with the Lord that is in question, and the implication is that man is completely unable of himself to attain such right standing."

The Bible does not necessarily condemn the claim of a man to be righteous. What is wrong is a claim to be able to make oneself righteous, i.e., to *earn* God's acquittal.

GENTILES,
JEWS, AND
RIGHTEOUSNESS

The meaning of righteousness is important to our understanding of what Paul says about Jews and Gentiles. In Romans 9:30-32, for example, we read: **What shall we say then? That the Gentiles, which followed not after righteousness, attained to righteousness, even the righteousness which is of faith: but Israel, following after a law of righteousness, did not arrive at that law. Wherefore? Because they sought it not by faith but as it were by works. They stumbled at the stone of stumbling.** If we were to take the word *righteous* in an ethical sense then we might misunderstand Paul to be saying: "The Jews were trying very hard to lead moral lives whereas the Gentiles were not trying at all. Then the Gentiles suddenly found themselves acting morally, whereas the Jews found that they couldn't." This is certainly not his meaning. He is referring to what was almost an obsession in some Jews, an obsession with the desire to procure an acquittal from God. They nonetheless failed to achieve this, because they tried to earn it through study and works of the Law. We must not suppose that the gentile converts (to whom Paul compares these Jews) had no interest at all in being right with God. In a characteristically Hebrew way, Paul indicates that the gentile interest was small in comparison to the Jews who were obsessed with it.[3] Nevertheless the gentile converts achieved a right standing before God because they sought it through faith and not through works.

On this passage of Romans Morris comments: "The forensic idea is very strong here. The Gentiles did not seek before God that righteous standing which the Jews sought by the way of works of merit. Nevertheless they attained to righteousness, namely the righteousness which is of faith. The Jews who were very anxious to establish themselves as righteous before God failed to do so because they came by the way of law works instead of by that of faith, which is the way God has appointed. It is quite clear that righteousness is being used to denote a standing, a status, a verdict of acquittal, and not an ethical quality" (p. 275).

In summary, therefore, several subjects dealt with in this book become clearer once we understand what the Hebrew meant by a righteous man. His primary meaning was not a man who lived up to a perfect moral standard, but one who had been acquitted in God's judgment.

NOTES

1. We are greatly indebted to Dr. Leon Morris who was kind enough to give us some valuable suggestions for amendments to this section, which is largely based on his work. We would also like to thank Tyndale Press for permission to quote so extensively from his book *The Apostolic Preaching of the Cross,* which is published by them.

2. The page numbers refer to the third edition, 1965.

3. Section 9 note 12 gives similar examples of this characteristically Hebrew use of an exaggerated comparison.

17

Word Study—Harden

The Authorized and Revised Standard Versions of Exodus both refer to God "hardening Pharaoh's heart." The object of this study is to try to clarify for the English reader the meaning and implications of this phrase in the original Hebrew.

The English phrase *hard-hearted* carries to many people overtones of cruelty or unrepentance. Thus "God hardened Pharaoh's heart" could be taken to mean that God prevented him from repenting. We are not saying that those who translated the AV, RV and RSV intended this, but rather

that the ordinary English reader could get this impression—
and in our experience often does! This puzzles him, for the
Bible clearly teaches that God is not willing that *any* should
perish, but desires *all men* to be saved and to come to a
knowledge of the truth. **Have I any pleasure in the death
of the wicked? says the Lord God: and not rather that he
should return from his way and live?**[1] God, we may be
sure, would rather that Pharaoh had repented than perished
in the Red Sea. We can never know what blessing God
would have wrought if Pharaoh had repented, nor how he
would have wrought it, but doubtless it could have been an
even greater blessing than was brought out of Pharaoh's
death. But, these things being so, how are we to explain
the paradox of God wanting Pharaoh to repent and yet
"hardening" him?

The paradox need not arise if we remember that a phrase
in one language should not be simply equated with a
phrase in another. English readers who see "hardened his
heart" may not understand the connotations of the Hebrew
phrase this represents. How may these connotations become
clearer to us?[2] One way is for us to see how the Hebrew
phrase is used elsewhere in Scripture. Let us note, however,
that we should not assume that the phrase is identical in
meaning in all its occurrences; this would be naive. Such
study is intended as a guideline to connotations, not as an
inflexible system of linguistic deduction.

We will compile, therefore, a table (see pages 158, 159)
of the verses in which the Bible uses the Piel form of the
Hebrew root *chazaq*[3] (the word usually used for the "hardening" of Pharaoh's heart). We have also listed the ways in
which the AV, RV, RSV, NEB, and JB render the word in each
case. This is not, of course, to pretend that some inflexible
meaning may be assigned to the Hebrew on the basis of
the English translations! It is simply to try to help the
English reader to grasp some of the associations of ideas
that might lie behind the Hebrew word. The English renderings are, in themselves, far less important than the contexts in which the word comes—and the reader might
profitably take time to look these up.

We notice from the table that when the object of the verb is (directly or metaphorically) personal, the rendering is nearly always "strengthen" or "make strong." The general concept is one of making firm, encouraging, etc. The Hebrew word should not be simply equated with any of these ideas, but the study may help the English reader to catch some of its undertones.

There is, however, a further complication in that the phrase is not "God (*chazaq*) Pharaoh" (as, e.g., in Daniel 10:18, 19), but "God (*chazaq*) Pharaoh's heart." It is, of course, linguistically possible for "(*chazaq*) Pharaoh's heart" to contain different connotations from *chazaq* when used on its own. Are there any other uses of the phrase as a whole in the Bible?

The answer to this is that the phrase as such is used only twice outside of Exodus. One is in Joshua 11:20, where the context is of battle, and God (*chazaq*) their hearts to continue fighting. Note that there is, of course, no question of repentance or unrepentance. The implication is that God gave them courage to resist when all was lost and battle seemed futile. Of itself, however, the verse does not make the connotations of the phrase clear enough. The other reference comes in Ezekiel 2:4, which again is not, of itself, sufficiently clear.

We find, therefore, that we have to consider similar though not identical phrases. One such phrase is "a (*chazaq*) forehead," and it is linked to the "(*chazaq*) heart" in Ezekiel 2:4 already mentioned. The latter speaks of "a (*qashah*) forehead and a (*chazaq*) heart." Ezekiel 3:7 switches this and speaks of "a (*chazaq*) forehead and a (*qashah*) heart." Thus the phrase using "forehead" seems similar to that using "heart."

The full text of Ezekiel 3:7-9 is: **But the house of Israel will not hearken unto you; for they will not hearken unto me: for all the house of Israel are of an hard (*chazaq*) forehead and a stiff (*qashah*) heart. Behold, I have made your face hard (*chazaq*) against their faces, and your forehead hard (*chazaq*) against their foreheads. As an adamant harder than flint have I made your forehead: fear**

Instances
of the Piel form
of *Chazaq*

Key:

(a) reference

(b) AV rendering

(c) NEB rendering

(d) JB rendering

(e) RV and RSV renderings where
different from AV.

° indicates that the object of
the verb is literally
or metaphorically personal.

Exodus	4:21°
	9:12°
	10:20°
	10:27°
	11:10°
	14:4°
	14:8°
	14:17°
Deuteronomy	1:38°
	3:28°
Joshua	11:20°
Judges	3:12°
	16:28°
1 Samuel	23:16°
2 Samuel	11:25°
2 Kings	12:5, 6, 7, 8, 12, 14
	22:5, 6
1 Chronicles	26:27
	29:12°
2 Chronicles	11:11
	11:12
	11:17
	24:5
	24:12
	26:9
	29:3
	29:34°
	32:5
	34:8
	34:10
	35:2°
Ezra	1:6°
	6:22°
Nehemiah	2:18°
	3:19
	6:9°
Job	4:3°
Psalms	64:5°
	147:13
Isaiah	22:21°
	33:23
	35:3°
	41:7a°
	41:7b
	54:2
Jeremiah	5:3°
	10:4
	23:14°
Ezekiel	13:22°
	30:24°
	34:4°
	34:16°
Daniel	10:18°
	10:19°
Hosea	7:15°
Nahum	2:1°
	3:14

b)	(c)	(d)	(e)
en	make obstinate	harden	
	"	make stubborn	
	"	"	
	"	"	
	"	"	
	"	"	
	"	"	
rage	encourage	give encourage-ment	
	encourage	encourage	
en	obstinate	stubborn	
gthen	rouse	give power over	
	give strength	give strength	
	give courage	encourage	
rage	tell to take heart	"	
c	repair	repair	
tain	upkeep	(paraphr.)	repair (RV)
strength	give strength	give strength	
y	strengthen	fortify	make strong (RSV)
strong	"	make strong	
gthen	"	added strength	
c	repair	repair	
	"	restore	repair (RV, RSV)
y	fortify	fortify	
c	repair	repair	
	help	help	
c	strengthen	strengthen	strengthen (RV, RSV)
	repair	repair	
d	strengthen	restore	restore (RSV)
rage	encourage	(paraphr.)	
gthen	assist	give assistance	aided (RSV)
"	encourage	encourage	" (RSV)
"	set about vigorously	(paraphr.)	
r	repair	repair	
gthen	greater energy	make stronger	
"	encourage	give strength	
rage	(paraphr.)	urge on	hold fast (RSV)
gthen	(paraphr.)	strengthen	
"	(paraphr.)	(paraphr.)	bind on (RSV)
"	hold firm	support	hold firm (RSV)
gthen	strengthen	strengthen	
rage	urge on	encourage	
n	fasten	fasten	
gthen	drive home	make firm	
harder	set hard	set hard	
n	fasten	fix	
gthen	encourage	abet	
"	strengthen	encourage	encourage (RSV)
"	"	strengthen	
"	encourage	make strong	
"	strengthen	"	
"	"	give strength	
"	"	"	
strong	brace yourselves	(paraphr.)	collect strength (RSV)
fy	strengthen	strengthen	strengthen (RV, RSV)

159

**them not, neither be dismayed at their looks, though they
be a rebellious house.**

This certainly helps our understanding of the phrase. The
chazaq forehead of the Israelites implies that they are firm
in the course they have chosen (i.e., rebellion and transgression—2:3 and 2:6). God says that he will make Ezekiel
just as firm as they are. He will make his forehead *chazaq*
against their foreheads. This does not, of course, mean
that God would make Ezekiel unrepentant or rebellious!
The phrase "a (*chazaq*) forehead" has no such connotations;
it simply implies "firmness" or "strength" or "stubbornness."
Thus the Lord follows his promise to Ezekiel with a command
not to fear them in spite of their hard-line rebellion. They
were rebellious, and were firm in this path, but the Lord
would make Ezekiel even more firm, more stubborn, in his
resolve to obey God's command to speak against them.
Therefore he need not fear.

This illustrates well the usage of the phrase "a (*chazaq*)
forehead." The phrase is, in itself, morally neutral. A person can have a "(*chazaq*) forehead" which makes him firm
to insist on his path of rebellion. A person can also have a
"(*chazaq*) forehead" which makes him firm to insist on
preaching God's truth in the face of opposition. The phrase
does not imply anything of guilt or unrepentance, but of
strength, firmness, stubbornness, to stay on some chosen
course. This is true, also, of the similar phrase "a (*chazaq*)
heart." It means a firmness to stick to some chosen course,
as reflected in the RV mg, JB and NEB renderings.[4]

Although one person may let his heart take courage, or
(as we might say in English) "steel his heart" to do evil,
another person may "steel his heart" to do what is right.
That phrase in itself is also morally neutral. The Hebrew
usage involves no suggestion of God acting on Pharaoh to
make him rebellious or unrepentant. The thought is one of
God's making Pharaoh firm—stubborn if you like—in his resolve to do what he had decided, even when the terrifying
plagues would have prompted a more prudent policy. In
section 11 we have seen how the significance of the plagues
became progressively more obvious. At first the magicians

competed on a limited scale.[5] Then they confessed that some power beyond them was at work: the "finger of God."[6] Then God distinguished between Israelites and Egyptians, showing the God of Israel to be the power behind the plagues.[7] After the plague of boils the Egyptian magicians could not even continue the unequal contest.[8] The Lord strengthened (*chazaq*) Pharaoh's heart, but followed this with a warning. He warned Pharaoh that it was he who had made him stand (made firm his resolve), and so he had better make sure that this was the path he wanted. There followed a form of hail hitherto unknown in Egypt, and the divine origin of the plagues was now clear beyond all doubt.[9] Pharaoh now recognized his sin, but still he did not repent. The last three plagues were terrifying. The locusts meant economic ruin, as Pharaoh's servants recognized in Exodus 10:7. The darkness signified total helplessness of the Egyptians against the God of Israel and showed how hopeless it was to resist. The death of the first-born reinforced this point with the certainty that God meant business. The complete futility of resistance against God became ever more apparent as the plagues progressed.

What would any normal unrepentant man in Pharaoh's position have done? Surely he would have given way through faintheartedness and fear. He may have still harbored the evil desire, but would have recognized the futility of trying to carry it out. But if Pharaoh had done this it would not have suited God's purpose, for it would have meant the end of his opportunity to show how he, the true God, was associated with Israel right from its birth as a nation. Therefore God gave Pharaoh the tenacity, the firmness of heart, to continue in his evil designs. He "made him stubborn" (JB) but this stubbornness relates to his refusal to grant the request to release the Israelites, not to the wider issue of repenting and getting right with God. If Pharaoh would not comply through repentance, God would act to stop him complying through expediency or fear. But this in no way contradicts the supposition that God would have preferred Pharaoh to repent. Have I any pleasure

in the death of the wicked, says the Lord God, and no
rather that he return from his way and live?

What, then, of Exodus 7:3 and 10:1, where the other two
Hebrew roots are used in connection with Pharaoh's heart?
The *qashah* root is used only twice: once with God as the
agent (7:3) and once with Pharaoh (13:15). Both references are to the process as a whole and not to a specific
time or instance of Pharaoh's heart being hardened. The
overall effect of God's actions was that Pharaoh was con-
firmed in his obduracy. The Lord knew Pharaoh and his
character, and knew what his reactions would be to Moses'
request. The Lord knew that the way his power would be
revealed little by little, as the plagues progressed, would
have the effect of stimulating Pharaoh into obduracy. God
was responsible for this process (in sending the plagues of
progressively more obvious origin) and Pharaoh was also
responsible (in making his unrepentant reactions to these).
It is the process, not any individual decision, which seems
to be meant. Also of interest in this matter is a passage in a
very useful analytical commentary on the Hebrew of Exodus
by Kalisch:

> As the external, often accidental, *occasion* of an
> event is mostly more obvious, even to the reflecting
> mind, than its primary cause or its true (often
> hidden) originator, it has become a linguistic pecu-
> liarity in most ancient, especially the Semitic, lan-
> guages, to use indiscriminately the former instead
> of the latter, so that the phrase "I shall harden the
> heart of Pharaoh" means: I know that I shall be
> *the cause* of Pharaoh's obstinacy; my commandments
> and wonders will be an *occasion*, an *inducement* to
> an increasing obduration of his heart. And the
> compassionate leniency of God, who, instead of
> crushing the haughtiness of the refractory king with
> one powerful blow, first tried to reform him by
> various less awful punishments, and who generally
> announced the time of the occurrence of the plagues
> by the words, "Behold I shall afflict tomorrow," in
> order to grant him time for reflection and repen-

tance; this clemency on the part of God increased Pharaoh's refractoriness; it was to him a cause of prolonged and renewed resistance.

If this is, as Kalisch implies, a Hebrew or Semitic trait, then it is little to be wondered that a similar line of interpretation is adopted by the great Hebrew-Christian scholar, Dr. Edersheim,[10] who writes:

> It is indeed most true that "God has no pleasure in the death of the wicked, but rather that he be converted and live;" and that He "will have all men come to the knowledge of the truth and be saved." But "he that being often reproved hardens his neck, shall be suddenly destroyed, and that without remedy." The same manifestation of God which to the believing is "a savor of life unto life," is to those who resist it "a savor of death unto death." As one has written, "the sunlight shining upon our earth produces opposite results according to the nature of the soil." In Scripture language: "the earth which drinks in the rain that comes oft upon it, and brings forth herbs meet for them by whom it is dressed, receives blessing from God: but that which bears thorns and briars is rejected, and is nigh unto cursing; whose end is to be burned." Or, as a German writer puts it: "It is the curse of sin that it makes the hard heart ever harder against the gracious drawing of the Divine love, patience, and long-suffering."[11]

These two Hebrew scholars, then, both take the implications of the words in Exodus to be along these lines. This, however, is often not realized by the average English reader. He may also be unaware that this is the earliest known Christian interpretation of the story of Pharaoh. Origen (c. 185-254 A.D.) is called by A. M. Renwick "one of the most brilliant teachers and writers ever known in the Christian Church."[12] In the early third century he wrote:

But since . . . we [regard God] as one who is at

the same time good and just, let us consider how the good and just God could harden the heart of Pharaoh. See, then, whether, by an illustration used by the apostle in the epistle to the Hebrews, we are able to prove that by one operation God has mercy upon one man while He hardens another . . . "The earth," he says, "which drinks in the rain that comes oft upon it, and brings forth herbs suitable for them for whom it is dressed, receives blessing from God; but that which bears thorns and briars is rejected, and is nigh to cursing, whose end is to be burned." As respects the rain, then, there is one operation; and there being one operation as regards the rain, the ground which is cultivated produces fruit, while that which is neglected and is barren produces thorns. Now it might seem a defamation for [the rain] to say, "I produced the fruits, and the thorns that are in the earth;" and yet, although a defamation, it is true. For, had rain not fallen, there would have been neither fruits nor thorns; but having fallen at the proper time and in moderation, both were produced. The ground, now, which drank in the rain which often fell upon it, and yet produced thorns and briars, is rejected and nigh to cursing. The blessing, then, of the rain descended even upon the inferior land; but it, being neglected and uncultivated, yielded thorns and thistles. In the same way, therefore, the wonderful works also done by God are, as it were, the rain; while the differing purposes are, as it were, the cultivated and neglected land, being [yet], like earth, of one nature.

And as if the sun, uttering a voice, were to say, "I liquefy and dry up," liquefaction and drying up being opposite things, he would not speak falsely as regards the point in question; wax being melted and mud being dried up by the same heat; so the same operation, which was performed through the instrumentality of Moses, proved the hardness of Pharaoh on the one hand, the result of his wickedness, and [proved] the yielding of the mixed Egyptian multitude who took their departure with the Hebrews . . . And it is not absurd to soften down such expressions in accordance with common usage: for good masters often say to their slaves when spoiled by their kindness and forbearance, "I have made you bad, and I am to blame for offenses of such enormity." For we must attend to the character and force of the phrase, and not argue sophistically, disregarding the meaning of the expression. Paul accordingly, having examined these points clearly, says to the sinner: "Or despise you the riches of His goodness and forbearance, and longsuffering: not knowing that the goodness of God leads you to repentance? but, after your hardness and impenitent heart, treasure up unto yourself wrath against the day of wrath, and revelation of the righteous judgment of God." Now, let what the apostle says to the sinner be addressed to Pharaoh, and then the announcements made to him will be understood to have been made with particular fitness, as to one who, according to his hardness and impenitent heart, was treasuring up unto himself wrath; seeing that his hardness would not have been proved nor made manifest unless miracles had been performed, and miracles, too, of such magnitude and importance.[13]

Even earlier than Origen, was Irenaeus, who lived about 130-200 A.D. Irenaeus wrote:

For one and the same God [that blesses others] inflicts blindness upon those who do not believe, but who set Him at naught; just as the sun, which is a creature of His, [acts with regard] to those who, by reason of any weakness of the eyes, cannot behold His light; but to those who believe in Him, and follow Him, He gives a fuller illumination of mind . . . If therefore, in the present time also, God, foreknowing the number of those who will not believe, since He foreknows all things, has given them over to unbelief and turned away His face from men of this stamp, leaving them in the darkness which they have chosen for themselves . . . As the Word spake to Moses from the bush "And I know that the king of Egypt will not give you leave to go unless compelled by a strong hand" (Exodus 3:19) . . . And for the reason that the Lord spake in parables, and brought blindness upon Israel, that seeing they might not see, since He knew the [spirit of] unbelief in them, for the same reason did He harden Pharaoh's heart.[14]

We have found, then, that both Hebrew scholarship and early Christian commentary point to a similar line of interpretation. This is, basically, that when it says God hardened Pharaoh, it simply implies that the effect of God's whole course of actions was to stimulate the unrepentance in Pharaoh. Our own conclusions would quite definitely be, therefore, that the uses of *qashah* in 7:3 and 13:15 refer to the effects of the whole process of God's dealings with Pharaoh. They do not refer to any specific action of God on his heart.

We must now turn to look at the meaning of *kabed* when associated with the heart. The root *kabed* is one of "weight," "thickness," or "heaviness," though words from it are used for various other forms of "greatness." The phrase "heavy (*kabed*) of heart" is obviously an idiomatic use of the word. What does it mean? We must, of course, deliberately ignore the English idiom "heavy of heart," for it is mere coincidence that this seems parallel to the Hebrew. There is absolutely no connection between them. The evidence about the Hebrew idiom is, unfortunately, scanty. It is used only of Pharaoh and once[15] in a comparison to Pharaoh. Some scholars, however, see a parallel in the following verses:

Zech. 7:11—"but they made their ears heavy that they should not hear" (see also Isaiah 6:10; 59:1)

Exodus 4:10—"for I am heavy of speech and of a heavy

tongue." In this case the meaning would have a common basis of "dull," or "hard to move," i.e., deaf (ears), unresponsive (heart), slow (tongue). This is, perhaps, the most plausible explanation—though we confess that we do not find it absolutely conclusive.

Whatever its meaning, *kabed* is used of Pharaoh's heart only once with God as the agent. This is in Exodus 9:34, 35; 10:1—**And when Pharaoh saw that the rain and the hail and the thunders were ceased, he sinned yet more, and hardened (*kabed*) his heart, he and his servants. And the heart of Pharaoh was strong, and he did not let the children of Israel go; as the Lord had spoken by Moses. And the Lord said unto Moses, Go in unto Pharaoh: for I have hardened (*kabed*) his heart, and the heart of his servants, that I might show these my signs in the midst of them.**

Pharaoh has received the solemn warning of 9:17 and has nevertheless "made heavy his heart" (9:34). It is immediately after Pharaoh has rejected this last chance and made heavy his own heart that the Lord's statement of 10:1 occurs.

There is a further nuance in the Hebrew which is not conveyed by the English. The meaning of the Hiph form of the verb, like the Piel, could consist of urging or causing others to do something. It may often be represented by such phrases as "to permit to," "to declare to," or "to help to."[16] This, perhaps, explains why Young in his literal translation gives "I have declared hard" as the sense in Exodus 10:1.[17] Perhaps Young understood by it that the Lord actively accepted, and would further and utilize Pharaoh's "heavy" heart for his own ends of revealing himself through increasingly wonderful signs.

Yet we would like to be cautious here, for this is obviously not a matter of word meaning but of grammar, and therefore discernible only to the expert. Both H. L. Ellison and D. F. Payne have informed us of their dissatisfaction with Young's rendering in this particular case (Exodus 10:1). Perhaps, therefore, the best we could do would be to quote the comment very kindly supplied by Mr. Payne on this:

I think that in general one could tell whether a specific causative verb was strictly causative or merely permissive, but perhaps not always. The fact that with the verb *chayah* ("to live") *both* causative conjugations can be used both in the sense of giving life and also of preserving life suggests to me that the Hebrew language structure did not make it easy to draw a distinction between causation and toleration. Ex. 9:16 confirms my judgment on this. All that I could personally deduce therefore from, e.g., Ex. 10:1 is that God actively desired and organized Pharaoh's obstinacy, that He was "behind it," if you like, and that the obstinacy was fully part of God's plan; I could not however deduce from the statement itself whether Pharaoh had any volition in the matter or not. I don't imagine it mattered to the Biblical author whether God caused Pharaoh to be obstinate or merely purposefully tolerated it. (Judg. 3:12 seems to be a rather similarly ambivalent statement, which could mean that God allowed Eglon to become strong.) But from the story as a whole I would certainly deduce, as you do, that Pharaoh was far from being an automaton.

PAUL'S TEACHING ON PHARAOH

In Romans 9 Paul refers to the story of God hardening Pharaoh, and we must consider briefly whether his words there should affect our interpretation of Exodus. The Greek word Paul uses is *sklērunō*. This is the word used by the Septuagint to render all three of the Hebrew words for "harden" that are linked to Pharaoh's heart. What does this Greek word mean? Did Paul intend to condone the LXX interpretation of Exodus?

The word means "stiffnecked," "stubborn," or "obstinate."[18] It never seems to be used in a neutral sense, but always hints that to be stiffnecked is, in itself, a bad thing. We do not consider it to be a very good rendering for the phrase "(*chazaq*) his heart" in Exodus, for the reasons already given. But, since the LXX was written 800-1,000 years after the compilation of the Exodus text, it could not be expected always to represent Hebrew nuances adequately. The Greek *sklērunō*, however, *is* close in meaning to the Hebrew *qashah*, and its use in Exodus 7:3 is much more appropriate since *qashah* (and not *chazaq*) is the word used there.

Paul, in Romans 9 (v. 17, 18), introduces the subject of Pharaoh with the main idea in Exodus: **For the Scripture says to Pharaoh, For this very purpose did I raise you up, that I might show in you my power, and that my name might be published abroad in all the earth.** After introducing the main concept in this way, he wishes to draw together and compare in summary God's dealings with the two key (and representative) figures of Moses and Pharaoh. What would he do but use the word familiar to his readers as used throughout the LXX rendering of Exodus? The context of Paul's reference is, after all, that of God's general dealings ("raising up" or "making to stand"), not of any specific act of God. Paul perhaps has in mind (if anything) the general reference of Exodus 7:3. He neither condones nor denies the LXX rendering of the passage as a whole. There seems no reason, therefore, for Paul's use of the Exodus passage to alter any of the ideas we have understood from it.

SUMMARY

The Bible does not teach that God made Pharaoh unrepentant. The main word used for the hardening of Pharaoh's heart is *chazaq*, and it seems to mean that God emboldened or encouraged Pharaoh's heart so that he had the stubborn courage to stand even in the face of very frightening miracles.

The verb *qashah* occurs only twice in the context of the hardening of Pharaoh's heart, and refers to the effects of the whole process of God's dealings and Pharaoh's reactions.

The phrase "made heavy" his heart is used only once with God as the agent of making heavy. This comes just after Pharaoh himself has rejected his final solemn warning, and has made his own heart heavy. It seems to indicate that God was actively involved in stimulating and allowing the process.

God never prevents anyone from repenting.

Have I any pleasure in the death of the wicked? says the Lord God: and not rather that he should return from his way and live?

POSTSCRIPT

After writing the above section we were much encouraged to find the following passage, which we quote in full from an excellent commentary on Exodus by Dr. G. A. Chadwick (pp. 112-117):

> When Moses received his commission, at the bush, words were spoken which are now repeated with more emphasis, and which have to be considered carefully. For probably no statement of Scripture has excited fiercer criticism, more exultation of enemies and perplexity of friends, than that the Lord said, "I will harden Pharaoh's heart, and he shall not let the people go," and that in consequence of this Divine act Pharaoh sinned and suffered. Just because the words are startling, it is unjust to quote them without careful examination of the context, both in the prediction and the fulfillment. When all is weighed, compared, and harmonized, it will at last be possible to draw a just conclusion. And although it may happen long before then, that the objector will charge us with special pleading, yet he will be the special pleader himself, if he seeks to hurry us, by prejudice or passion, to give a verdict which is based upon less than all the evidence, patiently weighed.
>
> Let us in the first place find out how soon this

dreadful process began; when was it that God fulfilled His threat, and hardened, in any sense whatever, the heart of Pharaoh? Did He step in at the beginning, and render the unhappy king incapable of weighing the remonstrances which He then performed the cruel mockery of addressing to him? Were these as insincere and futile as if one bade the avalanche to pause which his own act had started down the icy slopes? Was Pharaoh as little responsible for his pursuit of Israel as his horses were—being, like them, the blind agents of a superior force? We do not find it so. In the fifth chapter, when a demand is made, without any sustaining miracle, simply appealing to the conscience of the ruler, there is no mention of any such process, despite the insults with which Pharaoh then assails both the messengers and Jehovah Himself, Whom he knows not. In the seventh chapter there is clear evidence that the process is yet unaccomplished; for, speaking of an act still future, it declares, "I will harden Pharaoh's heart, and multiply My signs and My wonders in the land of Egypt" (vii. 3). And this terrible act is not connected with the remonstrances and warnings of God, but entirely with the increasing pressure of the miracles.

The exact period is marked when the hand of doom closed upon the tyrant. It is not where the Authorized Version places it. When the magicians imitated the earlier signs of Moses, "his heart was strong," but the original does not bear out the assertion that at this time the Lord made it so by any judicial act of His (vii. 13). That only comes with the sixth plague; and the course of events may be traced, fairly well, by the help of the margin of the Revised Version.

After the plague of blood "Pharaoh's heart was strong" ("hardened"), and this is distinctly ascribed to his own action, because "he set his heart even to this" (vii. 22, 23).

After the second plague, it was still he himself who "made his heart heavy" (viii. 15).

After the third plague the magicians warned him that the very finger of some god was upon him indeed: their rivalry, which hitherto might have been somewhat of a palliation for his obstinacy, was now ended; but yet "his heart was strong" (viii. 19).

Again, after the fourth plague he "made his heart heavy"; and it "was heavy" after the fifth plague (viii. 32, ix. 7).

Only thenceforward comes the judicial infatuation upon him who has resolutely infatuated himself hitherto.

But when five warnings and penalties have spent their force in vain, when personal agony is inflicted in the plague of boils, and the magicians in particular cannot stand before him through their pain, would it have been proof of virtuous contrition if he had yielded then? If he had needed evidence, it was given to him long before. Submission now would have meant prudence, not penitence; and it was against prudence, not penitence, that he was hardened. Because he had resisted evidence, experience, and even the testimony of his own magicians, he was therefore stiffened against the grudging and unworthy concessions which must otherwise have been wrested from him, as a wild beast will turn and fly from fire. He was henceforth himself to become an evidence and a portent; and so "The Lord made strong the heart of Pharaoh, and he hearkened not unto them" (ix. 12). It was an awful doom, but it is not open to the attacks so often made upon it. It only means that for him the last five plagues were not disciplinary, but wholly penal.

Nay, it stops short of asserting even this; they might still have appealed to his reason; they were only not allowed to crush him by the agency of terror. Not once is it asserted that God hardened his heart against any nobler impulse than alarm, and desire to evade danger and death. We see clearly this meaning in the phrase, when it is applied to his army entering the Red Sea: "I will make strong the hearts of the Egyptians, and they shall go in" (xiv. 17). It needed no greater moral turpitude to pursue the Hebrews over the sands than on the shore, but it certainly required more hardihood. But the unpursued departure which the good-will of Egypt refused, their common sense was not allowed to grant. Callousness was followed by infatuation, as even the pagans felt that whom God wills to ruin He first drives mad.

This explanation implies that to harden Pharaoh's heart was to inspire him, not with wickedness, but with nerve.

And as far as the original language helps us at all, it decidedly supports this view. Three different expressions have been unhappily rendered by the same English word, to harden; but they may be discriminated throughout the narrative in Exodus, by the margin of the Revised Version.

One word, which commonly appears without any marginal explanation, is the same which is employed elsewhere about "the cause which is too *hard* for" minor judges (Deut. i. 17, cf. xv. 18, etc.). Now, this word is found (vii. 13) in the second threat that "I will harden Pharaoh's heart," and in the account which was to be given to posterity of how "Pharaoh hardened himself to let us go" (xiii. 15). And it is said likewise of Sihon, king of Heshbon, that he "would not let us pass by him, for the Lord thy God hardened his spirit and made his heart strong" (Deut. ii. 30). But since it does not occur anywhere in all the narrative of what God actually did with Pharaoh, it is only just to interpret this phrase in the prediction by what we read elsewhere of the manner of its fulfillment.

The second word is explained in the margin as meaning *to make strong*. Already God had employed it when He said "I will *make strong* his heart" (iv. 21), and this is the term used of the first fulfillment of the menace, after the sixth plague (ix. 12). God is not said to interfere again after the seventh, which had few special terrors for Pharaoh himself; but from henceforth the expression "to make *strong*" alternates with the phrase "to make *heavy.*" "Go in unto Pharaoh, for I have made heavy his heart and the heart of his servants, that I might show these My signs in the midst of them" (x. 1).

It may be safely assumed that these two expressions cover between them all that is asserted of the judicial action of God in preventing a recoil of Pharaoh from his calamities. Now, the strengthening of a heart, however punitive and disastrous when a man's will is evil (just as the strengthening of his arm is disastrous then), has in itself no immorality inherent. It is a thing as often good as bad,—as when Israel and Joshua are exhorted to "Be *strong* and of good courage" (Deut. xxxi. 6, 7, 23), and when the angel laid his hand upon Daniel and said, "Be strong, yea, be strong" (Dan. x. 19). In these passages the phrase is identical with that which describes the process by which Pharaoh was prevented from cowering under the tremendous blows he had provoked.

The other expression is to make heavy or dull. Thus "the eyes of Israel were *heavy* with age" (Gen. xlviii. 10), and as we speak of a *weight* of honor, equally with the heaviness of a dull man, so we are twice commanded, "Make heavy (honor) thy father and thy mother"; and the Lord declares, "I will make Myself heavy (get Me honor) upon Pharaoh" (Deut. v. 16, Exod. xx. 12, xiv. 4, 17, 18). In these latter references it will be observed that the making "strong" the heart of Pharaoh and the making "Myself heavy" are so connected as almost to show a design of indicating how far is either expression from conveying the notion of immorality, infused into a human heart by God. For one of the two phrases which have been thus interpreted is still applied to Pharaoh; but the other (and the more sinister, as we should think, when thus applied) is appropriated by God to Himself: He makes Himself heavy.

It is also a curious and significant coincidence that the same word was used of the burdens that were made *heavy* when first they claimed their freedom, which is now used of the treatment of the heart of their oppressor (v. 9).

It appears, then, that the Lord is never said to debauch Pharaoh's heart, but only to strengthen it against prudence and to make it dull; that the words used do not express the infusion of evil passion, but the animation of a resolute courage, and the overclouding of a natural discernment; and, above all, that every one of the three words, to make hard, to make strong, and to make heavy, is employed to express Pharaoh's own treatment of himself, before it is applied to any work of God, as actually taking place already.

NOTES

1. Ezekiel 18:23; this plain teaching of Scripture is made null by some traditions. Thus one Reformer says: "It is true, God would not men should perish as touching his *signified will*, for he offered unto man a law, promises, threatenings, and counsels, which things, if he had embraced, he had surely lived. But, if we have respect unto that mighty and effectual will, doubtless we cannot deny, but God would have men to perish." We have examined this passage (from Calvin in Romans Tr. Sibson) in section 6.

2. How is one to go about finding the connotations of a word or phrase in an ancient language like Hebrew? The best way would obviously be to ask a cross section of ancient Hebrews or to consult a selection of dictionaries compiled by them. But such options are not open to us—so what can we do? It may often be illuminating to consult books by modern day experts, but if the experts should happen to disagree or to say little of a word's connotations, then what should we do? There would seem to be two main sources of a better understanding of the connotations of a Hebrew phrase used in a particular verse:

(i) Consideration of the contexts in which the same word or phrase is used elsewhere. This may suggest possible meanings to us, or help us to see connotations of the phrase.

This is not by any means infallible. A word cannot be assumed to be identical in meaning whenever used. Nevertheless if we were to reject altogether such considerations then it is difficult to see what basis there *would* be for us to study a phrase of a language written so long ago. In practice, we may even have to resort to guidance gleaned from uses of phrases that are similar (though not identical) to the one in question.

(ii) Consideration of the context in which the word or phrase is used in this particular verse in question. Some "translations" of a word (although valid elsewhere) may be seen to be meaningless in this verse. (One could, for example, rule out the "translation": "God repaired Pharaoh's heart"!) There may also be other renderings which would, in the verse in question, give a meaning contradicted by other Scriptures. Such renderings will be unacceptable to those of us who believe the Bible to be inspired and consistent—though we must, of course, be sure that it really is the Bible that it contradicts, and not merely our own preconceptions!

Such considerations may sometimes still leave us with several "possible" interpretations of the phrase, giving rise to several different understandings of the verse. One further consideration may help us in the difficult task of discernment. This is to ask ourselves whether an interpretation implies that the writer has put in an obscure or roundabout way what could have been put in a more simple and straightforward way. If it does, then we should be suspicious of it.

These two sources of understanding would not be infallible even if we were also to have a good knowledge of the language itself. In some cases it may be impossible to be certain of the meaning of a particular phrase, simply because of insufficient evidence. But, in the instance of an ancient language like Hebrew, it would seem that such evidence as there can be, may come through one of these two avenues of investigation.

3. The various conjugations of Hebrew verbs are not only spelled differently, but may have rather different meanings. To make this study easier for the English reader a Hebrew verb has always been signified by the root form (*chazaq, kabed,* etc.), whatever its conjugation. The latter is usually indicated somewhere in the text, but it seemed better always to give the root form for the sake of readers who may be unfamiliar with Hebrew.

4. One other interesting parallel is in Psalm 27:14—"Wait on the Lord. Be of good courage (*chazaq*) and he shall strengthen (*amats*) your heart." (This is AV, which renders the Hebrew the most obviously—though other renderings would not substantially alter our comment.)

We may see the similarity between the meanings of the roots *amats* and *chazaq* by comparing their use in Scripture: In Deuteronomy 31:6 they are parallelled, and we may also compare:

2 Samuel 22:18 with 2 Samuel 10:11

Proverbs 31:17 with Ezekiel 30:24, 25

2 Chronicles 13:18 with 2 Chronicles 27:5 and Daniel 11:7
It may seem, therefore, that Psalm 27:14 illustrates our point that to "strengthen" or "make firm" a person's heart is, in itself, a morally neutral act. Caution, however, is needed, for Psalm 27:14 uses the Hiphil conjugation of the verb, whereas the Piel form is used in connection with the heart of Pharaoh. It may be that this simply indicates intensity—as it would seem in Ezekiel 30:24, 25, where the Piel of *chazaq* is used in 24 and the Hiphil in 25. Nevertheless, it must be admitted that different conjugations of a Hebrew verb are not strictly comparable, and the parallel should not be pressed.

5. Exodus 7:22; 8:7
6. Exodus 8:19
7. Exodus 8:22; 9:4
8. Exodus 9:11
9. Exodus 9:24-27
10. Edersheim: *Bible History,* volume ii, p. 61
11. The remainder of this passage is well worth reading, but has been omitted for brevity here.
12. A. M. Renwick: *The History of the Church,* p. 45. Further comments on Origen are found in the appendix. Renwick makes the comment on Irenaeus that: "The importance of his work *Against Heresies* in saving the church from the doctrines of the Gnostics cannot be exaggerated."
13. The quotation is from the Greek version of Origen's *De Principiis* Bk 3 ch 1, the Greek being more reliable than the Latin translation of Rufinus.
14. Irenaeus, *Against Heresies,* ch xxix 1 & 2
15. 1 Samuel 6:6
16. See Gesenius, or other standard grammar.
17. Davidson's Hebrew Grammar (1956, 24th Edition, p. 95) specifically lists a declaratory meaning as a possible one for the Hiph form of verbs.
18. See, e.g., Souter's lexicon.

18

Word Study—Foreknowledge

The ultimate object of this study is to analyze what the Bible means when it talks of God's foreknowledge and predestination (or foreordination) of us. The earliest Christian commentators thought that it meant God foreknew something about us[1] and on this basis gave us the remarkable destiny of conformity to his Son. This is not the same conclusion we shall reach, but it is not unlike it. If this had been the only current view of the question, this word study might have been shorter or perhaps even omitted altogether.

There has arisen, however, a quite different view of foreknowledge, which has gained acceptance with a number of scholars and theologians. This is so markedly different from the early church view that it was decided to include here a study on the word. It is unfortunate that much of the study is a destructive analysis, for it is our own belief that this "new" view is unacceptable. This part is long and technical, and the following plan may help the reader:

(a) This part sets out seven shades of meaning of the word *ginōskō* (know) as we understand it to be used in Scripture.

(b) This part considers the suggestion that *ginōskō* can mean "choose," and the verses commonly cited to illustrate it. Our conclusion is that this meaning only ever occurs insofar as it is an integral part of a relationship.

(c) This part considers the use of the word *proginōskō*

(foreknowledge) as applied to subjects other than the church.

(d) (i) This part considers the "new" view of foreknowledge mentioned above and finds it unacceptable.

The last part, (d/ii), attempts to make a positive contribution to understanding the concept. Many readers may find this interesting even if they find the earlier parts too technical.

(a)
MEANINGS
OF *KNOW* IN
SCRIPTURE

The word *foreknowledge* is made up of the two Greek elements "previous" (*pro*) and "knowledge" (*ginōskō*). The Greek word *ginōskō* (like the English "know") can have many shades of meaning. It is not always possible from the context to distinguish between these. Nevertheless it will be beneficial if at the beginning of this study they are identified so that we may keep them clear in our minds. Then when we come to consider *fore*knowledge the various possibilities will be clear to us.

In part (a) therefore, we examine the various uses of the word *ginōskō* at the time of the apostles. Examples are given from the Greek New Testament, and also from the Septuagint (LXX) translation of the Old Testament. This Septuagint (or LXX) was the Greek translation of the Hebrew Old Testament which was familiar to the apostles and their contemporaries. It is not any more authoritative than any other translation, but will certainly help our understanding of what the Greek words concerned meant to the apostles:

(1) *Perceive* (usually knowledge of facts)

1 John 3:24—hereby we know that he abides in us . . .

Mark 13:28—you know that the summer is nigh

Luke 7:39—This man, if he were a prophet, would have perceived who and what manner of woman this is.

(2) *Understand*

John 8:43—Why do you not understand my speech?

John 10:6—But they understood not the things which he spoke

Acts 8:30—understand you what you read?

(In some cases this may be difficult to distinguish from (1); in other cases it may be closer to (6) below.)

(3) *Experience or follow*

Micah 3:1—is it not for you to know judgment? (LXX)

Micah 4:9—Why have you experienced calamities? (LXX)

Zephaniah 3:5—he knows not injustice by extortion (LXX)

Hebrews 3:10—But they did not know my ways

(4) *Acknowledge*

Deuteronomy 33:9—He acknowledged not his brothers and refused to know his sons (LXX)

1 Chronicles 28:9—And now Solomon my son, acknowledge the God of your fathers (LXX)

Job 19:13—My brothers have stood off from me and acknowledged strangers rather than me (LXX)

Jeremiah 3:13—Nevertheless acknowledge your iniquity (LXX) (See also Genesis 38:26; 1 Kings 10:24; Isaiah 33:13; 59:12; 61:9; Jeremiah 14:20; Daniel 4:22, 29, where "acknowledge" seems a preferable rendering.)

Sometimes it may be difficult to distinguish this from (5) or (6), e.g., in Acts 19:15—And the evil spirit answered and said unto them, Jesus I know (*ginōskō*), and Paul I know (*epistamai*); but who are you?

(5) *Recognize* (personal or impersonal objects)

Luke 24:35—how he was known of them in the breaking of the bread

Matthew 12:33—the tree is known by its fruit

1 Kings 20:41—And the king of Israel knew him, that he was one of the prophets. (LXX)

(6) *Knowledge of persons—implying understanding of them*

The word *ginōskō* can be used to imply thorough understanding of a person, knowledge about him. When used in this sense the object of the verb is a personal one, but there may be no relationship involved.

Matthew 25:24—I knew you that you are a hard man

John 2:24, 25—Jesus did not trust himself to them for that

he knew all men, and because he needed not that anyone should bear witness concerning man, for he himself knew what was in man

John 1:47, 48—Behold an Israelite indeed, in whom is no guile! Nathaniel said unto him, whence know you me?

John 5:42—I know you, that you have not the love of God in yourselves

Psalm 138(139):1, 2, 6:—O Lord you have examined me and known me. You know my sitting down and rising up; you understand my thoughts from afar . . . the knowledge of you is too difficult for me. (LXX)

Jeremiah 12:3—But you Lord know me (Heb: know and see me); you have examined my heart before you (LXX)

This knowledge or understanding of a person may, of course, be a result of personal acquaintance (e.g., Matthew 25:24). But equally well it may be without any acquaintance or relationship (e.g., John 2:24; 5:42). This is important. It shows that intellectual understanding and knowledge of a person may be all that is implied, even if the object of the verb is personal. There may be no implication at all of a relationship.

The Hebrew word for know (*yada*) seems also to be used in this way (e.g., 2 Samuel 3:25; 7:20; 17:8) but the LXX usually paraphrases this for clarity.

It may not be possible in all cases to separate this meaning precisely from the concept of an acquaintanceship, e.g., compare Nathaniel above to Genesis 29:5: Know you Laban. . . ? And they said, We know him. (LXX) Nonetheless there is a marked difference in some cases.

(7) *Knowledge of persons—special relationship*

1 John 2:4—He that says, I know him, and keeps not his commandments, is a liar, and the truth is not in him.

1 John 4:7—everyone that loves is begotten of God, and knows God

Matthew 7:23—I never knew you: depart from me, you that work iniquity. Every one therefore . . .

Deuteronomy 34:10—And there rose up no more a prophet in Israel like Moses whom the Lord knew face to face (LXX) (compare Exodus 33:11, 12, 17)

Hosea 6:3, 4—we shall arise and live before him and shall know him; let us follow on to know the Lord . . . (LXX) (see also Hosea 8:2)

It is, of course, also in the context of a special relationship that we have the following:

Genesis 4:1—And Adam knew Eve his wife and she conceived (LXX)

Luke 1:34—Mary said unto the angel, How shall this be, seeing I know not a man?

(b)
CAN *KNOW* MEAN TO CHOOSE?

In addition to the above meanings it has sometimes been suggested either that the Greek *ginōskō* has connotations of "election," or even that it could actually mean to *choose*. We have not yet found anyone claim to see such a usage in the secular Greek, but such allegations *are* made on the basis of Biblical usage. The suggestion is that the O.T. Hebrew *yada* (and thus the LXX *ginōskō*) evidences such a meaning, and that it has thus passed over into N.T. writings. It is, therefore, on the basis of Biblical literature and word usage that the suggestion must be assessed.

Some writers refer to "common" usage, others to "frequent" usage, and yet others to "very marked and very clear" usage. The impression one might get is that the use of "know" to imply election is common and clear in the O.T. and Bible generally. Our own belief is that this is not a justifiable impression. The Hebrew word *yada* (know) is used about 770 times in the O.T.—in about 500 of which the LXX used the Greek word *ginōskō* to translate it. In the N.T. the word *ginōskō* is used about 220 times. Yet advocates of this viewpoint[2] seem able to cite but few references in support. We have analyzed in the pages that follow the four most plausible O.T. and two most plausible N.T. verses usually cited in this way. Our own conclusion is that if ever there are implications of "choice" they form part of a special relationship. There can be no simple equation of "choice" with *ginōskō*.

Amos 3:2, 3—You only (or LXX "especially") have I known of all the families of the earth: therefore I will visit upon you all your iniquities. Shall two walk together, except they have agreed?

At first sight it would seem that a meaning for this verse could be preserved if one replaced "known" with "chosen." We know that Israel was the chosen nation, and "You only have I chosen . . ." would be a true statement. However, the context of Amos shows clearly that what is involved is not merely choice but a special relationship. A special relationship is, of course, usually set up as a result of a choice (i.e., perhaps the choice of the dominant party and the agreement of the other, e.g., in marriage). But a relationship itself is certainly more than a choice. The two concepts may not be equated.

In Amos 2:10-12 the Lord says: I brought you up out of the land of Egypt, and led you forty years in the wilderness, to possess the land of the Amorite. And I raised up of your sons for prophets, and of your young men for Nazirites. Is it not even thus, oh you children of Israel? says the Lord. But you gave the Nazirites wine to drink; and commanded the prophets, saying Prophesy not. The Lord is complaining that in spite of the special relationship he opened with them,[3] and in spite of his special care and protection for them as a nation, they have spurned his favors and broken the covenant. For this reason their judgment shall be the greater. He reiterates his theme in Amos 3:1-4 (compare 2:10)—Hear the word that the Lord has spoken against you, O children of Israel, against the whole family which I brought up out of the land of Egypt, saying, You only have I known of all the families of the earth: therefore I will visit upon you all your iniquities. Shall two walk together except they have agreed? Will a lion roar in the forest when he has no prey? . . . The Lord is referring to his personal knowledge of them, a relationship established when he brought them out of Egypt. The thought is similar to

Hosea 13:5 in many ways. It is because as a nation they have known God in this special way that the results of their sins are the more serious. The next verse seems to re-emphasize that this previous entry into a special relationship explains God's present special dealings with them. The Hebrew reads: "Shall two walk together unless they have met by arrangement?" The LXX reads: "Shall two walk together at all unless they know one another?" (The word *know* here is derived from *ginōskō* and means to "define the boundaries of their knowledge of each other.") What exactly does this mean? We notice that it is followed by a series of examples showing how one thing signifies previous occurrence of another; e.g., a trumpet sound means that trouble has come to a city. Similarly, we take it, two people do not walk along together (in friendship or relationship) unless it is by prior agreement. The Lord God has already defined his relationship with Israel, when they agreed to the covenant with him and he knew them in the wilderness. This explains his special interest in them now.

The prophet is, therefore, surely referring to a relationship. If he were merely talking of "choice," why should he go on to talk of two walking together by mutual agreement? To know someone in the sense of relationship does imply, of course, that some kind of choice has already been made. God knew Moses face to face because he had chosen Moses for a special position. But the word *know* in this sense certainly means much more than choice. Likewise, it must be insisted, the prophet refers in Amos 3:2 to their special relationship with God, and not merely to God's choice of them.[4]

Hosea 13:5—I did know you in the wilderness, in the land of great drought.

It would seem far more natural to take this to imply a relationship rather than merely a choice. Would the Lord really say: "I did choose you in the wilderness . . ." when, as we know, his choice of Israel was made long before that time? Surely he refers to his continual relationship with them there. The Septuagint, Syriac, Targum, and Vulgate all emphasize this by rendering it: "I tended you as a shepherd in the wilderness in an uninhabited land"—which is, incidentally, a better parallel to the next line. But perhaps the most important point to note here is that the whole book of Hosea is about a broken relationship (see, e.g., 8: 2, 3 also 6:3; 7:15; 11:1). Hosea and his unfaithful wife provide the object lesson for this (ch. 3), and God said that the Israelites had forsaken "knowledge" (*epignōsis*) of him (Hosea 4:1-6). All this constitutes very clear evidence that a broken relationship was what the prophet had in view. Again, this special relationship may imply that a choice had already been made, but it is much more than a choice. There seems no grounds for supposing a concept of "choice" outside that which is integral to a special relationship.

Genesis 18:17-19—And the Lord said, Shall I hide from Abraham that which I do; seeing that Abraham shall surely become a great and mighty nation, and all the nations of the earth shall be blessed in him? For I have known him, to the end that he may command his children and his household after him, that they may keep the way of the Lord, to do justice and judgment; to the end that the Lord may bring upon Abraham that which he has spoken of him.

The various versions appear to take this verse quite differently. The AV and Young seem to interpret it along lines similar to the Septuagint. The latter simply reads: "For I know that he will order his sons . . ." This makes sense of the text, and at first seems plausible, but in fact the Hebrew phrase used does seem to indicate purpose, i.e., "I have known him *to the end that* . . ."[5] What then is its meaning?

The RSV puts in a footnote that the meaning of the Hebrew word is "known," yet uses "chosen" in the text without further explanation. The NEB gives a more understandable rendering: "I have taken care of him on purpose that he may charge his sons . . ." Yet even this, perhaps, does not go far enough. What we must do is to consider verse 19 in the light of the whole context. The Lord's statement: **I have known him, to the end that he may command . . .** does not occur in a vacuum. It is given as the reason for God's decision to reveal to Abraham his plans about Sodom. If God were, as the RSV implies, merely referring to a *choice* of Abraham, why should this be any ground or reason for God to reveal his plans to him? The choice of a person is not necessarily any reason to confide in him. On the other hand a *special relationship* or friendship with a person *is* an obvious reason for confiding in him. This, surely, is what the Hebrew means here. Of course a person reveals his plans to his special friends—and Abraham is the "friend of God."[6] This, then, gives us the natural understanding of this verse. The Lord asks: "Shall I hide from Abraham what I do, seeing that I plan to bless the world through his descendants? For in order to bring this blessing through him I have 'got to know' him."[7] The Lord's reference is not so much to his choice of Abraham, nor even to the plan which that choice involved, but rather to the fact that during the course of that plan he has befriended Abraham—and therefore should confide in his friend. J. Skinner, in his commentary on Genesis, wrote: "Yahwe reflects, as it were, on the religious importance of the individual beside Him . . . *For I have known* (i.e., 'entered into personal relations with'; as Am. 3:2, Hos. 13:5) *him in order that,* etc."[8] Derek Kidner puts it very well: "The question *Shall I hide . . . ?* proves Abraham the 'friend' of God (Is. 41:8) by our Lord's own criterion (Jn. 15:15), and the expression *I have known him* (19, RV) reemphasizes it; it virtually means 'I have made him my friend.' "[9]

No one, of course, would say that God did not choose Abraham, nor that his friendship with Abraham was not a result of his own free choice. But it is one thing to say that God's "knowledge" of Abraham was a result of his "choice" of him; it is quite another thing to say (as the RSV) that his knowledge of him was *equivalent* to his choice. It is the friendship itself, and not the choice prior to the friendship, that is the ground for God's confiding in him. The words *For I have known him . . .* refer to the special relationship (friendship) and not merely to a choice.

Jeremiah 1:5-6—**Before I formed you in the belly I knew you, and before you came out of the womb I sanctified you:**

I have appointed you a prophet unto the nations. Then said I, Ah, Lord God! behold, I cannot speak: for I am a child. But the Lord said . . .

The sense of the word *know* here would seem to be similar to the sense in which Jeremiah himself uses it in 12:3— "But you Lord know and see me, you have examined my heart . . ." (see also (6) above). The LXX seems to indicate this sense when it translates the Hebrew word *yada* (know) not by *ginōskō* but by *epistamai*. The latter means to "understand fully" or "know through and through." The verse means, then, that God *fully understood* Jeremiah's nature, and on this basis "set him apart" (i.e., "sanctified" him) even before his birth. Why does the Lord begin his words to Jeremiah by assuring him that he fully understood his nature even before he was born? The answer is seen in Jeremiah's immediate reaction to God's words about "appointing him as a prophet." Jeremiah exclaims: "Ah, Lord God, behold I cannot speak!" Surely, says Jeremiah, there must be some mistake—I would be hopeless at such a task! How gracious of the Lord to begin his message to Jeremiah with the personal reassurance that he knows him better than he knows himself, that his appointment has long been planned on the basis of that knowledge.

God did, of course, choose Jeremiah before his birth—for a choice is involved in the sanctification. But his knowledge is the *basis* of the choice (sanctification). It is by no means to be *equated* with it.[10]

SUMMARY
(OLD TESTAMENT)

This study has been to analyze in what sense we might see some connection between "election" and the Hebrew word *yada*, and thus what implications could be passed on to the Greek *ginōskō*. Out of 770 uses of *yada* in the O.T. the four most commonly cited were considered. Our own conclusion was that three of them clearly refer to a special relationship and the fourth to a thorough understanding rather than a choice. Further, although the LXX uses *ginōskō* 600 times to translate *yada*, in only one of these four (Amos 3:2) is *ginōskō* used.[11] In that one it definitely seems to mean a special relationship.

Would we be justified, then, in speaking of the word *ginōskō* having a "common" and "very clear" implication of electing grace in the O.T.? Surely not if we meant by this that the O.T. usage might have led Paul to use *ginōskō* to mean "choice"—even if he meant that this choice would later lead to a relationship. If, on the other hand, we intended only to imply that *ginōskō* could mean a special relationship which might *involve* a choice, then this would be true enough. But we must be sure to remember that it is the special relationship, rather than merely the choice, that is meant by *ginōskō*.

NEW TESTAMENT USE OF GINŌSKŌ

We may look now at the two Pauline references most commonly cited to connect *ginōskō* with election. Both are plays on words, and we must look very carefully at their contexts to grasp their meanings.

1 Corinthians 8:1-4—**Knowledge puffs up, but love edifies. If any man thinks that he knows anything, he knows not yet as he ought to know; but if any man loves God, the same is known of him. Concerning therefore the eating of things sacrificed to idols . . .**

This is one of the few verses, if not the only one, out of the 221 times *ginōskō* is used in the New Testament, that would still have an apparent sense if "known" were replaced by "chosen." There are, however, two questions we should ask. First, would Paul have expected the word to convey "chosen" to his readers? Surely not, for it is not the usual secular Greek usage, and, even in the LXX, there seems no clear instance of it being used thus. Second, is there some common meaning for "know," which better fits the context? We believe that there is. Paul is explaining how a Christian may *know* that meat sacrificed to idols is no different from other meat, but there is no reason to be puffed up with this knowledge. Paul emphasizes that any action in such external matters cannot, of itself, commend or "discommend" anyone to God (v. 8). It is not a person's own knowledge that matters, but that if he loves God then God recognizes (knows) him. Other men may be impressed by someone's knowledge about external rituals, but God recognizes a true servant by his love. This point is repeated elsewhere in Scripture, e.g., **he is a Jew, which is one inwardly; and circumcision is that of the heart, in the spirit, not in the letter; whose praise is not of men, but of God.**[12]

We accept, therefore, the NEB rendering: "But if a man loves, he is acknowledged (or 'recognized') by God." (AB is similar). This use of *ginōskō* is found elsewhere (see (4) and (5) above). There seems no reason to suppose that Paul meant us to go beyond this simple meaning to add a concept of "election."

Galatians 4:8, 9—At that time, not knowing God, you were in bondage to them which by nature are no gods, but now that you have come to know God, or rather to be known of God, how turn you back again to the weak and beggarly elements?

Whatever its meaning this verse does not, in fact, seem relevant to the present discussion. The line of argument seemingly used from it runs: "knowledge" in Galatians 4:9 means "election" or "marking out" and similarly "foreknowledge" means "chosen in advance." Yet the verse implies that their present state of knowing and being known by God has replaced a former state of non-knowledge. If God "fore-knew" them all along (in this supposed sense of election), how could Paul imply that the present state of mutual knowledge replaced a former state where neither "knew" the other? Yet he does say this, and thus whatever the sense of "know" here, it must be different from that in God's "fore-knowledge" of Christians.

But what *could* be the sense of know in this verse? The

Galatians were putting themselves under regulations of service to "elements" or "elemental spirits" imagined to be of more concern in daily living than faith in God working by love.[13] Paul seems to be contrasting the bondage they sought under "weak and beggarly elements" with the fact that as Christians God himself showed interest in them. Not only had they come to know God, but he had likewise come to acknowledge them. This showed how inferior to true faith was the service of no-gods. Paul's word-play is given well by the NEB: "Formerly when you did not acknowledge God, you were the slaves of beings which in their nature are no gods. But now you do acknowledge God—or rather now that he has acknowledged you— how can you turn back to the mean and beggarly spirits of the elements?"

This interpretation is both contextually satisfying and in accord with general use of *ginōskō*. Sometimes, of course, the word *acknowledge* may imply some selection of the acknowledged one, but the idea does not seem particularly relevant here. In any event, as we have seen, the word *knowledge* must be meant differently here from its use in "fore-knowledge."

SUMMARY

We remember that there are 770 instances in the O.T. of the Hebrew *yada*, and 600 LXX and 220 N.T. instances of *ginōskō*. Out of these we have considered the six verses most frequently and most plausibly cited to illustrate the suggestion that "know" has connotations of election or even that it can actually *mean* election. What should we conclude?

We can see no evidence that any of these (or indeed any other) verses ever use *ginōskō* to mean "chosen." We can, in other words, find no place in the Bible where it seems to us that the sense intended by the writer would not be radically changed by putting "chosen" instead of *yada* or *ginōskō*. The question of whether the word might have *connotations* of election is more difficult. From the verses considered we would conclude that there could (e.g., in

Amos 3:2) be such connotations, but that they would come as an integral part of a special relationship—not as a concept separate from one or prior to it.

(c)
FOREKNOWLEDGE

The Greek word *foreknowledge* (*proginōskō*) is made up of the two Greek elements "previous" (*pro*) and "knowledge" (*ginōskō*). In general Greek literature it simply means "knowledge in advance," or sometimes "prognosis" in the medical sense.[14]

In the early church the term was sometimes used as another word for prophecy.[15] When used of God it seems always to mean knowledge in advance—usually of events.[16]

Sometimes it is connected with his full understanding of us, e.g., in Clement: "For He has foreknowledge of all things and knows what is in our hearts."[17]

Also Justin: ". . . until the number of those foreknown by Him as good and virtuous is complete" and "For He foreknows some about to be saved by repentance."[18] The early church was, we note, emphatic in its denial that foreknowledge implied any predetermination of events. Thus Justin Martyr says: "So that what we say about future events being foretold, we do not say it as though they came about by fatal necessity; but God foreknowing all that shall be done by all men, and it being His decree that the future actions of men shall all be recompensed according to their value, He foretells by the Spirit of prophecy that He will bestow meet rewards . . ." and "But if the word of God foretells that some angels and men shall be certainly punished, it did so because it foreknew that they would be unchangeably wicked, but not because God had created them so."[19]

Origen says: "I shall take from the Scriptures the predictions regarding Judas, or the foreknowledge of our Savior regarding him as the traitor . . ." and then proceeds to argue that this foreknowledge in no way implied compulsion.[20]

Jerome, not-withstanding his withering attack on the Pelagians, is also clear on this point: "For Adam did not sin because God knew that he would do so; but God, inasmuch as He is God, foreknew what Adam would do of his own free choice."21

We can find no hint in any of the early church writings that "foreknow" was ever interpreted in the sense of the theologians whose views are cited in note 2. It may be useful to bear such background in mind, for the evidence on the word from the Bible itself is small. In the Old Testament (LXX) it is not used at all, though the LXX does use it five times in the apocrypha.22

In the New Testament it is used only seven times, and these we must now consider. We may begin by looking at the five times when it is used of subjects other than the church:

2 Peter 3:17—You therefore, beloved, knowing these things beforehand, beware lest, being carried away with the error of the wicked, you fall from your own steadfastness.

The meaning of "known" here is clearly that of (a/1) above, the knowledge of events. This is the sense of the word common in secular and early church writings. Peter is telling his readers to beware, for they know in advance that people will try to give Paul's writings strange and devious meanings.

Acts 2:23—Jesus . . . being delivered up by the determinate counsel and foreknowledge of God, you by the hand of lawless men did crucify and slay.

This use of the word is similar to (1) in referring to foreknowledge of events. God made his plans in the light of what he knew would happen. God's plan to deliver up his Son to them was made in the knowledge that they would crucify him.23

1 Peter 1:18-20—you were redeemed . . . with precious blood, as of a lamb without blemish and without spot, even the blood of Christ: who was foreknown indeed before the foundation of the world, but was manifested at the end of the times for your sake . . .

This verse is, unfortunately, the subject of strong, misleading traditions. Peter does not use the Greek word for "foreordain" (*prooriz*ō) but the word for "foreknow" (*pro-gin*ō*sk*ō). There is no indication either in secular or in Biblical literature that readers would take this word to mean foreordain.[24] Scholars who take it in this way would seem to do so on philosophical rather than linguistic grounds. As a straight translation the RV is surely the correct rendering (whatever philosophical implications may be advocated).

Literally the Greek reads: "were ye redeemed . . . with precious blood, as of a lamb unblemished and unspotted—Christ's—foreknown, indeed, before the foundation of the world, and manifested in the last times because of you."[25] Peter's grammar here is not entirely consistent, and his exact meaning is unclear. From the sentence structure it would seem that the "foreknowledge" would naturally refer back to the noun "blood"; but in fact Peter makes its Greek form agree with the word *Christ's!* Does he mean, then, that God foreknew Christ before the world began? The Father did, of course, have a relationship with the Son before the creation—and to interpret Peter to mean this would be quite consistent with the present word study. It does seem, however, that there would be little point in Peter stating this truth here.

The context of his words may help us. He has been saying that the suffering and death of Christ (which achieved our salvation of faith) was something that prophets of old dimly saw and sought to understand (v. 10, 11). Even angels desire to look into such matters. It is with this in mind (he says) that we should set our own aim and hope—*knowing* that we were redeemed by Christ's blood, for which the Old Testament sacrificial lamb was merely a picture. He follows this with the words: "foreknown, indeed, before the world, but manifested in these last times for you." God foreknew the redemptive function of the Messiah[26] before history began, but its actual manifestation did not come until the New Covenant. This we take to be Peter's meaning.

Paul similarly talks of a manifestation of God's method of redemption by Christ's blood, implying that God foreknew it all along.[27] The epistle to the Hebrews further indicates that God established the sacrifices in Israel as a foreshadow of the redemption by blood which he foreknew would come.[28] John, in the Revelation, emphasizes that the redemption through the blood "as of an unspotted and unblemished lamb" was always in God's mind, by calling Christ the "lamb slain from the foundation of the world."[29]

This is, therefore, how we would understand Peter's words in 1 Peter 1:20. It is certainly linguistically possible that he refers to a prior relationship of Father and Son, but this seems unlikely to have been his intention. In any event there is certainly no reference here to "foreordination" or "predestination."

Romans 11:2—God did not cast off his people which he foreknew.

This is the first verse we have considered in which the object of the "previous-knowledge" is a personal one. It could mean either of the following:

(i) When God made the promises to Israel he knew that most of the nation would fall at the time of Christ. In spite of this knowledge, God made the promises and so will not go back on them now.[30] This would be to interpret knowledge in the sense of (a/6) above i.e., a knowledge of persons that does not necessarily imply a relationship, but an understanding of their thinking and reactions.

(ii) God entered into a personal relationship with Israel before their later unbelief to which Paul refers. Thus God "foreknew them" or "knew them of old." This is a possible meaning but we should note three things about it. First, it is not necessarily implied by the fact that the object is personal (see (a/6) above and (5) below). Second, if it is true, it does not mean that God entered in some former time into a relationship with the Israelites of today; it means that he entered a (two-way) relationship with the Israel that existed in early Old Testament times, and he regards the present Israelites as integral with it. Third, there would be no reason to bring in a concept of choice other than that which is an integral part of a special relationship.

Acts 26:4-5—My manner of life then from my youth up, which was from the beginning among mine own nation, and at Jerusalem, know all the Jews; having knowledge of me from the first, if they be willing to testify, how that after the straitest sect of our religion I lived a Pharisee.

Paul's manner of life was well known to all the Jews. He adds, therefore, "pre-knowing me from the first . . . how that . . . I lived a Pharisee." He does not here, of course, imply that all the Jews knew him in the sense of being on personal terms. Indeed, since he was brought up in Tarsus it is not likely that *all* the Jews at Jerusalem would have known him personally! The point was that they knew all about him, the sense of know being similar to (a/6) above. Here foreknowledge implies knowledge about the manner of life he lived from his earliest days.

This example of the use of the word *foreknowledge* is important. We note that the grammatical object of the verb is a personal one (i.e., Paul), yet it does not imply any special relationship with that person. "They foreknew me" means "they previously knew about me." A special relationship is not in view, and there is certainly no idea of election.

(d)
GOD'S
FOREKNOWLEDGE
OF THE CHURCH

1 Peter 1:1, 2—to the elect . . . according to the foreknowledge of God the Father.[31]

Romans 8:28-30—We know that in everything God works for good with those who love him, who are called according to his purpose. For those whom he foreknew he also predestined to be conformed to the image of his Son, in order that he might be the first-born among many brethren. And those whom he predestined he also called; and those whom he called he also justified; and those whom he justified he also glorified. (RSV)

God's foreknowledge of those in the church predates their election and predestination. Since God chose them, in Christ, before the creation (Ephesians 1:4), it would seem that they were foreknown even before the world began. What, therefore, does "foreknow" mean here? Theologians have suggested two alternatives. It means:

(1) God had a special relationship with them or "chose" them.

(2) He foreknew them in the sense of knowing about them and understanding all their reactions and characters. Let us consider these:

Special Relationship or Choice. The various versions of this view are linked by the common assumption that the term *foreknowledge* implies not just passive understanding but some action on God's part. It is based on the idea that as *ginōskō* can mean "choose" or "set apart," so *proginōskō* implies some kind of "setting apart beforehand" or "election."

How are we to interpret this? If it were taken to imply a setting apart prior to a special relationship, then Romans 8:29 would make sense. It could, in fact, be taken quite consistently with our own view of election—provided that the setting apart were viewed as a collective action on those *in Christ*. If, however, the word *foreknow* is taken in this way to imply a choice other than as an integral part of a special relationship, then there is the difficulty of finding a single verse to support this (out of 770 cases of *yada* and 820 of *ginōskō* in the Bible). Admittedly in some verses *yada* or *ginōskō* is used of a special relationship where there could be connotations of election. But it would surely be unacceptable to deduce from this that *ginōskō* could mean "choice" other than as an integral part of such a relationship. Paul could surely never have expected such a meaning to be read into "foreknow" by his Romans readers? If this had really been his meaning then surely he would have said "fore-elect" or "foreconsecrated" rather than "foreknow."

The alternative interpretation of the view would be to take it that the suggested connotations of election are accompaniments of the kind of special relationship represented in verses like Amos 3:2. This is not to say that this is necessarily the interpretation intended by those scholars who make the allegation, but that it is the only interpretation of the view which seems justifiable from O.T. usage of *yada* and *ginōskō*. While linguistically justifiable, however, there would seem to be great difficulties in making the interpretation conceptually meaningful. This is basically because it would imply that God set up a special relationship with us before the world began, which raises a number of problems.

For one thing, if God set up a relationship with some people before the world began, he must presumably first have selected them. In this case his "foreknowledge" of them would have depended on his choice. But Peter does not say "foreknown according to the election of God"; he says "elect according to the foreknowledge of God." Thus such a view of foreknowledge would seem to invert the apostolic teaching.

Second, if God has always been linked with us in a special relationship, how was this changed by our new birth? The Bible seems to regard us as enemies and strangers who, being reconciled by the blood of Christ, have been born again into a living relationship with God. How can this be so if God always had a personal relationship with us? One possible answer is that God's relationship was broken off when we were born—but this seems a rather devious explanation! Surely Paul would not have wrapped up in the one word *foreknowledge* a doctrine not given anywhere else in the Bible.

But there is a more serious difficulty. This becomes apparent if we ask when it is that a human being comes into existence. Is it conception, birth, or some other moment? Surely no Christian would say that human beings existed before the world began. He might, perhaps, say that they existed in God's thoughts. But if God had a relationship with "his thoughts about them," this is certainly not the same as having a relationship with *them*. Yet Paul's reference is to "those whom he foreknew . . ."; he says that God foreknew the Christians, not that God foreknew his thoughts about the Christians. If one is to interpret foreknow to imply a special relationship, then it must be with Christians—not with thoughts about Christians. But if they did not exist, then God must have had a relationship with entities that did not exist! But surely the word *relationship* implies that two people *do* exist, to be (personally) related to each other. Personal relationship implies a two-way action-reaction. If foreknowledge were really taken in this sense, then we must have known and reacted to God before we existed. This whole line of thinking seems self-contradictory.[32] The words "to have a two-way relationship with a non-existent person" do not even state an *impossibility*. They do not state anything at all. They are simply a collection of words in a meaningless series.[33]

This is an important distinction. Jesus said: "With God all things are possible,"[34] but Scripture tells us of things that God cannot do.[35] So we must not apply these words blindly. Such things as changing water into wine are impossible to man, but there is nothing *meaningless* about a liquid's properties changing in this manner. Many similar things are possible to God but not to man. But to "have a two-way relationship with a non-existent person" is not an impossibility; it is a meaningless word series. To put "God can" in front does not make it meaningful. Linguistic analysts have long been aware of such word series, which look like sentences but are without meaning. One famous one is "Socrates is identical." In our former book we gave another example: "God can make a tripod with four legs." The words "a tripod with four legs" are meaningless, and to prefix them with "God can" does not alter this.

The whole line of thinking, therefore, that interprets foreknowledge in terms of a special relationship seems to us to be conceptually meaningless. Unless Paul wished to imply the preexistence of the human spirit (which would be an incredible doctrine to wrap up in one word without further mention), we cannot see how that could be his meaning.

In summary, there would seem to be three basic ways to take the word *proginōskō* in Romans 8:29.

The first sense is an active one, implying a unilateral act by God in "choosing" or "marking out" some people with whom he would later start a relationship—but *without* implying any reaction from them at that time. Our own conclusion was that this interpretation of *proginōskō* was conceptually meaningful, but linguistically could not be justified on the basis of the Biblical usage of the word *ginōskō*.

The second sense is also active, but implying a two-way action-reaction in a relationship in which there might be connotations of election. This interpretation seems to be linguistically justifiable from Biblical usage of *ginōskō* (e.g., in Amos 3:2), but it is conceptually meaningless since it implies a relationship with someone non-existent.

It may be that there is some way around such difficulties which we have not seen; but as a contribution to the concept we would like to explore the possibility of a third interpretation of *ginōskō* in Romans 8:29. This is one of a "passive" sense, i.e., as implying a thorough understanding but not an action on God's part.

Knowledge Without Relationship. J. B. Phillips renders Romans 8:29—"God, in his foreknowledge, chose them (i.e., those who love him) to bear the family likeness of his Son . . ." In other words, God has set the destiny of those who love him in the full light of his foreknowledge of them and their characteristics.

But is an interpretation of this kind admissible? Objections to it might be raised on the grounds that since the grammatical object is a personal one (i.e., *those whom* God foreknew), more is implied than knowledge *about* those concerned. This objection is, we feel, nullified by Biblical usage in verses where the grammatical object of the verb *ginōskō* is personal, but where no more is implied than a thorough understanding of a person and his character. Several examples of this are given above in (a/6). Moreover, the word *proginōskō*, though used only seven times in all, is used at least once in this sense. Compare Jesus' words: "I know you, that you have not the love . . ." with Paul's: "they foreknew me . . . how that after the straitest sect . . ." In both cases the grammatical object is personal, but "knowledge" implies no more than thorough knowledge *about* the person concerned.

There seems, therefore, no grammatical objection to a similar interpretation where God is the subject: "those whom he foreknew . . ." could mean no more than a knowledge of their characters and reactions. It does not necessarily imply any relationship.

Thus interpretation (2) is grammatically in accord with Biblical usage, and avoids the impossible implications of interpretation (1) above. It also fits well into the context of Romans 8:29, as we may now consider.

In the first few chapters of Romans, Paul describes the two streams of humanity, the repentant and the unrepentant. He establishes that whether a person is Jew or Gentile is irrelevant to this, and in chapter 3 that the basis of anyone's acceptance with God is the faithfulness and death of Christ. Chapters 5-7 deal with the way in which the Christian is freed from the power of sin—through Christ's death. Chapter 8 begins with the Christian's freedom from condemnation, and how thus the Spirit breaks sin's power over him. Then Paul talks of walking in the Spirit, and the Spirit's method of operating in Christians. From 8:17 we begin to see the future task for which Christians are intended —their revelation as sons of God, which will release creation. In verse 23 he notes that we also, though we have the Spirit of adoption, wait as eagerly as the creation for the future time of adoption (or "son-placing") when we shall be revealed as sons. As we wait we "groan" inwardly, longing for the coming time when goodness and beauty will triumph (v. 23). Yet we do not know how to pray as we ought, how to express these groanings and longings for our world. So the Spirit partakes in and shares our prayers, with groanings too deep to be put into words (v. 26). God understands the Spirit's "groanings" because the Spirit intercedes on our behalf according to God's own designs (v. 27). For we know that God's Spirit works in everything for good, together with those who love God and are called (or named or given a calling) according to his purpose (v. 28).[37] Verse 29 begins with "because" (Grk *hoti*) referring back to the previous verse and giving the grounds for our knowledge: "Because these whom he foreknew, he also predestined to be conformed to the image of his Son . . ."

We must be sure to bear in mind, here, to whom Paul is writing, whom he has in mind, and why. Briefly, he is writing to Christians, about Christians, and to reassure them of God's love for them and God's desire for them to cooperate with his Spirit in working for good and in overcoming all tribulation.

We may see this by looking back at the context. In verses 16-26 Paul continually refers to "us," meaning the children of God who are awaiting Christ's return and working for good with God and in prayer. Between verse 26 and 27 Paul changes from using the first person "us" to the third person "the saints." Yet he is making an identical statement about both these subjects, i.e., that the Spirit intercedes on their behalf. Further, his conclusion in verse 31 is again in the first person: "If God be for *us* . . ." Obviously, then, his use of the third person is merely stylistic, and he has in mind himself and his Christian readers. This also applies to verse 28, where he refers to "those" who love God and are given a calling (or role) according to God's own purpose. Verse 29, as we have noted, is giving a reason for our confidence in the knowledge of verse 28: "We know . . . because these whom He foreknew, He also predestined to be conformed to . . ." Paul is speaking of the fact that as Christians they have this destiny of cooperating with God to release the creation by their being revealed in the likeness of his Son.

Are we doubtful whether our inner groanings in prayer are of any use? Does God really want us to cooperate with his Spirit in working for good? It is astounding but we know that it is true. But how may we be sure of this? Because although he foreknew us, although he understood all about us and our weaknesses, yet he gave us this great destiny and task of helping him to set his creation at liberty.

201

This passage of Paul's letter may be set out in a table to help to bring out the structure and pattern of thought:

> **Creation** groans and travails together until now (v. 22)
>
> (not only so but also)
>
> **We** ourselves, groan within ourselves as we wait for this adoption (i.e., our "son-placing," or revealing as sons of God)
>
> (likewise)
>
> **The Spirit** also takes share in our weakness (for we know not how to put our groaning into words) by himself supplicating on our behalf with groanings which cannot be put into words
>
> (But)
>
> **God** (who knows our hearts)
>
> *Knows* what the Spirit means by these groanings (v. 27)
>
> *Because* it is *according to God's own will* that the Spirit makes his intercessions on our behalf (v. 27)
>
> (And)
>
> **We**
>
> *know* that in everything the Spirit works for good in cooperation with us (those) who love God and are positioned (called) according to his purpose. (v. 28)
>
> *because* **us** (those whom) he foreknew, he gave the destiny of conformity to the image of his Son (v. 29)
>
> (and) **us** (these whom) he predestined he also gave a calling
>
> (and) **us** (these whom) he called he also declared right with him
>
> (and) **us** (these whom) he declared right, he also glorified (i.e., will certainly glorify, v. 18)

What then shall we conclude?

That (i) if God be on our behalf who can oppose us? (v. 31)

(ii) if he even gave us his Son for us, will he
not give us (with Christ—as his co-heirs v. 17)
all things? (v. 32)

Let us note that in this passage Paul is not at all concerned
with the question of why or how they became Christians,
nor with why anyone else did not. He is talking to them,
as Christians, of the future plans of God for them. He is
saying that these plans were made in full knowledge of
them and all their weaknesses.

Some have taken Paul to be referring to God's foreknowledge of some specific feature of them, e.g., of "loving
God" (from v. 28). Our own feeling is that, if this had
been his meaning, he would have made it clearer. He
does not so much seem concerned with some specific feature that God foreknew, but that God did understand (or
know) them utterly and yet gave them this destiny. Paul
is not concerned to find some distinguishing feature that
explains how or why believers have received something unbelievers have not. He is concerned to assure them, as believers, that God (so to speak) knew what he was letting
himself in for, when he pledged himself to bring them to
conformity to the image of Christ. In a sense we might say
that he has pre-destined us in spite of his foreknowledge,
rather than because of it—though this may be going too far!

Here, as we know, Paul is assuring those who love God
that he has a destiny for them, and wants to cooperate with
them. What then of unbelievers? Are they excluded from
God's plans? Did God predestine only believers?

This question is not so simple as Christians sometimes
assume. We should remember two things here. First, the
Greek word *proorizō* (predestine) does not mean an in-
evitable fiat. It may be a predetermination in the sense of a
"marking out beforehand."[38] Beet has remarked, "The boy
marked out for one trade may enter another,"[39] and such
a meaning is not precluded by the word *predestine* in this
context. Second, when Paul makes a statement in a context of speaking of the church, he does not necessarily mean
that it may not apply to unbelievers also. Thus in Romans

3:23 he says: "All have sinned . . ." meaning all those who are justified. But we know that all those outside the church have sinned as well.[40] Likewise when Paul says that God foreknew those who love him, he does not mean that God did not foreknow others also in this way. Moreover, when Paul says that God had marked out a destiny for those who love him, he need not necessarily be saying that such a destiny was not intended for all men. Indeed we have seen how Luke tells us that God did have plans for a group of unbelievers, which they rejected for themselves.[41] Perhaps these plans included the marking out of a destiny in Christ, which they failed to obtain because they rejected Christ. Paul does not specifically say this, for he rarely uses the word *proorizō*, and only in a context of believers. But his words by no means rule it out.

In any event he makes it clear in Ephesians 1 that this destiny is marked out for us *in Christ*. We have seen how our election was not as individuals, but was an election in Christ, the elect One. Ephesians 1:4, 5 might be literally rendered: "He chose us in Him before the foundation of the world that we should be holy and blameless before Him; in love, predestinating us to the son-placing through Jesus Christ to Himself." The destiny marked out for us is obtained by those in Christ, and is obtained through Christ. Romans 8 also reflects this, for Paul begins in verse 1 by referring his comments to those "in Christ." Ephesians also shows us that, even if God marked out this destiny for all men, the inheritance is obtained only in Christ; Ephesians 1:11 reads: "in whom also we obtained an inheritance, being predestined according to the purpose of Him who energizes all things according to the counsel of His will."

In brief, whatever destiny God has for man, it is achieved only in Christ. God did not simply select people to receive a destiny. His whole eternal purpose is accomplished only in Christ.[42] Our inheritance is obtained and our destiny worked out in Christ, and this destiny was set out by God in the full light of his foreknowledge of those who would receive it.

SUMMARY
(NEW TESTAMENT)

In looking at Romans 8:29, we must be clear to whom Paul is talking, of whom he speaks, and why. He is not dealing with questions about how anyone came to be converted, nor with why anyone else did not. He is writing to *Christians* about *their own* position. The foreknowledge he has in view implies a complete understanding of them, of their characters, their weaknesses, and their reactions. He is saying that God completely understood those to whom he gave the destiny of being conformed to the image of Christ. Nevertheless he gave them this destiny, he wants to cooperate with them now to bring in good, and he wants to give them all things as Christ's fellow-heirs. The whole context is one of their own destiny, as Christians, in the creation and in its liberation.

With this great destiny in store, a destiny made in a full understanding of our natures and weaknesses, we may indeed see that **nothing shall separate us from the love of God which is in Christ Jesus our Lord.**

NOTES

1. Origen, for example, said that it was our "character and fitness" (*Philocal.*, xxv.2).

2. F. F. Bruce puts forward one version of the view in his commentary on Romans. Sanday and Headlam are another authority who adopt it. They criticize Gifford's suggestion that God foreknows the believers "as those who love God," because they think that Gifford "does not sufficiently take account of the O.T. and N.T. use of *ginōskō*. They describe this use as "very marked and very clear" in the instances in which it means "to take note of" or "fix the regard upon." To show this "very marked and very clear" use, they quote five verses, including the usual Amos and Hosea ones and including (surprisingly!) Matthew 7:23—"Depart from me for I never fixed my regard upon you" (?). John Murray is another commentator who voices this view, and who also refers to "frequent" Scriptural use of the word *know* to mean "set regard upon." To support this reference, he cites more verses than most others—giving the six we have examined and another six (e.g., 1 John 3:1) which seem to us even less convincing.

Other writers are less careful and more direct in their statement of the view. Peake's commentary (1967) simply says: "Foreknow means 'chosen in advance'—a Hebraic use of 'know,'" and cites in support only Jeremiah 1:5 and Amos 3:2. J. I. Packer gives a similar comment in the *New Bible Dictionary*: "The Hebrew verb *yada*, 'know,' which is used of various acts of knowing that, in idea at least, imply and express affection (e.g., relations between sexes and the believer's acknowledgement of God), is used to denote God's election (i.e., his taking cognizance of persons in love) in Gn. xviii.19 (see RV); Am. iii.2; Hos. xii.5 The Gk. *prōginōskō*, 'foreknow,' is similarly used in Rom. viii.29, xi.2 to mean 'forelove' (cf. also the use of *ginōskō* in 1 Cor. viii.3 and Gal. iv.9)" (p. 357). We note, of course, that the verses cited are the usual five. Rudolf Bultmann gives a similar comment in *Gnōsis*: "The corresponding reference to divine knowledge as meaning election, characteristic of the Old Testament, occurs a few times in the New Testament, most clearly at ii Tim. ii, 19 (from Numb. xvi.5; cf. Matt. vii.23), but also at 1 Cor. viii.3; xiii.12; Gal. iv.9."

The view is, of course, held by some other scholars and theologians —though by no means all. But enough have been quoted to show that the same few verses are always referred to. Most of these verses are examined in the present study.

3. God "made Himself known to them" in Exodus 2:25; 25:22; 29:42; 30:6; 30:36; Numbers 12:6; 17:4; Deuteronomy 9:24; LXX. The Hebrew sometimes differs.

4. This is the interpretation of Amos 3:2 and Hosea 13:5 indicated in the Skinner commentary quoted below.

5. The phrase which the RV renders "to the end that" does sometimes have a weakened meaning, e.g., Isaiah 44:9; Hosea 8:4; Psalm 51:4, and so the LXX rendering may be just possible. The weakened sense is, however, very much the exception, and this is not the most natural way to take the verse.

6. Abraham is called the "friend of God" more than once in the Bible. In James 2:23 the description is applied to him because he believed that promise which the Lord mentioned in Genesis 18:19—and matched his belief with action.

7. We mean "got to know" in its colloquial sense and not, of course, in the sense of compulsion!

8. J. Skinner, *Genesis* (ICC, 1912) p. 304.

9. Derek Kidner, *Genesis* (IVF, 1967) p. 132.

10. There may, perhaps, be a good parallel between Jeremiah 1:5, 6 and John 13:18—"I know whom I have chosen." Christ's appointments, like his Father's, were made with a thorough understanding of the ones appointed.

11. The LXX paraphrases Hosea 13:5; in Genesis 18:19 it uses *oida* and interprets it entirely differently; in Jeremiah 1:5 it uses *epistamai*.

12. Romans 2:29; see also John 5:44; 12:43; 1 Corinthians 4:5; 2 Corinthians 10:18; 1 Peter 3:4.

13. Galatians 5:6

14. See, e.g., Thucydides ii.64.8; Plato, *Rep* iv 426 c; Aristotle, *N. Ethics* 6.2; the noun *prognōsis* came to mean a prediction based on a diagnosis.

15. e.g., Justin Martyr (*Dial* 39.2) and Clement (*Strom* ii. 12. 54.1).

16. e.g., Clement of Rome: 2 Clem 9.9
Irenaeus of Gaul: *Ag. Heresies* xxiv ch 2
Justin Martyr: *Apol* 1 xliv
Hermas: *Commands* 4,3,4
Origen: *Ag Celsus* Bk. 2. ch. 20
(see also Josephus *Ant* 8.8.5.10 & 15.10. 5.4-5)

17. 2 Clement 9.9

18. Justin: *Apol* 1 xlv & xxviii

19. Justin: *Apol* 1 xliv and Dial cxli

20. Origen: *Ag Celsus* Bk. 2 ch. 20

21. Jerome: *Ag Pelagius* Bk. 3; Jerome, of course, wrote in Latin.

22. These five apocryphal uses are as follows:

(i) Wisdom 6.13: The most difficult of the five. Literally it would read: "She (wisdom) goes before those desiring to be known before." The meaning would seem to be: "She goes before those who desire her, making herself first known to them," but it is difficult to glean very much from this.

(ii) Wisdom 8.8: "She (wisdom) foresees (or foreknows) signs and wonders and the issues of seasons and times."

(iii) Wisdom 18.6: "That night was made known beforehand to our fathers . . ."

(iv) Judith 9.6: "all your ways are prepared, and your judgments are in your foreknowledge."

(v) Judith 11.19: "for these things were told me according to my foreknowledge."

Apart from the first one (the meaning of which is difficult to determine), all of these uses indicate a simple knowledge in advance.

23. Linguistically compare Judith 9.6; "Your judgments are in your foreknowledge."

24. In this we concur with H. A. Meyer, who concluded that *proginōskō* "never in the N.T. (not even in Romans 11:2, 1 Peter 1:20) means anything else than *to know beforehand.*"

25. Young's Literal Translation, which shows very fairly the sentence structure.

26. To Peter's Jewish readers of the Dispersion, the word *Christ* perhaps still implied "Messiah."

27. Romans 3:25

28. Hebrews 9:7

29. Revelation 13:8; AV, RV, Phillips

30. Among scholars, Beet, for example, takes it thus. Sanday and Headlam give the alternatives but call this the "natural" meaning.

31. Cf. Judith 9.6 LXX: "all your ways are prepared and your judgments are in your foreknowledge."

32. Paul himself, of course, uses this method of exposing erroneous teaching by showing its self-contradiction, e.g., 1 Corinthians 15:12, 29, etc.

33. Although mindful of the serious nature of the question, one cannot help being reminded of the rhyme:

As I was coming up the stair I met a man who wasn't there,

He wasn't there again today, I wish that man would go away.

34. Luke 18:27; the context is of salvation of those engrossed in the world

35. 2 Timothy 2:13; Hebrews 6:13, 18; James 1:13

36. See section 6, especially note 16.

37. We have given reasons in section 2 note 25, for accepting either the NEB or RSV rendering of this verse.

38. This meaning is given in lexicons such as Liddell and Scott, Green and Bagster. The word *proorizō* is found only in Acts 4:28; Romans 8:29; 8:30; 1 Corinthians 2:7; and Ephesians 1:5, 11. It is formed of the two Greek elements *pro* and *horizō*. The latter is from the same root as the word *boundary*, and is reflected in the English word *horizon*. A rather poetical rendering of *proorizō* might even be to say that God has "preset our horizons"!

39. J. Agar Beet commentary on Romans, p. 257

40. Christians often use Romans 3:23 (with good effect!) in reference to unbelievers. In its context, however, the words "All have sinned . . ." refer to "all them that believe" (v. 22) who are "justified freely by His grace" (v. 24) Paul is speaking of believers and emphasizing that in the church Jews and Gentiles are on an equal footing—but he does not, of course, mean that there are some outside the church who have not sinned.

41. Luke 7:30; see also section 6.

42. Ephesians 3:11

Subject Study—Jewish Ideas of Works and Righteousness

This study concerns rabbinical teaching during the first century. Why is such a study important? We suggest:

(a) The Christian gospel first spread among the Jews scattered throughout the Roman Empire. The early church included a great number of Jews and "God-fearers" schooled in the rabbinic thought associated with the synagogues. I we know nothing of their background and way of thinking, parts of the New Testament will be obscured to us: What, for example, did Paul mean when he attacked the idea that a man could be "justified by works"? Why was the concept of unmerited grace so hard for many Pharisees to accept?

(b) The main opposition to Paul's teaching came from Pharisees and those who, like them, supported rabbinical teaching on "works" and the superiority of Israel over the Gentiles. Paul had not only to meet with such leanings in the church (Acts 15:5), but sometimes with *public* contradiction and objections (Acts 13:45). Thus, in his systematic treatise of Romans 1:17—11:36, Paul continually imagines the objections that would be thrown up by such an antagonist (Romans 3:1; 3:5; 3:9; 6:1; 6:15; 7:7; 9:14; 9:19; 11:1; see also 2:17; 7:1). If we know nothing of rabbinical thought then we will understand little of the implications behind these "objections."

In Romans 9-11 such considerations became especially important since Paul was dealing specifically with the Jewish question. Why had God chosen the Jews—was it because of their "merits" as some rabbis taught? What did it mean to be the "chosen nation"—were the rabbis right in taking it that "all Israel shall have a part in the world to come"? Did the Christian gospel mean that God had cast off his people the Jews, so that they were no longer the chosen nation? To the early church these were not academic quibbles; they were questions that affected its whole being. To Paul, whose heart yearned for his people, they were absolutely vital to answer, and he does so systematically in Romans 9-11. Thus, unless we understand something of the beliefs of the rabbis on such questions, we shall find it very difficult to understand these chapters of Romans.

Before commencing the study we must outline something of the different groupings in Israel in the time of Christ:

(a) *Essenes*: These were a religious group who believed the Jerusalem priesthood to be apostate. Their influence within the land of Israel at that time was strong, but they need not concern us in the present study.

(b) *Sadducees*: These held a majority in the highest Jew ish civil and religious body, the Sanhedrin. The High Priest was a Sadducee. Their opposition to Jesus was mainly on the utilitarian ground that they wished to avoid any disturbance that might provoke Rome. Their teaching, as such seems to have exerted little influence in the early church.

(c) *Scribes/Lawyers/Rabbis*: These were the experts in the Jewish Law—both the written Pentateuch and the oral traditions of the elders. The words *scribe* and *lawyer* were synonymous; the term *Rabbi* was honorific at the time of Christ but later came to be the standard word for a lawyer.[1] In this study, for convenience, we have used the word to apply to lawyers of Christ's time as well.

(d) *Pharisees*: These were a "lay" society, and "while the Scribes were the interpreters of the law, the Pharisees made it their aim to live according to the letter of the law."[2]

Christians have sometimes suggested that the religion of the scribes and Pharisees was an empty and hypocritical legalism, thoroughly wicked in its thinking. There are, we believe, two main reasons why such a suggestion is both wrong and misleading:

The first is the wide divergence of opinion among rabbis. Thus, e.g., the two schools of Hillel and Shammai were often in disagreement. Some rabbis had little sympathy for the Pharisees. Some, like Gamaliel, advocated a liberal approach to those of dissident viewpoint.[3] Some did not wholeheartedly accept legalism, but set down some good thoughts.[4] There were, in short, many different strands of thought within rabbinicism.[5]

Second, some in all the strata of Jewish society were waiting in humility for the kingdom of God. Nicodemus was a Pharisee, Joseph of Arimathea was a member of the highest Jewish civil and religious body, and both were disciples of Jesus.[6] We should also note that at least one lawyer found no conflict between his rabbinical studies of the Law and Jesus' interpretation of it; Jesus told him that he was not far from the kingdom.[7]

It seems, therefore, unjust to portray rabbinicism or Pharisaism as empty or wicked. But what, on the other hand, are we to think of the attempts made in recent years to completely "rehabilitate" the Pharisees? These attempts have generally proceeded either by saying that the N.T. is inaccurate and Jesus differed little from the Pharisees, or else by saying that he only criticized a minority of them.[8] The former suggestion is unacceptable to anyone who believes the N.T. to be authoritative, and on the latter we entirely agree with H. L. Ellison: "It is quite out of the question that mainly non-Jewish readers of the Gospels could have been expected to have known so much about the Pharisees that, without guidance, they could have divided them into two groups to the major of which our Lord's words did not apply."[9]

We must, then, fully recognize the differences between Jesus and the rabbinic party. In Matthew 23 he repeatedly says: "Woe unto you, scribes, Pharisees, hypocrites!" We may, perhaps, carefully note Ellison's argument that the word *hypocrite* in Matthew lacked the implications of conscious deceit it has today.[10] Nevertheless Jesus' words to them are couched in the strongest terms. He said all their works were for men's praise, and he called them "sons of hell," fools, and blind.[11] He said that they had omitted judgment, mercy, and faith, and merely kept the trivial details of the Law.[12] He called them whitewashed tombs, full of uncleanness and iniquity. He called them serpents and vipers, warning them of their impending judgment.[13] He blamed them for the persecution of God's prophets and the righteous men.[14] This is not the language of minor disagreement, but of fundamental antipathy. Jesus seems to be saying that the mainstream of rabbinic practice was entirely wrong. What was it in their teaching that provoked such strong reaction in the "Prince of Peace"? This we will discover only by looking at the rabbinic teaching on various subjects. There is, of course, little rabbinic literature dating from the time of Christ. The teaching of rabbis before and during that time were, however, preserved orally and set down by the end of the second century. Later they were included (and commented on) in the Talmud. These details, however, need not concern us, for Ellison writes: "The

211

case for a distinction between Pharisaic religion and the Rabbinic religion of the Talmud is strongly argued by A. T. Robertson but we consider that this theory has been fully answered by Lukyn Williams (*Talmudic Judaism and Christianity*, ch. 11) and that his conclusion, 'The outlook and attitude of Talmudic Judaism is identical with that of Palestinian Rabbinic Judaism of the first century' is unassailable. Development there was, but it was in the same direction."[15]

With this reassurance we may now consider the rabbinic teaching on various topics, and compare it with that of Christianity.

ON AN INDIVIDUAL LEVEL

Sin. The rabbinical view of the effects of sin differed from the Christian view in two main ways:

(a) *The power of sin.* The Christian believes that when a man commits any sin he puts himself in sin's power. He cannot, then, (in his own strength) break loose from that power, nor undo the spiritual death it has wrought in him. The rabbis, on the other hand, taught:

It is in the power of each wholly to overcome sin and to gain life by study and works.[16]

If he has sinned he is always able to find his way back . . . he can hallow and purify himself again, he can make atonement.[17] It is true that Christianity also speaks of "purifying yourselves"[18] and even "saving yourselves."[19] But, nevertheless, it is much more clearly stated in Christianity that such phrases urge us to appeal for unmerited help from God, not to strive for justification by moral effort.

(b) *The judicial consequences of sin.* As Christians we believe that a man falls short of God's standards even if he has committed only one sin.[20] We believe that (without the atonement of Christ) a man would have to be absolutely sinless to be acquitted at God's bar of judgment. The rabbis did not claim to be sinless[21] but rather denied that such a sinless life was necessary for a man to obtain acquittal by God. They believed that though a man might do evil deeds these could be outweighed by his good ones —and it was the overall balance which decided God's verdict. This concept of a "treasury of merits" formed a well-defined element in the religious thought of that milieu into which Christ and Paul came.[22]

> It was a postulate of Rabbinic thought that a man by his obedience to the Torah (Law) could obtain merit.[23]

> Every good deed was thought to have a certain quantity of merit attached to its performance, while similarly every evil deed incurred a corresponding portion of demerit.[24]

> From this first principle of intrinsic merit in certain actions the rabbis go a stage further, postulating that God keeps an exact record of the merits and transgressions of each individual. On this view, every action which is not ethically neutral must increase either the credit or the debit balance in a man's heavenly bank account, and a man stands finally judged by whichever happens to be in excess of the other.[25]

> The final judgment represented a weighing up of the merits and demerits acquired by a man during the course of his lifetime, and this is often represented as a weighing in the scales. If the good deeds outweighed the bad, then the man was adjudged righteous, and entered into blessedness, whereas, if the bad deeds predominated, Gehenna was his portion.[26]

It is worth including here, a translation of some of the opening words of volume iv of Strack-Billerbeck's great work:

> So, thanks to God's love, the Israelites are God's children; as such, they have received the most precious Divine possession—the Law—through which also the world was made. Just as the Law gave

213

life to the whole world, it also means especially life for Israel. For the Law was only given to Israel so that they could gain reward and merit by it. To that end the study of the Law should be above all; for from study there naturally follows observation. Here the question is raised as to whether man, i.e., the natural man, has not only the power to decide for good in a formal and rational way, but also possesses the moral strength to carry out his decision for good to a full extent through the fulfillment of the Law. The old synagogue affirmed this. It had to, for the whole system of Pharisaical "salvation" stood or fell with the capability of man to fulfill the will of God revealed in the Law. . . the old synagogue was quite seriously convinced that man possessed the complete moral freedom and power in every way to fulfill the commandments of the Law. . .

Every commandment fulfilled means a merit for the Israelites, earned in the sight of God, while on the other hand every transgression brings on him a portion of guilt in God's eyes. Merits through fulfillment of commandments, and guilt through transgressions, are both entered in the book of heaven. Thus the Israelite has an account with God. The relationship, measured by numbers and value, which exists between merit and guilt, reveals the position of a man regarding judgment before God: if the merits weigh heavier, then God looks upon the man in question as a righteous man and declares him righteous; if the transgressions weigh heavier then the man is regarded as a transgressor. If merit and guilt are equally balanced in the end, then the man in question is "average." Everything is decided by the number of deeds . . . No man during his life on earth has any insight into the state of his account with God. So there is no certainty of salvation on earth for the righteous since his account can alter at any time . . .

Accordingly, the old Jewish religion is a religion

of complete self-redemption. It has no room for a Savior-Redeemer who dies for the sins of the world.[27]

The Apostle Paul also makes striking comments on this. Perhaps the best examples of these are in Romans and Galatians. Galatians 2:16 reads: "a man is not justified by the works of the Law, but only through the faithfulness of Jesus Christ,[28] even we had faith in Christ Jesus, that we might be justified by the faithfulness of Christ, and not by works of the Law." By works of the Law here, we must understand Paul to mean the works of the Torah by which Pharisees thought they obtained merit. By justified, of course, he means declared-righteous or acquitted by God. What he is saying, therefore, is that the rabbinic doctrine of merits is completely wrong. A man cannot be justified by building up a credit balance of good deeds. He can be justified only on the basis of what Christ has done, not on the basis of what he himself has done.

Study. The study of Torah (Law) is extolled above all other means of obtaining merit.[29] Reverence for the Torah almost rivals that for God himself, so it is not surprising to find God sometimes represented as a kind of super rabbi.[30] God is believed to pray, to study Torah for three hours a day, and to conduct a heavenly academy for study.[31] The decisions of earthly rabbis are binding even in heaven, and on occasion one may be summoned to heaven to settle a dispute between its members—including, of course, God himself.[32] Oesterley and Box remind us that to "Oriental ears hyperbolic utterance is the normal way of expressing things" but such notions certainly illustrate the importance to the rabbis of study. Even the great and gentle Rabbi Hillel had a maxim: "The ignorant (Am-ha-arez) cannot be pious."[33] The New Testament reflects this attitude as expressed rather more scornfully by some Pharisees: "this multitude which knows not the Law are accursed."[34]

Ceremonial Observance. Some rabbis, and the majority of Pharisees, placed great emphasis on meticulous observance of all laws. There are two good illustrations of this in Mark's Gospel. In chapter 7 we find "the Pharisees and *some* of the rabbis [scribes]" criticizing the disciples for not adhering to the washing ceremony prescribed by the "traditions of the elders."[35] Jesus replied that it is what is in a man's heart that counts, not what external regulations he keeps.

A more significant incident is found in Mark 3. In chapter 2 Christ had claimed to forgive sins (v. 5) and this had caused questionings among some rabbis (scribes) though the Pharisees are not mentioned. In 2:16, some "rabbis who were Pharisees" questioned his eating with common people. In 2:24 the Pharisees questioned his disciples' plucking of ears of corn on the Sabbath. It was, however, in 3:1-6 that the crisis came. It was because Christ healed on the Sabbath that the Pharisees decided that he must be killed! (3:6)[36] It is little wonder that Jesus was grieved at their hardness of heart (3:5).

Alms, Fasting, Prayer. Jesus himself attacks the "play-actors" who gave alms, fasted, and prayed in order to receive men's praise.[37] (They also thought it gave them merit in heaven.) Jesus implies that they love to stand and pray in synagogues and on street corners,[38] and they sometimes use vain repetitions.[39] He also speaks of the long "play-acting" prayers of the scribes.[40] Edersheim explains how the Pharisee would literally stop in the market place and bend right over to pray.[41] Of course not all the scribes[42] or even the Pharisees were like this, but this tendency was often seen. Edersheim claims that when more closely examined even *repentance* "as preceding the free welcome of invitation to the sinner, was only another form of work righteousness."[43]

ON A NATIONAL LEVEL

We have already noted the extreme reverence of the rabbis

for the Torah (Law). They also believed that Israel's destiny as a nation was indissolubly bound up with it. It was the Torah which marked off Israel as God's chosen nation, distinct from all others. This was also connected in some way with the doctrine of merits.

When we come to consider further the exact relationships between God, the Torah, and Israel and relate this to "merits," our task is not easy. Rabbis often disagreed, and on many questions of importance to us there is no authoritative rabbinic teaching.[44] Nevertheless, consideration of a few ideas of different rabbis may help us to understand their general climate of thought.

We have already mentioned the "doctrine of merits" in its application to individuals. It was also applied collectively and nationally. Marmorstein writes of the rabbinical views about

> the merits which were believed to have caused the creation of the world, which secure the existence of the universe, and wrought the miracles as well as safeguarded the life of Israel as a religious community during its historical course. There must be a merit for everything. Without work nothing can be achieved. A reason has to be found, why the world was created. It was made for some purpose or aim. For whose sake? There are different theories trying to give a more or less plausible answer . . . Who or what are the moral pillars of this world? The scribes were even more deeply interested in the third problem. It was not an accident, it was not blind chance that God had chosen the fathers, had selected Israel among the nations, had redeemed the children of Abraham from Egypt, had divided the sea, given them manna and quails in the wilderness, made them cross the Jordan, inherit the Holy Land and so on. They must have had merits; what were they?[45]

Let us consider first the deliverance from Egypt. Marmorstein writes:

Most significant for the whole doctrine of merits is the saying of R. Matja ben Cheresh. The time had come when God had to redeem the oath which he swore unto Abraham to deliver his children, but they had no observances to observe in order that they might be redeemed. They were naked of all commandments. God therefore gave them two observances: the blood of the Paschal offering and the blood of the circumcision, in order that they might be redeemed. There is, namely, no reward without work.[46]

Few rabbis might have agreed with ben Cheresh that it had to be the Israelites *own* merit, but it seems to have been a common assumption that *some* kind of merit was needed. Some rabbis held it to be Abraham's or Jacob's merit. Others suggested that it was Moses' and Aaron's merits, or that of the twelve tribes, or of the pious Israelite women.[47]

A similar division of the rabbis occurred over whose merits caused God to divide the Red Sea. Davies writes:

The first discussion on the question of merits in the Rabbinic literature occurred between two Rabbis of the first century B.C., namely R. Shemaiah and R. Abtalion. The specific question with which they dealt was, "What merit did the Israelites possess that God divided the sea before them?" Shemaiah taught: "Sufficient is the faith, with which Abraham their father believed in Me that I should divide the sea before them, as it is said: 'And He believed in God and He counted it unto him (i.e., at the sea) for (doing) charity (with his children)'" (Genesis 15:6).

Abtalion says:

Worthy is the faith they (the Israelites themselves) believed in Me so that I shall divide the sea before them, as it is said: "And the people believed" (Exodus 4:31).[48]

Other rabbis suggested it was the merits of Abraham, Jacob, Joseph, or the twelve tribes, which caused the Red Sea to part.[49] One rabbi specifically ascribed it to circumcision.

Forgiveness for the golden calf episode is likewise ascribed to "merits," usually those of Abraham and the patriarchs.[50]

Of special interest are the different rabbinical views as to why God created the world. One view was that it was for his own name's sake, another that it was for man's sake. Other rabbis believed that:

> God had created the world on account of Israel, and for their merit, making preparation for them long before their appearance on the scene, just as a king who forsees the birth of his son; nay Israel had been in God's thoughts not only before anything had actually been created, but even before every other creative thought. If these distinctions seem excessive, they were, at least, not out of proportion to the estimate formed of Israel's merits. In theory the latter might be supposed to flow from "good works," of course, including the strict practice of legal piety, and from "study of the law." But in reality it was "study" alone to which supreme merit attached.[51]

Other rabbis believed creation was because of the Torah. Here Stewart's distinction may be helpful.[52] He distinguishes two slightly different meanings of "Torah"—reflected in Paul's use of "Law" in Romans 2-3. Sometimes the word denotes the written and oral laws as actually imparted to Israel at Sinai. In this sense the rabbis said that "the Torah was conceived by God not only after, but for the sake of, His people Israel, who must therefore take precedence."[53] But rabbis sometimes used "Torah" in a wider sense, referring to the supposedly eternal reality of which the Sinai code was the embodiment. In this sense they said the Torah existed 2,000 years before the creation[54] and the world was created for its sake.[55] The Torah had been known

and studied by the patriarchs.[56] It had also been offered
to all the other nations but refused.[57]

Oesterley and Box write:

> We have seen that the *Torah* was believed to
> have been offered to all men originally but that
> Israel alone, among all the nations of the world,
> accepted it. It was this fact that constituted the
> children of Israel the "Chosen People" of God. The
> titles "Chosen People," "Peculiar treasure," the "Peo-
> of God," had their *raison d'etre* in the fact that
> the Israelites were the people of the *Law*. By their
> acceptance of the divine revelation at Sinai the
> Israelites believed themselves to be a *holy* nation
> in a sense in which it was impossible for any other
> nation to be.[58]

Davies writes:

> It was the Gentiles themselves who were responsible
> for their miserable lot: they too had had the oppor-
> tunity of accepting the Torah but had refused it.
> Rabbi Jose ben Simeon said (A.D. 120-190): "Ere you
> stood at Sinai and accepted my Torah you were
> called Israel, just as the other nations e.g., Sabtek-
> hah, Raamah, are called by simple names without
> addition. But after you accepted the Torah at Sinai
> you were called "My people," as it says, "Hearken,
> O my people, and I will speak." Moreover, not only
> had the Gentiles failed to keep the Torah revealed
> on Mount Sinai. Adam had been given six command-
> ments that were binding on all nations. One other
> commandment had been added to these and all
> seven were again given to Noah so that his de-
> scendants—the Gentiles—should obey them, but all
> in vain: the Gentiles did not accept even these.[59]

Edersheim writes:

> Well might "the earth tremble," for, if Israel had
> not accepted the Law at Sinai, the whole world

would have been destroyed, while it once more "was still" when that happy event took place, although God in a manner forced Israel to it. And so Israel was purified at Mount Sinai from the impurity which clung to our race in consequence of the unclean union between Eve and the serpent, and which still adhered to all other nations.[60]

He also says:

[The Talmudic writings] are full of references to the merits of the just, to the "merits and righteousness of the fathers," or else of Israel in taking upon itself the Law. And for the sake of those merits and of that righteousness, Israel, as a nation, expects general acceptance, pardon, and temporal benefits, nor do they need to get them from heaven, since they can and do work them out for themselves.[61]

A widely accepted idea was that: "All Israel has a share in the world to come."[62] As long as one did not become obviously wicked or heretical, being an Israelite was a guarantee of eventual salvation. As for the Gentiles, in theory a Gentile might also achieve "merits," but in practice there was little hope for him unless he became a Jewish proselyte.[63] This explains, of course, Peter's surprise that a man like Cornelius (who was not a full proselyte) could be considered "clean."[64]

Edersheim says of the final judgment:

We must here once more make distinction between Israel and the Gentiles, with whom, nay, as more punishable than they, certain notorious sinners, heretics, and all apostates, were to be ranked. Whereas to Israel the Gehenna, to which all but the perfectly righteous had been consigned at death, had proved a kind of purgatory, from which they were all ultimately delivered by Abraham, or according to some of the later Midrashim, by the Messiah, no such deliverance was in prospect for the heathen nor for the sinners of Israel.[65]

One last point needs to be brought out. The rabbis believed that God's actions were often determined by men. The doctrine of merits illustrates this well, for (as we have seen) many of God's actions at the birth of the nation were imagined to have been determined by someone or other's merits. There is also a sense in which rabbis thought that: "by giving the Torah at Sinai God had yielded up something of his own authority."[66] If man follows its precepts then he is bound to experience God's grace. Moreover, God is said to be "subject to the authoritative decisions of the Rabbis concerning the precepts of the Torah."[67] Very telling in this connection is an incident when Rabbi Joshua G. Hananiah (A.D. 80-120) had a dispute with Rabbi Eliezer ben Hyrkonos. R. Eliezer finally appealed to heaven and a heavenly voice expressed support for him. R. Joshua, however, would not accept this, and R. Jeremiah said "The Law was given us from Sinai. We pay no attention to a heavenly voice. For already from Sinai the Law said, 'By a majority you are to decide.'"[68] Man, in other words, had spheres in which his decision was authoritative even before God.

PAUL
AND THE
RABBIS

Some of these aspects of rabbinical teachings should undoubtedly be borne in mind in studying Romans, especially 9-11. It will be profitable to contrast briefly here the rabbinic and Pauline teachings on four topics:

Why Was Israel Chosen? A common rabbinical answer might have been that Israel was chosen for her merits, or that the Torah was given her to enable her to obtain merits and that this in itself set her apart. We have also noted the idea that Israel became the chosen nation through accepting the Torah when all other nations had refused it. Paul answers this: "Rebecca also having conceived by one, even by our father Isaac—for (the nations) being not yet born, neither having done anything good or bad, that the purpose of God according to election might stand, not of works, but of him that calls, it was said unto her, The elder shall serve the younger. Even as it is written, Israel (or Jacob) I loved, but Edom I hated."[69] Paul is saying that the choice of Israel could not be for "merits" or for accepting the Torah or whatever—for the choice was made before any of this. He is not, of course, necessarily denying that there was some reason for God to choose Israel. He is denying that the choice was "according to works." God's strategy is determined by God's wisdom, not by man's works.

What Did Election Imply? The rabbis believed that the very fact of being in the chosen nation would guarantee anyone's salvation provided that he was not exceptionally wicked. Paul carefully argues against this in Romans 2-3, etc. He argues that the Bible records instances both of Gentiles *and* of Jews being under sin.[70] He argues that both justification *and* condemnation will come "to the Jew first and also to the Gentile."[71] He also argues that a large part of Israel will *not* be saved,[72] because they seek to be saved by "works." Contrary to rabbinical thought, the "lump" which is the nation of Israel will *not* be treated as one unit, but is divided into a vessel for honor and one for no honor.[73]

What Was The Place of the Law? The rabbis believed that the possession of the Law marked Israel off as the chosen nation. They thought it would enable them through "works of the Law" to acquire enough merit to be saved. Even Montefiore and Loewe say: "From one point of view the whole purpose of the Law with its large number of enactments was to enable the Israelites to acquire 'merit' and through 'merit,' reward."[74]

This background seems vital if one is to understand Paul's writings fully. The epistle to the Romans, for example, is full of references to it, for Paul speaks "to those who know the Law."[75] Note especially: "Now we know that whatever the Law says to those who are under the Law, it says in order that every mouth may be stopped, and all the world might be brought under the judgment of God: because by the works of the Law shall no flesh be justified in His sight: for through the Law comes the knowledge of sin. But now apart from the Law a righteousness of God has been manifested, being witnessed by the Law and the Prophets; even the righteousness of God through the faithfulness of Jesus Christ unto all them that have faith; for there is no distinction; for all have sinned and fall short of the glory of God; being justified freely by His grace through the redemption that is in Christ Jesus."[76] Paul is saying that if a man puts himself "under the Law" then its only function can be to bring him condemnation because he has sinned and falls short of God's standards revealed there.[77] The Law simply brings a clearer understanding of sin, and so makes it "exceeding sinful."[78] A man is not justified through what *he* has done but through what *Christ* has done. This is the "faithfulness of Christ to them [whether Old or New Testament] who have faith." It is the only basis of justification by God's standards for anyone at any time. This is the "righteousness of God" (Romans 3:22) to which Israel refused to subject themselves but sought rather to establish their own righteousness (Romans 10:3). Christ, in his faithfulness, has done all that is necessary, and a man simply has to accept it in faith. In section 6 we mentioned a suggestion we have heard, that unless God forces us to accept salvation, our acceptance of it is a "work."[79] Such a suggestion would have been quite unintelligible to Paul, who meant by "works of the Law" the rabbinical idea of merit obtained through works of the Torah. Paul specifically says: **Now to him that works, the reward is not reckoned as of grace, but as of debt.**[80] To assert that accepting grace is a work is to stand Paul on his head. When Paul attacks works he means the notion that the possession of the Torah in itself enabled Israel to acquire enough merits to be saved.

Paul's own attitude to the Torah may be too complex to examine properly here. He says that the Law is good and yet sin used it to overcome him.[81] Sin is always sin, but does not count where there is no law, so the coming of the Law made sin "exceedingly sinful."[82] But the Law brings condemnation only to those who are "under the Law" (see above). To those who approach it in faith it has a rightful place. Faith does not make void the Law but establishes it, because the righteousness of the Law can be fulfilled only in those who do not walk according to the flesh but according to the Spirit.[83] But it is only when a man reckons himself dead to the Law (through Christ), that he is able to attain the Law![84] Thus the Law has a place, but certainly not the place the rabbis imagined.

The Acts in Israel's History. We have already seen how some of the rabbis ascribed the redemption from Egypt, forgiveness for making the golden calf, etc., to "merits." Paul picks this out to comment on in Romans 9:14-18. He picks out the two clear places where God emphasized that it was *he* who determined his strategy. His hand was not forced by anyone's merits. He said that he could not go down among the people lest he consume them.[85] There is certainly no hint here of anyone's merits compensating for their sin. Moses saw God's glory (as God showed mercy to whom he would show mercy). Then Moses said: "If now I have found favor (or 'grace') in Your sight, O Lord, let the Lord I pray go in the midst of us . . ."[86] He did not appeal to merits but to God's strategic decision—and in a sense the appeal was granted. Since Moses had seen the glory, his face shone, and *in him* God went in the midst![87]

Likewise in the incident with Pharaoh we see God acting freely, strategically, and unconstrained by human will or merit.

God's actions in Israel's history are free and strategic. To Israel he shows special dealings in a manner he has determined. To Pharaoh he gives the stubborn determination to carry on with his defiance. And it is not man's works but God's strategy that decides God's actions in this respect. None of this is to deny that God's actions do sometimes depend on what man chooses to do. God refers to such a "dependence" in Jeremiah chapter 18. But the point is that man's merits never force God's hand. In Jeremiah 18 God is saying what he *will* do, not what he *has* to do.

225

Moreover, Israel's election does not even come into this category. It is a choice completely in the free strategy of God.

BOOKS REFERRED TO OR QUOTED

Davies, *Paul and Rabbinic Judaism* (1948)
Edersheim, L. & T: *Life and Times of Jesus the Messiah*, vols. i & ii (1901) S.J.L.: *Sketches of Jewish Social Life* (1876)
Ellison, *Jesus and the Pharisees* (1959)
Grant, *Ancient Judaism and the New Testament* (1961)
Herford, *Judaism In the New Testament Period* (1928)
Jocz, *The Jewish People and Jesus Christ* (1949)
Keith, *The Social Life of a Jew in the Time of Christ* (1959)
Marmorstein, *The Doctrine of Merits in Old Rabbinic Literature* (1920)
Montefiore & Loewe, *Rabbinic Anthology* (1938)
Moore, *Judaism*, vol. ii (1927-30, Revised Ed. 1958)
Morris, *The Apostolic Preaching of the Cross* (1965)
Oesterley and Box, *Religion of the Synagogue* (Revised Ed. 1911)
Robertson, *Pharisees and Jesus* (1920)
Schürer, *The Jewish People at the Time of Jesus Christ* (1885)
Stewart, *Rabbinic Theology* (1961)
Strack-Billerbeck, *Kommentar zum Neuen Testament aus Talmud und Midrasch* (1928)
Williams, *Talmudic Judaism and Christianity* (1933)

NOTES

1. See the *New Bible Dictionary*, Oesterley p. 232; Schürer, Div ii vol. iv p. 313-5, etc.
2. Oesterley, p. 233
3. Acts 5:34-39
4. e.g., in *Pirke Aboth* 1.3, Antigonus of Soko says we should be like servants who serve their master for the service and not for reward—"and let the fear of heaven be upon you" (*Living Talmud*, Mentor Books, p. 48). It is interesting to see how scholars' comments on this saying reflect their general thesis about rabbinicism. Moore's work is really an apologetic for the rabbinical tradition and (though worth reading from this point of view) seems to select the better strands of it. Of the above saying, he writes that it "stands at the head of . . . the Pharisaic tradition" (p. 96). Schürer, on the other hand, is much more critical of rabbinicism and says that it is "by no means a correct expression of the keynote of Pharisaic Judaism, which was in fact like the servants who serve for the sake of recompense." Third, Edersheim, being himself a Hebrew Christian, is prepared to be critical of rabbinicism while recognizing better strands within it. He points out that this saying of Antigonus was made in times of persecution. "These were dark times, when God's persecuted people were tempted to think that it might be vain to serve him." (i p. 95) One

might add that the connection between Antigonus and later rabbis is indistinct, and his saying dates back several centuries before those scribes and Pharisees whom Jesus criticized.

Perhaps more noteworthy is the saying of the first century Rabbi Simeon (*Pirke Aboth* 2): "Be alert in reciting the Shema and the prayer. When you pray, do not make of your prayer something automatic, but a plea for compassion, a supplication before God, blessed be He."

There is no reason to deny that some of the rabbis said some true and beautiful things; all that we need to note is that the general trend of rabbinic/Pharisaic thought had some unfortunate tendencies.

5. See also note 44.

6. John 19:38, 39 and chapter 3; Luke 23:50

7. Mark 12:34

8. Ellison mentions one such (p. 39), and Jocz mentions several (pp. 18-21)

9. Ellison, p. 40

10. Ellison, p. 113. The basic argument, originally stated by Williams in an appendix, is that the Pharisees' motive for whatever they did was not deceit, and so they were not "hypocrites" in our sense of the word. This may be supported to a certain extent by Paul's words in Romans 10:2, 3: he did not deny the reality of their zeal, he said that the zeal was misplaced in trying to be right with God on a basis of "self" righteousness. Yet Williams certainly seems to overstate his case, for the gospels imply that prayers might be made (as a pretense) to conceal greed and unkindness (Mark 12:40; also Matthew 23:27, 28). It is also hard to read Jesus' words about "whited sepulchres" which are "full of rottenness," without feeling that they must have had at least some consciousness of concealing wickedness with a pious exterior. The Lord's words may not necessarily apply to *all* scribes and Pharisees of his time, let alone all rabbis of all times, but we should note their real severity. It is an unfortunate feature of any system (whether in church or in synagogue) which emphasizes the external, that hypocrites (in our sense) often appear within it.

11. Matthew 23:5; 23:15-17

12. Matthew 23:23, 24

13. Matthew 23:27, 33

14. Matthew 23:34

15. Ellison, p. 37; Williams, p. 55; Marmorstein tries to bring out these "developments," though the average reader may find his work rather difficult and repetitive.

16. Edersheim L & T, vol. i p. 167

17. Jocz, p. 278

18. 2 Timothy 2:21

19. Acts 2:40

20. Romans 3:23

21. The rabbis taught that a person who never sinned would never die—and very few had that distinction. (Edersheim L & T, vol. i p. 166)

22. This is a semi-quotation from Davies, p. 272. The idea is dealt with by, e.g., Davies, Marmorstein, Montefiore, Stewart, Eder-

sheim—and even Moore (though his emphasis on it is, predictably enough, rather different!). It would be foolish to believe that all rabbis took the doctrine crassly literally—but its importance is hard to doubt.

23. Davies, p. 272

24. Morris, p. 267

25. Stewart, p. 128

26. Morris, p. 267

27. This is a translation from Strack-Billerbeck iv pp. 3-6: *Das Soteriologische der Alten Synagogue.*

28. Although incidental to our theme, we will briefly state why we depart from the usual renderings of Galatians 2:16 (those interested might also look at an article by G. Hebert in the monthly journal *Theology,* October 1955). The AV renders the Greek the most accurately: "Knowing that a man is not justified by works of the law, but by the faith of Jesus Christ, even we have believed in Jesus Christ, that we might be justified by the faith of Christ, and not by the works of the law." Paul does not use the usual phrase for "faith in Christ," but *pisteōs Christou,* i.e., "faith of Christ" or "faithfulness of Christ." The more modern versions unfortunately fail to indicate this, interpreting it as an "objective" rather than a "subjective" genetive, and rendering it freely. On the question of whether it is objective or subjective the view of grammarians is expressed by J. N. Moulton (*Grammar of N.T. Greek,* vol. 1 p. 72): "It is as well to remember that in Greek the question is entirely one of exegesis, not of grammar." The question, then, must be decided from the context, and we note the following:

(a) Paul uses a very similar phrase "faithfulness of God" in Romans 3:3.

(b) Paul uses this phrase *only* in Romans 3:22, 26; Galatians 2:16; 2:20; 3:22; Ephesians 3:12; Philippians 3:9. In every case he could easily have used the ordinary phrase to say "faith in Christ" had he wished—but he would have had no other way of saying "faithfulness of Christ."

(c) There is a connection between Jesus and the "aman" or faithful one in the Old Testament. In Revelation 3:14 Jesus is called the "Amen, the Faithful the True." In 2 Corinthians 1:18-20 Paul says that God is faithful and that all the promises of God are yes and amen in Christ. Christ is not only called "Faithful and True" (Revelation 3:14; 19:11) but a faithful High Priest and faithful to God. (Hebrews 2:17; 3:2). Paul himself says: "if we are unfaithful yet he (Jesus) stays faithful" (2 Timothy 2:13). The similarity of this verse to Romans 3:3 can leave us in little doubt that the concept of Christ's "faithfulness" is one that would have quite possibly occurred to Paul in Romans 3:22.

(d) In all the verses (see b) in which the phrase is used, the rendering "faithfulness of Christ" makes good sense (see AV which renders these verses the most strictly). On the other hand, if we remember that the Greek word rendered *believe* is just the verbal form of "faith," the rendering "faith in Christ" often makes the verse strangely repetitive (as in Galatians 2:16) and obscure.

(e) The general context in which Paul usually used the phrase again points to the rendering "faithfulness of Christ." It is natural for Paul to compare justification through what a man himself does ("works of the Law") with justification through what Christ has done for him (the "faithfulness of Christ"—which is appropriated through faith in him).

(f) We might also note that Romans 3 is talking of faith in general—not specifically of New Testament faith *in Christ*. He has been speaking of the two streams of humanity—those with faith and those without—and of God's treatment of them. He has established that works of the Law cannot be a way to earn God's acquittal, for no one has ever kept them perfectly. In Romans 3:21 he is introducing, for the first time, an indication of the basis on which God establishes men as "right before Him" (justified). If Paul really suggested "faith in Christ" as such a basis, then he would have completely omitted to tell us how the Old Testament believers could be right before God. It is surely incredible that Paul should have made such an omission in such a systematic treatise. Surely we must read verse 22 in its most straightforward way: "the righteousness of God through the faithfulness of Jesus Christ for *all* who have faith." This covers Old and New Testament men who have faith—and we may then suppose Paul to begin talking specifically of the church in Romans 5:1, etc., and not before.

29. Stewart, p. 127, Morris, p. 267

30. Oesterley and Box, p. 189; Stewart, p. 31

31. Stewart, p. 31; Oesterley and Box, p. 70, 189; Keith, p. 54; Edersheim L & T, vol. i p. 106, ii p. 15 *et al.*

32. Oesterley and Box, p. 189; Edersheim i p. 106; Keith, p. 54

33. *Pirke Aboth* ii 5; Edersheim L & T, i p. 508; Schürer, Div. ii vol. 2 p. 44 *et al.*

34. John 7:49

35. The mention of the "tradition of the Elders" and Jesus' angry reply makes it clear that not personal hygiene but ceremony was at issue.

36. This point must be made in answer to Jocz' suggestion that the Pharisees' main objection was to:

(a) His claim to the messiahship and interpretation of what this meant.

(b) His teaching that, in themselves, all men were equally incapable of achieving righteousness before God.

These undoubtedly were points of difference, but it was *not* his claim to forgive sin which made them plot to kill him—it was his healing on the Sabbath (compare Mark 2:6; 3:5, 6). John also says: "For this cause did the Jews persecute Jesus, because he (healed) on the sabbath" (John 5:16). His claims of equality with God (John 5:17) only made them seek *the more* to kill him (John 5:18). See also Schürer Div. ii vol. ii p. 104; Davies p. 73.

37. Matthew 6

38. Matthew 6:5

39. Matthew 6:7; see also note 4.

40. Luke 20:47

41. Edersheim S.J.L., p. 214

42. The other side to the prayer of the rabbis is stressed in the chapter on prayer in Moore's work—though his account is itself one-sided. See also note 4 above.

43. Edersheim L & T, vol. i p. 509

44. Jewish theology divided into two branches: the Halakhah and the Haggadah (see especially Herford pp. 52-58, also Stewart p. 6 et seq, the introduction in *The Living Talmud*, and Edersheim L & T, vol i p. 11). The former were purely legislative—establishing exactly what one should do in prescribed circumstances. Rabbis did not always agree on these, but, once laws were agreed, they were fixed and authoritative. The Haggadah, on the other hand, "was only the personal saying of the teacher, more or less valuable according to his learning and popularity . . . (it) had no absolute authority" (Stewart). This being so we often find disagreement amongst rabbis on precisely those wider issues in which we are interested. This, of course, makes it all too easy to present a onesided view by careful selection of quotations. The picture presented by "apologists" for rabbinicism (e.g., Marmorstein, Moore, and his later admirer Grant) differs markedly from that of those who are "middle of the road" (e.g., Edersheim) and bears no resemblance to that of hostile critics (e.g., Robertson). We have done our best to pick our way through the maze of different standpoints!

45. Marmorstein, pp. 4, 5

46. Marmorstein, p. 143

47. Davies, p. 270; Marmorstein throughout.

48. Davies, p. 269; see also Marmorstein, p. 37, etc., who points out that at this stage "faith" was the "merit" in view—though it seems that soon "merit" came to imply works of the Law.

49. Marmorstein, p. 144, etc.; Davies, p. 270

50. Marmorstein, p. 103. Rabbi Abun is the only one cited by Marmorstein who believed the Exodus a result just of God's grace. Yet this same rabbi thought Moses invoked "merits" over the golden calf. See also Davies, p. 271.

51. Edersheim L & T, vol. i p. 84; see also Marmorstein.

52. Stewart, p. 38

53. Stewart, p. 38

54. Stewart, p. 35; Oesterley & Box, p. 163; Edersheim L & T, vol. i p. 86

55. Stewart, p. 38

56. Edersheim L & T, vol. i p. 85; Oesterley and Box (p. 169) write: "The Rabbis utter all kinds of queer examples of how the patriarchs and other heroes of old showed forth their piety by obedience to the Torah."

57. Edersheim L & T, vol. i pp. 85, 166; Oesterley and Box, p. 164, 170; Marmorstein, p. 70; Davies, p. 64, 65 *et al.*

58. Oesterley and Box, pp. 170, 171

59. Davies, pp. 64, 65

60. Edersheim L & T, vol. i p. 90

61. Edersheim L & T, vol. ii p. 290

62. It is noteworthy that Professor Goldin chooses this maxim to preface his translation of *Pirke Aboth*.

63. See, e.g., Davies, p. 63. He also says: "To accept the Torah meant not merely initiation into a religion . . . but incorporation into a nation."

64. Acts 10:28, etc.

65. Edersheim L & T, vol. ii p. 440

66. Ellison, p. 44

67. Sandhedrin 39a, cited in Oesterley and Box, p. 189

68. Davies, pp. 214, 215; Ellison says of this: "This means quite simply that the rabbis believed that God had so delivered Himself into the hands of men by the revelation of the Law, that it was for them to decide how He was to be served, provided that the decision was consistent with the Law" (p. 43).

69. Romans 9:10-13. We have already noted that Genesis 25:23 emphasizes that it is "Two nations are in your womb"—the children as such are *not* in view.

70. Romans 3:9-18

71. Romans 2:9-10

72. e.g., Romans 9:27

73. Romans 9:21

74. Montefiore and Loewe, p. 219

75. Romans 7:1

76. Romans 3:19-24. This seems to us to be a more likely rendering of this verse than the usual one—though it is of little importance to our present theme. See also note 23.

77. Romans 3:23

78. Romans 7:13

79. See especially section 6, p. 37, and the Appendix.

80. Romans 4:4

81. Romans 7:12, 13

82. Romans 7:13

83. Romans 3:31; 8:2-4

84. Romans 6:11, etc.

85. Exodus 33:3

86. Exodus 34:9

87. Exodus 34:29, 35

Subject Study—
Causes of Jewish Unbelief

In Romans 11:7-11 Paul writes: **What then? That which Israel seeks for, that he obtained not; but the election obtained it and the rest were hardened: according as it is written, God gave them a spirit of stupor, eyes that they should not see, and ears that they should not hear, unto this very day . . . Did they stumble that they might fall? God forbid: but by their fall salvation is come unto the Gentiles, for to provoke them to jealousy.** We know that there were those, like Paul himself, who turned, because of Israel's unbelief, to preach with renewed vigor to the Gentiles.[1] But do Paul's words imply that Israel's unbelief was irresistibly ordained by God in order to stimulate such preaching? Is Paul's opponent making a reasonable point when he asks in Romans 9:19—"Why does he still find fault, for who can resist his will?" Paul, in Romans 9, angrily repudiates such misrepresentation of God. In Romans 11 he talks of Israel's blindness, but his own actions demonstrate that this blindness is not irresistible. He is intending to stimulate some of them to repentance by emphasizing his ministry to the Gentiles. His object is that *all* Israel shall come in.[2] What did the apostle intend then, by his quote from Isaiah about the blindness that was sent on Israel?

It may help our understanding of this if we look at the way in which the Lord himself used the same quote. It came at a crucial point in Christ's ministry to Israel, at the time when he first began to use parables in his teaching. His disciples asked him why he had begun to use parables, and the Lord used the quote from Isaiah in his reply. All three synoptic Gospels record the incident:

And the disciples came and said unto him, Why speak you unto them in parables? And he answered and said unto them, Unto you it is given to know the mysteries of the kingdom of heaven, but to them it is not given. For whosoever has, to him shall be given, and he shall have abundance; But whosoever has not, from him shall be taken away even that which he has. Therefore speak I unto them in parables; because seeing they see not, and hearing they hear not, neither do they understand. And unto them is fulfilled the prophecy of Isaiah, which says, By hearing you shall hear, and shall in no wise understand; And seeing you shall see, and shall in no wise perceive: For this people's heart is waxed gross, And their ears are dull of hearing, and their eyes they have closed; lest haply they should perceive with their eyes, And hear with their ears, And understand with their heart, And should turn again, And I should heal them. But blessed are your eyes, for they see; and your ears, for they hear. For verily I say unto you, that many prophets and righteous men desired to see the things which you see, and saw them not; and to hear the things which you hear, and heard them not (Matthew 13:10-17).

And when he was alone, they that were about him with the twelve asked of him the parables. And he said unto them, Unto you is given the mystery of the kingdom of God: but unto them that are without all things are done in parables; that seeing they may see and not perceive; and hearing they may hear and not understand; lest haply they should turn again, and it should be forgiven them (Mark 4: 10-12).

And his disciples asked him what this parable might be. And he said, Unto you it is given to know the mysteries of the kingdom of God: but to the rest in parables; that seeing they may not see, and hearing they may not understand (Luke 8:9, 10).

As may be seen, Matthew gives the fullest account, Mark's is an edited version of the incident, and Luke gives little more than a passing reference.

It may come as a surprise to some of us to discover the reason given by the Lord for his use of parables. It is not, as might have been supposed, to clarify his meaning, but to disguise it! Let us look more closely at what he says:

What Is Disguised? Jesus says that he is veiling the "secrets of the kingdom of heaven." He is not concealing the need for repentance. He is not concealing the way to a relationship with God. He is not concealing something that would enable them to go to heaven instead of to hell. He says, in fact, that many prophets and **righteous men**[3] longed to know these secrets, but could not. It cannot, therefore, be necessary to know them in order to be right with God. They are the secrets about the kingdom of heaven and they concern what God is doing now in history and what he will do in the last times.

From Whom Is It Disguised? The Lord's meaning was disguised from anyone who did not come to him to ask what he meant. From Mark we discover that there were others, besides the twelve, who came to ask him about his meaning. He explained it to those who asked, but the general populace were not interested. Jesus implies that they had already suppressed knowledge of the need for repentance. His words about them might be paraphrased: "This people's heart has grown cold; they have closed their eyes in order to avoid having to recognize and understand that they need to turn and be healed." The secrets of the kingdom of heaven are veiled[4] to those who will not recognize their need to repent.

Why Is It Disguised? Jesus gives the principle here: **For whosoever has, to him shall be given, and he shall have abundance; but whosoever has not, from him shall be taken away even that which he has.** The Lord is being rather cryptic here, for one cannot literally take from someone who has nothing. His meaning is that those who already have a relationship with God will receive also the secrets of the kingdom. Those who are without God will soon be in an even worse position than they are at present.

This does not fully explain Jesus' motives in using parables, and some clues are found elsewhere. He had already instructed them: **neither cast your pearls before the swine, lest haply they trample them under their feet, and turn and rend you.**[5] These words apply particularly to Jesus at that time. What would have happened if he had openly claimed to be the Messiah and the chief heir in the kingdom of heaven? This pearl would have been trampled underfoot, and then they would have turned on Jesus himself— such a claim would almost certainly have brought arrest and trial. To avoid this happening before his hour came, the Lord disguised the pearls he taught and kept his enemies uncertain of his meaning. Thus, for example, in John 10 we find them divided over what he meant.[7] They came to him and asked him directly if he was the Messiah.[8] His reply was again equivocal, but he implies that those who are right with God will understand his meaning.[9] The Lord makes the same point after his reference to the swine and the pearls: **Ask and it shall be given to you; seek and you shall find . . . for everyone that asks receives.**[6] Anyone who went to Jesus to ask his meaning was given it. In short, his followers learned Jesus' meaning from his own lips[10] or perhaps from God their Father,[11] and his enemies did not understand it at all.

From these references we may learn two important facts. First, the reason for Jewish unbelief was that they closed their own eyes in case the truth were uncomfortable. Second, the Lord taught in parables so that the spiritual among his hearers would be stimulated to inquire about his meaning, while the truth would be concealed from his enemies and from the disinterested.

In the Gospel of John we find this theme coming out strongly. Only those in Israel who are spiritually discerning are able to understand what Jesus is teaching. As early as John 3 a hint of it is contained in Jesus' cryptic reply to Nicodemus. The latter says he knows that Jesus has come from God because of the signs he does (v. 2). Jesus' reply is that a man cannot even see the signs unless he is born again, that is, one must be born again to **see the kingdom of God** (v. 3) and (in the language of Matthew) to "understand its secrets." In John 4 the Lord talks in parables of spiritual things and even his followers do not understand. He talks of "living water" (v. 10) and "his meat" (v. 32) and the "harvest" (v. 35), and his hearers are puzzled.

In chapter 6, things begin to come to a head. First, the people misunderstand the sign of the feeding of the five thousand (see vv. 14, 15, 26, 27). Jesus goes on to explain that he is the true bread of life. (v. 35) At this saying the Jews **murmured concerning him.** (v. 41) They were still looking at the subject in an earthbound sense, examining Jesus' human ancestry and not understanding the spiritual truths. Jesus therefore tells them: **Murmur not among yourselves. No man can come to me, except the Father which sent me draw him; and I will raise him up in the last day. It is written in the prophets, And they shall all be taught of God. Everyone that has heard from the Father and has learned, comes unto me.**[12]

To understand the thought here, we must remember the situation in Israel at that time. Broadly speaking there were two groups of people: One group were seeking to establish their own righteousness without regard to faith or to the mind of God on the question. The other group contained those who had received John's baptism of repentance, and in faith were waiting for God to reveal his coming kingdom. The epitome of this latter attitude is seen in Simeon who was, according to the Bible, **righteous and devout, looking for the consolation of Israel: and the Holy Spirit was upon him.**[13] This was truly one who was taught by God and learned from him. We know, of course, what happened: the Father *drew* him to Jesus and he knew that this was the Messiah. An interesting parallel is found later in the story of Lydia. She was one who worshiped the true God, and Paul found her at a place of prayer. Just as

Simeon knew that the Messiah had come at last, so the Lord opened the heart of Lydia to Paul's message, and she knew that he brought tidings of God's anointed, the Savior of the world.[14] Cornelius is, perhaps, an even more striking example of a righteous person whose prayers were acceptable to God, and who was therefore led by him to seek and accept Christ.[15]

The same type of principle applied during Jesus' ministry. As Isaiah prophesied, all the Jews were given God's teaching, but only those who listened to God and learned from him would be drawn to Jesus. What Jesus is saying to his hearers is this: "Don't murmur among yourselves and try to analyze what I say. Go to God and let him teach you my meaning. If you do this then he will give you understanding and draw you to accept me." This is one of Jesus' continuing themes throughout John 6 and 7, and it shows similarities to the topic we have already covered in Matthew 13. Those who come to Jesus will have the meaning explained to them; those who go to God will hear and learn from him. Those who are disinterested or enemies of Christ and the Father will simply be unable to understand his meaning.

The pattern continues from John 6:47 throughout the rest of the chapter and beyond. They are still using their own minds and strength to try to understand him. Jesus explains that it is the Spirit and not the flesh which brings life and understanding (v. 63—one must be born of the Spirit to see the Kingdom). Christ knows, of course, that some do not believe and that Judas will betray him. He says therefore: **But there are some of you that believe not . . . For this cause have I said unto you, that no man can come unto me, except it be given unto him of the Father.**[16] Jesus knows that some of them do not believe, and this is his reason for telling them to go to the Father and learn from him of the truth.

Many of those who have been following him turn back at this point because they cannot understand him. His own brothers do not understand that his strategy is to conceal his mission because his hour is not yet come.[17] All Jerusalem is in a turmoil because of the difficulty of comprehending the veiled allusions in his teaching. Then Jesus begins to speak in the Temple: **My teaching is not mine, but his that sent me. If any man wills to do his will, he shall know of the teaching, whether it be of God or whether I speak from myself . . .**[18] This is the point. The difficult sayings and parables over which they are murmuring are not really those of Jesus; they belong to God. If anyone really wanted to do the will of God, then God would show him what the teaching meant. Those Jews who are really seeking God's will for their lives will be drawn by God to come to Christ. Later, Jesus adds: **He that is of God hears the words of God: for this cause you hear them not, because you are not of God.**[19]

Jesus is continually using a veiled manner of teaching, and this makes the book of John difficult to comprehend. Perhaps it is partly because of this that misunderstandings have sometimes arisen over a few of the verses in John 6. They have sometimes been supposed to have some connection with the election of the church. One may see, however, that in their context the concern of the references to the Father "drawing people to Jesus" is with pious Jews at that time. This helps to explain the paradox that many Jews rejected their own Messiah. They rejected him because they had closed their eyes and came neither to Jesus nor to the Father for explanation of his teachings.[20]

Later in the Gospel of John we find another reference to the Isaiah 6 passage quoted in Matthew: **But though he had done so many signs before them, yet they believed not on him: that the word of Isaiah the prophet might be fulfilled, which he spake, Lord who has believed our report? And to whom has the arm of the Lord been revealed? For this cause they could not believe, for that Isaiah said again, He has blinded their eyes and he has hardened their heart; Lest they should see with their eyes and perceive with their heart, And should turn, And I should heal them.**[21]

There is a difficulty in interpreting this passage, for the second of the apostle's quotes does not appear as such in any of our versions of Isaiah. The first words "He has blinded their eyes . . ." may have been taken from Isaiah 29:9-12. In that particular context God is said to have confused the minds of the nation's seers and prophets because they honoured him with their lips but not in their hearts. The following verse, Isaiah 29:13, is particularly relevant to the Jews at the time of Christ. It may be, therefore, that John is quoting this passage and adding to it the words from Isaiah 6:10 which we have already examined. This may be the correct interpretation, but it does leave the following problem: The text says: "He has blinded . . . lest . . . I should heal them." Why should it change from the third person to the first person if God is the subject in both cases? This might be explained if we adopt another possible interpretation. In verse 31 of the same chapter John has been talking about the "Prince of this world." It may be that *he* is the agent who is blinding their eyes. Some support is given to this view by what is said by Paul: **But their minds were hardened, for until this very day at the reading of the old covenant the same veil remains unlifted; which veil is done away in Christ. But unto this day whenever Moses is read, a veil lies upon their heart. But whensoever a man shall turn to the Lord, the veil is taken away . . . But and if our gospel is veiled, it is veiled in them that are perishing: in whom the god of this world has blinded the minds of the unbelieving . . .**[22] The blindness in this context is blindness to the meaning of the prophecies of the old covenant—blindness to the Messiahship of Jesus. Paul makes it clear, however, that the blindness does not remove the individual's responsibility in the matter. They are unable to recognize Jesus as their true Messiah, but the basic lack in their lives is not *insight* but *repentance*. When any of them repents, when he turns to God, then the Lord will remove the veil; the flood of enlightenment will come. The cure for blindness is repentance.

The same principles apply today. The Bible tells us to repent and believe. If we repent, God will help us to see and believe in his Son. We may be sure that John agrees with Paul on this point, even if we are not entirely certain of some of his meaning. It is clear that John 12:40 does not mean that God has made it impossible for the Jews to believe in Christ, for, having said that their eyes are blinded, John then adds: **Nevertheless even of the rulers many believed on him;** it was clearly their own fault if they did not understand and accept Jesus, for their hearts were far from God.[23]

In summary then, the reason for Jewish unbelief was that they themselves closed their eyes lest they should see the uncomfortable truth. Since their hearts were far from God, the secrets of the kingdom and the Messiah's task were hidden from them. Only those who were "of God" learned from the Father (or from the lips of the Savior himself) the meaning of his words and coming.

The cure for those who did not understand was not more study, but that they should turn to the Lord. When a man turned to the Lord, the veil was removed and he was healed.

POSTSCRIPT

It is interesting to note the two main contexts in which Isaiah 6:10 is quoted in the New Testament. In Matthew 13 it is quoted at the time when Jesus changed from teaching openly to using parables. Because of people's unbelief, Jesus began to disguise his teaching so that only those who were of God would seek and find understanding. It was a time when, as it were, he turned away from the nation as a whole to teach only those who were spiritually discerning.

The other great turning point at which Isaiah 6:10 is quoted is Acts 28:26-28. Paul, like Christ, quotes the text in full, upbraiding them for closing their eyes to avoid understanding. "Very well," he seems to say, "then know that God's salvation is sent unto the Gentiles, they will listen to it." This seems to mark the time when he turned from his countrymen to a more intensive ministry to the Gentiles. Not that he does this in malice, but in the hope that they will be made jealous and so be led to repent.

Both Christ himself and his servant Paul lay the blame for unbelief with the unbelievers themselves. Both imply that since these have closed their eyes they will also lose the privilege of receiving the message of the kingdom. It will be given to those whose hearts seek God. Only when a man turns to the Lord is the veil removed and the secrets of God's kingdom revealed.

God's wrath came upon many Israelites because they would not repent. Nonetheless, God's wrath was not for its own sake, for he had another purpose in view. As we have elsewhere noted, he used them as a vessel of no-honor to demonstrate to the world the results of rejecting him. He endured with much longsuffering the vessels of wrath fitted for destruction in order that he might make known the riches of his glory upon the vessels of mercy. **For God has shut up all unto disobedience, that he might have mercy upon all.**

O the depth of the riches both of the wisdom and the knowledge of God! how unsearchable are his judgments, and his ways past tracing out! For who has known the mind of the Lord? or who has been his counselor? or who has first given to him, and it shall be recompensed unto him again? For of him, and through him, and unto him, are all things. To him be the glory for ever. Amen.

NOTES

1. In spite of his call as the apostle to the Gentiles (Acts 9:15; Galatians 2:8), throughout Acts Paul preached to the Jews first. His words in Acts 28:26 show that the paucity of their response stimulated him to turn to preach to the Gentiles. There is also another way in which the unbelief of the Jews may indirectly have increased the impact of the gospel on the Gentiles. As a result of the Wrath which came on the Jews the Temple was destroyed and the nation dispersed. This helped to destroy the power of those who taught that converts must become "Judaized" to be saved, and thus a stumbling block to potential converts was removed.

2. Romans 11:26
3. Matthew 13:17
4. Cf. p. 194
5. Matthew 7:6
6. Matthew 7:7
7. John 10:19

8. John 10:24
9. John 10:25-30
10. Mark 4:10-20
11. John 6:45
12. John 6:43-45
13. Luke 2:25
14. Acts 16:13-15
15. Acts 10:30-32
16. John 6:64, 65
17. John 7:4-6
18. John 7:16, 17
19. John 8:47
20. This also explains the paradox that the purpose of Jesus' mission was to "give repentance to Israel" (Acts 5:31; Cf. Acts 11:18). This saying of the apostles could only be taken by their hearers to mean that the *whole nation* of Israel were given the gift. Their words to the council are barbed: "You killed Jesus, but God raised him up to give all Israel (including you as its head) repentance." The gift was, of course, refused by many—especially by those who Luke says rejected for themselves God's plan for them to receive the baptism of repentance (Luke 7:30)—but it was offered to all. See also, in the appendix, the comment (p. 206) of Clement of Rome c. 96 A.D., and note 60 (p. 227).

21. John 12:37-40
22. 2 Corinthians 3:14—4:4
23. It is thus that we understand 1 Peter 2:8. The people were disobedient to God, and so were appointed by him to stumble at Jesus.

Appendix
Early Teaching
on God's and Man's Will

The earlier studies in this book deal with various topics of
Bible background and language, and are intended to aid our
understanding of the Bible. The present study has been
appended to the book with a rather different aim: to help
us to understand *ourselves* as we approach the Bible.

In section 6 we commented on the clear teaching of the
Bible that men can and do reject God's will and plan for
them, and on the various influences that may lead us to
overlook such teachings. The present study examines the
earliest Christian teaching available on this subject and
tries to find some clue as to how these influences have
arisen. As Christians we stand, either consciously or un-
consciously, in a long Christian tradition, and are influenced
by its thinking. We may well find it useful to see the origins of some of our own ideas and presuppositions about
Bible teaching.

The early church had the task of interpreting and eluci-
dating the New Testament writings. What was implied often
had to be made explicit. Sometimes new words (like "trinity") were coined. One of the earliest of these words was

"free-will." The early church noted the Scriptures (such as Matthew 23:37) which indicated that man sometimes defied and disobeyed God's will. They may also have noted verses (e.g., John 7:17) which indicate that man's will is not automatically forced to be what God wants it to be. They therefore coined the term "free-will" to describe the will of man. This was to emphasize the Bible's teaching that man's will was free to choose not to do the will of God. We may not like the expression "free-will" for it is not used in the Bible, and was later misused by the Pelagians. But like "trinity," it was part of the early Christians' attempt to define apostolic teaching more clearly.

The doctrine of "free-will" seems to have been universally accepted in the early church. Not a single church figure in the first 300 years rejected it and most of them stated it clearly in works still extant. We find it taught by great leaders in places as different as Alexandria, Antioch, Athens, Carthage, Jerusalem, Lycia, Nyssa, Rome, and Sicca. We find it taught by the leaders of all the main theological schools.[1] The only ones to reject it were heretics like the Gnostics, Marcion, Valentinus, Manes (and the Manichees), etc. In fact, the early Fathers often state their beliefs on "free-will" in works attacking heretics. Three recurrent ideas seem to be in their teaching:

1. The rejection of free-will is the view of heretics.

2. Free-will is a gift given to man by God—for nothing can ultimately be independent of God.

3. Man possesses free-will because he is made in God's image, and God has free-will.

We have, below, set out some passages from writings of leading early church figures. Each is accompanied by a very brief explanation of who the writer was, but for further explanation the reader should see any standard work.[2] One word of prior explanation (given by Smith) may be useful: "The writers who tried to put the Christian case are often called the "Apologists," from the Greek apologia, a speech for the defense. In English this is a misleading term, because it implies that they were apologizing for something. They were not. Some of their work was more of a frontal attack on contemporary paganism. Much of it was an explanation of what Christians were and why they were innocent of the charges laid against them."[3]

JUSTIN MARTYR
(c. 100–165 A.D.)

Renwick calls Justin "the greatest of the early apologists, a most earnest Christian and a true lover of learning." Quasten calls him "the most important of the Greek apologists of the second century and one of the noblest personalities of early Christian literature."[4]

As a philosopher, Justin had sought the truth in various schools but remained unsatisfied. Then in Ephesus he met an old man who talked to him about the Lord. He says that "it seemed as if a fire was kindled in him." Still wearing his philosopher's cloak, but now on fire for the Lord, he won many with his testimony. Finally, a rival (anti-Christian) philosopher accused him to the city Prefect of being a Christian. The Prefect threatened Justin with flogging and execution, and jeeringly asked him if he thought he would ascend to heaven. Justin replied: "I don't *think* so, I know and am fully persuaded of it." Thus he received martyrdom.

The "soundness" of Justin's teaching is examined later in this section. He mentions "free-will" in several works, e.g., in *The Sovereignty of God,* but here we will quote only one instance:

> *Dialogue CXLi*: God, wishing men and angels to follow His will, resolved to create them free to do righteousness. But if the word of God foretells that some angels and men shall certainly be punished, it did so because it foreknew that they would be unchangeably (wicked), but not because God created them so. So if they repent all who wish for it can obtain mercy from God.

IRENAEUS
OF GAUL
(c. 130–200)

Irenaeus was the first of the great Fathers of the period 180-250. He was a disciple of Polycarp of Smyrna who was a disciple of Saint John. The importance of his work *Against Heresies* in saving the church from the doctrines of the Gnostics cannot be exaggerated.[5]

> *Against Heresies XXXVII*: This expression, "How often would I have gathered thy children together, and thou wouldst not," set forth the ancient law of human liberty, because God made man a free (agent) from the beginning, possessing his own soul to obey the behests of God voluntarily, and not by compulsion of God. For there is no coercion with God, but a good will (toward us) is present with Him continually. And therefore does He give good counsel to all. And in man as well as in angels, He has placed the power of choice (for angels are rational beings), so that those who had yielded obedience might justly possess what is good, given indeed by God, but preserved by themselves . . .
>
> 4) If then it were not in our power to do or not to do these things, what reason had the apostle, and much more the Lord Himself, to give us counsel to do some things and to abstain from others? But because man is possessed of free-will from the beginning, and God is possessed of free-will in whose likeness man was created, advice is always given to him to keep fast the good, which thing is done by means of obedience to God.

ATHENAGORAS
OF ATHENS
(2nd century)

Athenagoras was an Athenian philosopher who became a Christian. He was by far the most elegant, and certainly at the same time one of the ablest, of the early Christian Apologists.[6] The *Embassy* was written in about 177 A.D.

> *Embassy for Christians XXIV*: Just as with men who have freedom of choice as to both virtue and vice (for you would not either honor the good or punish the bad; unless vice and virtue were in their own power, and some are diligent in the matters entrusted to them, and others faithless), so is it among the angels.

THEOPHILUS OF ANTIOCH
(2nd century)

Theophilus became Bishop of the important town of Antioch about 169 A.D. He wrote an apology for Christianity, addressed to Autolycus. He seems to have been the first writer to have used the term "trinity" to refer to the Godhead. "His works were highly thought of and before long were studied in the West. Ireneus and Hyppolytus made use of them before Tertullian."[7]

> *To Autolycus xxvii*: For God made man free, and with power over himself . . . now God vouchsafes to him as a gift through His own philanthropy and pity, when men obey Him. For as man, disobeying, drew death on himself; so, obeying the will of God, he who desires is able to procure for himself life everlasting.

TATIAN OF SYRIA
(flourished late 2nd century)

Tatian was at first Justin's pupil. Soon, however, he became independent. This is seen in that, unlike Justin, he condemned all pagan philosophy as totally evil. He returned to Syria as a missionary, and composed the *Diatessaron*, a harmony of the Gospels. This work, and his influence, were of great importance in early Syriac Christianity. His followers followed a very strict rule of life and soon split off from the Greek church. Smith says: "Perhaps one of his (Tatian's) converts was Bardaisan who was born in Edessa and was converted about 179. Bardaisan was strongly against the determinism of much Greek philosophy, and he strongly attacked Marcion. He is also the first known Syrian hymn writer. Like Tatian he was an enthusiastic missionary, and the Syriac churches probably owed much of their strength to leaders like these. Despite the fact that they came under the suspicion of Greek Christian writers, these men were probably orthodox Christians with a number of odd ideas."[8]

> *Address*, xi: Why are you "fated" to grasp at things often, and often to die? Die to the world, repudiating the madness that is in it. Live to God, and by apprehending Him lay aside your old nature. We were not created to die, but we die by our own fault. Our free-will has destroyed us; we who were free have become slaves; we have been sold through sin. Nothing evil has been created by God; we ourselves have manifested wickedness; but we, who have manifested it, are able again to reject it.

BARDAISAN OF SYRIA
(c. 154–222)

As already mentioned, Bardaisan was probably mainly orthodox, but was not accepted by Greek writers. Eusebius says: "Bardaisan, a most able man and highly skilled disputant in the Syriac language, composed dialogues against the followers of Marcion . . . At an earlier stage he had belonged to the school of Valentinus, but later he condemned it and refuted many of its fanciful ideas . . . For all that the taint of the old heresy stuck to him to the end."

> *Fragments*: "How is it that God did not so make us that we should not sin and incur condemnation?" —if man had been made so, he would not have belonged to himself but would have been the instru-

ment of him that moved him; . . . And how, in that case, would a man differ from a harp, on which another plays; or from a ship, which another guides: where the praise and the blame reside in the hand of the performer or the steersman . . . they being only instruments made for the use of him in whom is the skill? But God, in His benignity, chose not so to make man; but by freedom He exalted him above many of His creatures.

CLEMENT
OF ALEXANDRIA
(c. 150–215)

Clement was a presbyter of tremendous learning, both of the Bible and of secular literature. He was for some time head of the Alexandrian school of Christian scholars, and is one of the most famous early Christian writers.[9] He has sometimes been accused of placing too much stress on the intellect[10] but we find this criticism hard to accept. For one thing, most Christian theologians and apologists place emphasis on right belief, especially in arguing against heresies. For another, Clement repeatedly makes it clear that faith is a moral issue, and a matter of decision for Christ. In *Stromata*, Bk ii ch 2, for example, he argues strongly that "faith is not established by demonstration." Faith involves a choice and "choice is the beginning of action." Shortly after we read:

Stromata, Bk ii ch. 4: But we, who have heard by the Scriptures that self-determining choice and refusal have been given by the Lord to men, rest in the infallible criterion of faith, manifesting a willing spirit, since we have chosen life and believe God through His voice.

Stromata, Bk iv ch. 12: But nothing is without the will of the Lord of the universe. It remains to say that such things happen without the prevention of God; for this alone saves both the providence and the goodness of God. We must not therefore think that He actively produces afflictions (far be it that we should think this!); but we must be persuaded that He does not prevent those that cause them, but overrules for good the crimes of His enemies.

TERTULLIAN
OF CARTHAGE
(c. 155–225)

Tertullian was the first Latin theologian, and one of the greatest early Christian writers of the west. He later tended toward the "rigorist" views of the Montanists, though his Montanism did not prevent him from remaining dogmatically orthodox in most respects. His apology is one of the ablest ever written.[11] He was strikingly different from Clement,[12] and emphasized man's inherited sinfulness.[13]

Against Marcion, Book II ch. 5: I find, then, that man was by God constituted free, master of his own will and power; indicating the presence of God's image and likeness in him by nothing so well as by this constitution of his nature . . .

—you will find that when He sets before man good and evil, life and death, that the entire course of discipline is arranged in precepts by God's calling men from sin, and threatening and exhorting them; and this on no other ground than that man is free, with a will either for obedience or resistance.

. . . Since, therefore, both the goodness and purpose of God are discovered in the gift to man of freedom in his will . . .

NOVATIAN
OF ROME
(c. 200–258)

Novatian was the first Roman theologian to write in Latin. Smith says "Novatian was brilliant. He was a competent theologian, and a work on the doctrine of the Trinity survives to give an idea of his prowess. Even his enemies had to admit that he was blameless in his life, and had been a zealous worker."[14] Novatian lost the election for the bishopric of Rome, and separated from the "official" group on the issue of whether lapsed believers might be received back into fellowship. His followers, called "Puritans," were excommunicated by the Catholic church.[15] Bruce says: "In doctrine they were strictly orthodox; Novatian himself, indeed, was one of the chief exponents of pure trinitarian theology in the third century."[16]

> *On the Trinity, ch. 1*: He also placed man at the head of the world, and man, too, made in the image of God, to whom He imparted mind, and reason, and foresight, that he might imitate God; and although the first elements of his body were earthly, yet the substance was inspired by a heavenly and divine breathing. And when He had given him all things for his service, He willed that he alone should be free. And lest, again, an unbounded freedom should fall into peril, He laid down a command, in which man was taught that there was no evil in the fruit of the tree; but he was forewarned that evil would arise if perchance he should exercise his freewill in the contempt of the law that was given.

ORIGEN
(c. 185–254)

Renwick calls Origen "one of the most brilliant teachers and writers ever known in the Christian Church. The son of a martyr, and reared in a fine spiritual atmosphere, he became head of the catechetical school at the age of 18 and raised it to its highest fame in spite of persecution. He loved the Scriptures and showed remarkable ability in interpreting them."[17] Bruce says: "Greater still than Tertullian and Novatian was the Alexandrian theologian Origen, the greatest scholar and thinker of the church in the first three centuries."[18]

Origen sometimes gave expression to some wild speculations, which later brought criticism on him. He did, however, distinguish clearly between his speculations and his teaching of established doctrines. Renwick says: "He claimed that he was loyal to the rule of faith adopted by the Church, while exercising ample liberty of expression on matters not covered by the accepted creed."[19] Let us, therefore, note carefully his words:

> *De Principiis, Preface*: Now it ought to be known that the holy apostles, in preaching the faith of Christ, delivered themselves with the utmost clearness on certain points which they believed to be necessary to everyone . . . This also is *clearly defined in the teaching of the church* that every rational soul is possessed of free-will and volition.
>
> *De Principiis, Bk 3 ch. 1*: There are, indeed, innumerable passages in the Scriptures which establish with exceeding clearness the existence of freedom of will.[20]

METHODIUS
OF OLYMPUS
(c. 260–martyred 311)

Methodius was a bishop in Lycia, Asia Minor, known chiefly as an antagonist of Origen.[21] But, although he attacked Origen's speculations, there was one point on which he (like all early Christians) agreed:

> *The Banquet of the Ten Virgins xvi*: Now those who decide that man is not possessed of free-will, and affirm that he is governed by the unavoidable necessities of fate . . . are guilty of impiety toward God Himself, making Him out to be the cause and author of human evils.
>
> *Concerning Free-will*: I say that man was made with free-will, not as if there were already existing

some evil, which he had the power of choosing if
he wished . . . but that the power of obeying and dis-
obeying God is the only cause.

ARCHELAUS

Cyril, Epiphanius, and Jerome record a disputation (in
277) between the heretic Manes (founder of Manichaeism)
and the orthodox Archelaus. The dialogue, as we have it,
was probably set down by a later writer, but does show us
differences between orthodoxy and heresy at that time.

The Disputation with Manes: For all creatures that
God made, He made very good, and He gave to every
individual the sense of free-will in accordance with
which standard He also instituted the law of judgment. To sin is ours, and that we sin not is God's
gift, as our will is constituted to choose either to sin
or not to sin.

ARNOBIUS
OF SICCA
(c. 253–327)

Arnobius wrote a brilliant Christian apology about 300
A.D.[22]

Against the Heathen: 64. I reply: does not He free
all alike who invites all alike? or does He thrust
back or repel any one from the kindness of the
Supreme who gives to all alike the power of coming
to Him—? To all, He says, the fountain of life is
open, and no one is hindered or kept back from
drinking . . .

65. Nay, my opponent says, if God is powerful,
merciful, willing to save us, let Him change our
dispositions, and compel us to trust in His promises.
This then, is violence, not kindness nor the bounty of
the Supreme God, but a childish and vain strife in
seeking to get the mastery. For what is so unjust

as to force men who are reluctant and unworthy, to reverse their inclinations; to impress forcibly on their minds what they are unwilling to receive, and shrink from . . .

CYRIL OF JERUSALEM
(c. 312–386)

Cyril was a Bishop of Jerusalem with little claim to fame, but he shows us what the ordinary churchman believed:

Lexture IV 18: Know also that thou hast a soul self governed, the noblest work of God, made after the image of its Creator, immortal because of God that gives it immortality, a living being rational, imperishable, because of Him that bestowed these gifts: having free power to do what it willeth.

20. There is not a class of souls sinning by nature and a class of souls practicing righteousness by nature; but both act from choice, the substance of their souls being of one kind only and alike in all.

21. The soul is self-governed: and though the Devil can suggest, he has not the power to compel against the will. He pictures to thee the thought of fornication: if thou wilt, thou rejectest. For if thou wert a fornicator of necessity then for what cause did God prepare hell? If thou wert a doer of righteousness by nature and not by will, wherefore did God prepare crowns of ineffable glory? The sheep is gentle, but never was it crowned for its gentleness; since its gentle quality belongs to it not from choice but by nature.

GREGORY OF NYSSA
(c. 335–395)

Gregory was one of the most acute intellects of the fourth century, having great influence in the eastern churches.

He was at the council of Constantinople (381) and was nominated by Theodosius I as a norm of orthodoxy.[23]

On Virginity (368) ch. XII: Being the image and the likeness . . . of the Power which rules all things, man kept also in the matter of a free-will this likeness to Him whose will is over all.

JEROME
(c. 347–420)

Jerome was one of the four great doctors of the western church and the most learned of the Latin Fathers.[24] He was an expert on Hebrew and Greek and his Latin translation of the Bible (the Vulgate) was far better than other Latin versions of the time. His attitude to "free-will" is important for three main reasons. First, he stands, like Augustine, in the Latin tradition and was a strong critic of Origen and the Alexandrian heritage. Second, as a Bible translator he had a deep and firsthand knowledge of New Testament writings. Third, he wrote against the Pelagians, whose teachings had brought disrepute on the word *free-will*. The orthodox Christian view of the first three centuries had been that God gave man a free-will to obey or to disobey God's commands to trust him, to accept or reject grace. Some Pelagians seem to have taken free-will to imply that man could (of his own will) decide to live a moral life. There is a world of difference between these two ideas, and it is a pity that this is not always realized. The early church view was that man had free-will to accept or reject God's offer of free pardon and grace to live a holy life. It was always understood that conversion was a spiritual rebirth accomplished by God's power, and that a man could live a holy life only in Christ. The Pelagians replaced regeneration with self-effort, and their view was rightly condemned.

Jerome strongly attacked the Pelagians, but wanted to distinguish the Pelagian concept of free-will from the orthodox and biblical one:

Letters CXXXIII: It is in vain that you misrepresent me and try to convince the ignorant that I condemn free-will. Let him who condemns it be himself condemned. We have been created endowed with free-will; still it is not this which distinguishes us from the brutes. For human free-will, as I said, depends upon the help of God and needs His aid moment by moment, a thing which you and yours do not choose to admit. Your position is that once a man has free-will he no longer needs the help of God. It is true that freedom of the will brings with it freedom of decision. Still man does not act immediately on his free-will but requires God's aid who Himself needs no aid.

Against the Pelagians, Book III, 10: But when we are concerned with grace and mercy, free-will is in part void; in part, I say, for so much depends upon it, that we wish and desire, and give assent to the course we choose. But it depends on God whether we have the power in His strength and with His help to perform what we desire, and to bring to effect our toil and effort.

JOHN
CHRYSOSTOM
(347–407)

Bruce writes: "In the east there is none to match John of Constantinople." Renwick calls him: "a saintly man, an outstanding scholar, and one of the greatest orators of all time . . . His faithfulness in preaching repentance offended the empress Eudoxia and he . . . died through ill-treatment on his way as a prisoner to Pityus."[25] He is eloquently clear on the topic of free-will:

On Hebrews, Homily 12: All is in God's power, but so that our free-will is not lost . . . It depends therefore on us and on Him. We must first choose the good, and then He adds what belongs to Him. He

does not precede our willing, that our free-will may
not suffer. But when we have chosen, then He af-
fords us much help . . . It is ours to choose beforehand and to will, but God's to perfect and bring to
the end.

Thus we find striking agreement among early church
leaders over the issue of free-will. The same teaching was
held by mainstream and fringe groups, by scholars and
ordinary ministers, by the Greek, Latin, and even Syrian
traditions—by everyone, in short, except total heretics. We
may not like the phrase "free-will," which today has connotations of Pelagianism, but as used by true early Christians
it expressed their universally held belief that God made
man free to accept or reject his offer of free pardon and
grace. As we have seen in section 6, many verses in the
Bible seem to imply this, and early church teaching was
simply a clarification of it, just as their teaching on the
"trinity" helped to clarify that issue.

THE NEW THEOLOGY— AUGUSTINE (354–430)

It may seem surprising that after such universal agreement
among early Christian writers there should be a change.
Nevertheless there was, and it is interesting to see how
this came about.

What was the exact point of the change, insofar as it
may be identified? Some words of a great Reformation
scholar are relevent here. But Ambrose, Origen, and Jerome
were of the opinion that God dispenses his grace among
men according to the use which he foresees that each will
make of it. It may be added that Augustine was for some
time also of this opinion; but after he had made some
progress in knowledge of Scripture he not only retracted
it as evidently false, but powerfully confuted it.[26]

Augustine himself wrote:

> I labored indeed on behalf of the free choice of the human will, but God's grace overcame, and I could only reach that point where the apostle is perceived to have said with the most evident truth, "for who makes you to differ? and what do you have that you have not received? Now if you have received it why do you glory as if you received it not?" And the martyr Cyprian was also desirous of setting forth . . . Faith then, as well in its beginning as in its completion, is God's gift; and let no one have any doubt whatever, unless he desires to resist the plainest Scriptures, that this gift is given to some, while to some it is not given.[27]

We should note three things from this passage. First Augustine notes his change of view. The view for which h formerly labored was the orthodox early Christian view, bu he was "overcome" with these new ideas.

Second, Augustine does not himself seem entirely awar of his break with the early Christian view. He here cite Cyprian, but although Cyprian was probably the least clea on the issue of all the leading early Christians, we can fin no statement by him that faith is an irresistible gift. In th passage Augustine cites, Cyprian is speaking in as general sense as Paul himself and does not state Augustine's view Yet Augustine may have believed that Cyprian really hel such views (he himself seems to have known little abou early Christian writings).[28] Thus he may not have realize the extent of his novelty.

Third, it is important to note that the issue is *not* one o whether salvation is of works or of faith; it is one o whether faith itself is an irresistible gift. This is important for the two issues are frequently confused. Most Christian have never read a word of Augustine's writings, but thei views are generally affected by the ideas of Christia scholars. Among many of the latter there is an unfortunat tradition to think in terms of the early church having "poor understanding" of Pauline doctrines, which were "re stored" by Augustine. The spell of this idea is so strong that it produces statements like the following comment in a recent (and generally good) book on church history. It refers to the letter from the church at Rome to the church at Corinth, written about A.D. 96 and generally ascribed to Clement. The comment is: "Salvation is seen to be based on faith and works; for example Rahab is said to have been saved by faith and hospitality. Perhaps the particular situation called for emphasis on faith being accompanied by suitable actions, but it does seem that Paul's doctrine of salvation through the grace of God alone was not well understood."

Now Paul wrote to the Roman church in about A.D. 58 and Clement's epistle was sent from Rome in about A.D. 96. It would seem almost certain that some of the original recipients of the epistle to the Romans would still have been in that church. Are we seriously to believe that they failed to understand the central teaching of the epistle Paul wrote them?

When, moreover, we look at the first epistle of Clement, our amazement at the allegation increases. In 1 Clement 4.5-6 we read:

> Let us look steadfastly to the blood of Christ, and see how precious His blood is in the sight of God: which being shed for our salvation, has obtained the grace of repentance for all the world. Let us search into all the ages that have gone before us; and let us learn that in every one of them our Lord has still given place for repentance to all such as would turn to Him.

In 1 Clement 14.20-1 we read:

> And we also being called by the same will in Christ Jesus, are not justified through ourselves, neither by our own wisdom, or knowledge, or piety, or the works which we have done in the holiness of our hearts: But by faith by which God Almighty has justified all men from the beginning; to whom be glory for ever and ever, amen.

Could Paul's doctrine be more firmly or clearly stated? Even in the passage referring to Rahab we later read that the spies: "gave her, moreover, a sign: that she should hang out of her house a scarlet rope; showing thereby, that by the blood of our Lord, there should be redemption to all that believe and hope in God." We might, even, compare the clarity of this emphasis on the efficacy of faith through Christ's blood, with the analyses in some of the books in the New Testament itself. Clement refers to Rahab being saved by "faith and hospitality;" James mentions neither faith nor grace but simply says: **"was not Rahab the harlot justified by works, in that she received the messengers and sent them out another way?"**[29] If we are to view Clement as one who "did not understand" Paul's doctrine of grace, then surely James must be classed as one who did not understand it at all?[30] Even worse, on this basis the parable of the sheep and the goats[31] must surely be classed as heresy.

Unthinkable as such ideas are to the Christian, they are no more indefensible than the accusations made against Clement and the early church. Yet such accusations are made on the basis of passages in early Christian writings for which there are parallel (or "worse") passages in the Bible itself. The accusations are perhaps the worst when directed against writers like Justin Martyr. Through reading some commentators one might almost get the impression that Justin was a "liberal" theologian, barely Christian. The truth is that Justin's writings are intensely biblical. He shows good knowledge of both the Septuagint and the Hebrew Old Testament, as well as the New. His love for Christ shows through in every paragraph, and he is quite clear on the necessity of Christ for salvation. He shows deep understanding of Paul's ideas, and his defense of Christ's divinity from the Old Testament is outstanding. Christians sometimes criticize him for his quotation of pre-Christian philosophers, but in doing so they seem to forget to whom he addressed himself. Justin addressed the intelligent pagan—unlike the apostles whose recorded words were mainly to Jews or Christians and so needed no such quotations. Acts 17 is perhaps the only passage in the New Testament in which the intelligent pagan is addressed—and in this passage Paul himself quotes with approval two pre-Christian philosophers on the nature of God. If we are to frown on Justin for such activities then shall we also frown on Paul? Justin, like Paul, is often misunderstood. Take, for example, his teaching on the "Word." John 1:9 was taken seriously by Justin (compare Augustine, whose rather bizarre interpretation is given below). Justin says:

> We have been taught that Christ is the first-born of God, and we had declared above that *He* is *the Word* of whom every race of men were partakers; and those who lived *reasonably* are Christians . . . as among the Greeks Socrates . . . and among the barbarians Abraham . . .[32]

At first sight it would seem that Justin is suggesting salvation through our own reason, but this is not so. The common rendering "reasonable" should strictly read "with the Word" (*meta logou*), i.e., with Christ as the pre-existent Word of God. Justin is saying that Socrates, like Abraham, was justified through his association with a Savior whom he never knew by name. Whether or not we personally agree with him on this, it has been the belief of many orthodox Christians and we can hardly fault him for it.[33]

Let us now, then, look at some of Justin's words in his dialogue with Trypho, who was a Jew and possibly a rabbi. We may compare them with the apostolic teaching, especially with that of Paul. Justin says:

> (1) I purpose to quote you Scriptures, not that I am anxious to make merely an artful display of words; for I possess no such faculty, but God's grace alone has been granted to me to the understanding of His Scriptures, of which grace I exhort all to become partakers . . . (*Dial* lviii).
> (2) And you deceive yourselves while you fancy that, because you are the seed of Abraham after

the flesh, therefore you will inherit the good things announced by God to be bestowed through Christ. For no one, . . . has any thing to look for, but only those who in mind are assimilated to the faith of Abraham (xlvi, cf. Romans 4:12).

(3) But though a man be a Scythian or a Persian, if he has knowledge of God and of His Christ, and keeps the everlasting righteous decrees, he is circumcised with the good and useful circumcision, and he is a friend of God . . . And we, who have approached God through Him, have received not a carnal but a spiritual circumcision, which Enoch and those like him observed. And we have received it through baptism, since we were sinners, by God's mercy; and all men may equally obtain it (xxviii and xliii, cf. Romans 2, etc.). "What need, then, have I of circumcision, who have been witnessed to by God?" (xxix, cf. Galatians 4:9).

Justin, however, like Paul, does not object to Jewish Christians keeping the Law, provided that they neither seek salvation through it nor compel Gentiles to keep it (xlvii).

(4) For Isaiah did not send you to a bath, there to wash away murder and other sins, which not all the water of the sea were sufficient to purge; but as might have been expected, this was that saving "bath" of olden time which followed (was for) those who repented, and who no longer were purified by the blood of goats and of sheep . . . but by faith, through the blood of Christ, and through His death, who died for this very reason, as Isaiah himself said, when he spake thus: "The Lord shall make bare His holy arm in the eyes of all the nations, and all the nations and the ends of the earth shall see the salvation of God" (xii).

Justin continues with a moving quotation of Isaiah 53. What firmer statement of Paul's doctrine of justification by faith could there be? He later adds:

As Isaiah cries, we have believed, and testify that the very baptism which he pronounces is alone able to purify those who have repented; and this is the water of life. But the cisterns which you have dug for yourselves are broken and profitless to you. For what is the use of that baptism which cleanses the flesh and body alone? (xiv).

Compare this with 1 Peter 3:21—"Baptism now saves you, not as the removal of dirt from the body, but as an appeal to God for a clear conscience through the resurrection of Jesus Christ."

One may compare Justin's clear fidelity to New Testament baptism, with the view of Augustine (see below) that babies are saved against their will by baptizing them. Justin also mentions the Isaiah passage again to Trypho: "that you have crucified Him, the only blameless Man, through whose stripes those who approach the Father by Him are healed . . ." (xvii).

(5) For the whole human race will be found to be under a curse. For it is written in the Law of Moses, "Cursed is everyone who continues not in all things that are written in the book of the Law to do them." And no one has completely done all, nor will you venture to deny this . . . If, then, the Father of all wished His Christ for the whole human family to take upon Him the curses of all, knowing that, after He had been crucified and was dead, He would raise Him up, why do you argue about Him who submitted to suffer these things according to the Father's will, as if He were accursed, and do not rather bewail yourselves? (xcv).

(6) And you yourselves . . . must acknowledge that we, who have been called by God through the despised and shameful mystery of the cross . . . and endure all torments rather than deny Christ even by word, through whom we are called to the salvation prepared beforehand by the Father, are more faithful to God than you . . . (cxxxi). . . . you hate

and murder us who have believed through Him in the God and Father of all, as often as you can. And you curse Him without ceasing, as well as those who side with Him; while all of us pray for you, and for all men, as our Christ and Lord taught us to do, when He enjoined us to pray even for our enemies, and to love them that hate us, and to bless them that curse us (cxxxiii).

This was no idle boast from one who was later flogged and martyred. Jesus told us to recognize his true followers by their fruit. These passages from Justin help us to see both his personal character and his strict acceptance of Pauline teachings. His *Dialogue* continually refers to the cross as God's method of dealing with sin,[34] to the spiritual circumcision of heart which Christ gives to those who believe in him,[35] to faith,[36] to repentance,[37] to forgiveness of sins through being washed in his blood,[38] to the healing through Christ's stripes,[39] and so on. Above all he urges Trypho and his fellow-Jews to repent[40] and to "become acquainted with Christ" their Messiah.[41] Yet in the recent book already mentioned we read this of Justin: "To Justin, conversion was mainly an ethical and rational thing, concerned with a change of attitude and behavior." What basis is there for this remark? There seems little basis in the *Dialogue*, for Justin's plea to Trypho is for repentance, not for a change of ethical code. Could it be his use of rational argument? But then we read time and time again in Acts that the apostles argued and disputed with the Jews.[42] Could it be that he quotes pre-Christian philosophers? But so does the Apostle Paul when he addresses the type of person for whom Justin wrote in his *Apology*.[43] Could it be his belief that the Christian does not find God's commandments a burden? But the Apostle John says almost this very thing.[44] Surely to Justin, no less than to the New Testament writers, conversion was a *moral* and *spiritual* thing, involving repentance, divinely wrought regeneration, forgiveness on the basis of the blood of Christ, and a new relationship with the only One through whom men could come to God. Early church figures like Clement and Justin fully accepted the doctrine of salvation by faith.

What, therefore, was the real issue between Augustine and the early church? The latter did *not* believe that man had "free-will" to keep the Law and so earn salvation by works.[45] Their beliefs were far removed from the rabbinical ideas that Paul meant by "works." In Augustine's day some Pelagians held views not unlike the rabbis, but their views were not those of the early church. It may, therefore, be useful to summarize the three alternative views:

(1) *Works.* The Pelagian view, which Augustine stated thus: "the law being given, the will is of its own strength sufficient to fulfill that law, though not assisted by any grace imparted by the Holy Spirit in addition to instruction in the Law."[46] He also stated it as: "the grace of God is bestowed in proportion to our own deserts."[47]

(2) *Faith.* The early church view, and Augustine's own earlier view. He stated it as: "For it is ours to believe and to will, but it is His to give to those who believe and will the power of doing good works through the Holy Spirit . . ."[48]

(3) *Irresistible gift of faith.* Augustine's later view (which triumphed in the church) was that faith itself was an irresistible gift given by God to a few people whom he had selected on some basis known only to himself.[49] God could have given it to others had he so chosen[50] for it is "rejected by no hard heart."[51] Without it no man could perform any good, whether in thought, will, affection, or action.[52]

Views (1) and (2) are seldom properly distinguished in Augustine's writings. This may have been partly due to the unfortunate practice in his day of referring to the "merit of faith" and the "merit of conversion."[53] This led or enabled Augustine to regard faith as a form of "work"; he says: "The apostle, therefore, distinguishes faith from works, just as Judah is distinguished from Israel . . . though Judah is Israel itself."[54] This is a totally un-Pauline idea, and it fails to understand the Hebrew background to Paul's writings. Paul always sets faith and works in antithesis. He makes it clear that if salvation is of works then it is earned, but if of faith then it is unearned: "Now to him that works, the reward is not reckoned as of grace, but as of debt. But to him that works not, but believes on him that justifies the ungodly, his faith is reckoned for righteousness."[55] Paul does not say that unless the faith itself were irresistible it would be works! The words: "to him that *works not* but *has faith* . . ." would be sheer nonsense if faith itself were a work. Paul simply assumes that faith is not a "work of the Law," it earns nothing, it merits nothing. God would be quite just to damn anyone who has faith—it is of his own free grace that he declares them righteous. The reward for works is a payment of a debt, but for faith there is no such debt; God "reckons it as righteousness." This is always the case in Pauline terms. He contrasts grace and works, or faith and works, but never faith and grace, for faith is never a work.

Augustine could find nothing at all in Paul to support a claim that faith could be a work. The best he could do was Jesus' words: "This is the work of God, that you believe on him whom he has sent."[56] This parallel is very unconvincing. Christians today talk of doing "the Lord's work" without in the least implying that they expect to earn salvation by doing it. The question to Jesus does not concern "works of the Law" (as a way to salvation) but the "works of God." When Paul used the term *works* he always used it technically to mean works of the Law—i.e., in an entirely different context. In any case, the reply Jesus gave is intentionally cryptic and turns the questioner back to the true priority—before doing the Lord's work we must be right with the Lord!

The conclusion must be that in Pauline terminology faith could never be classed as a work, and the practice in Augustine's day of thinking of it as such was misleading. Thus the early church view (2) has to be clearly distinguished from the Pelagian view (1). The latter amounted to saying that salvation was of works, while the former did not. Paul clearly rejected views like the Pelagian one, but they were no less clearly rejected by Justin, Clement of Rome, and other early church figures. Thus, though we may rule out the Pelagian view, we still have to decide whether

Augustine or the early church represents the true Pauline doctrines.

We must, therefore, see what Scriptures Augustine advanced to demonstrate his assertion that faith is an irresistible gift. First, however, we might clarify a few points about his approach.

Of Hebrew, he told Memorius in a letter, he knew nothing, and relied either on the LXX or the Latin. He also wrote in his *Confessions* of his early dislike for Greek, which prevented him from developing overmuch in it. He had, further, little concern to ensure the accuracy of translations used. In about A.D. 394 he wrote to Jerome begging him not to waste his time in translating the Hebrew; for, if the Hebrew was obscure then no one had any hope of understanding it, and if it was plain then surely the LXX translators must be right. Jerome was a first-rank, internationally famous scholar, and his somewhat withering counter to this attack on his life's work brought Augustine to modify his views. Nonetheless, Augustine's underlying attitude seems to show in his frequent use of translations without reference to the original—even where the latter does not support his argument at all.

Augustine also accepted as inspired what we today call the Apocrypha and so uses verses from Wisdom, Ecclesiasticus, etc., to support important doctrines.

Last, he is apt repeatedly to quote a verse to "prove" his case without being careful as to the original context. Thus, for example, he repeatedly quotes Jesus' words "You have not chosen me . . ." in a passage dealing with the election of believers—without apparently seeing that the words are addressed to the apostles (see section 15).

VERSES QUOTED
BY AUGUSTINE

(1) 1 Corinthians 4:7—**"What have you that you did not receive?"**

This is the verse that he says brought him to believe his new doctrine that faith itself is a gift, and he cites it many times. The problem is that Paul nowhere specifically applies it to the commencement of faith. One cannot, of course, take Paul's words crassly literally—for if they have nothing that they have not received from God, then presumably their party spirit and proneness to boast are also gifts of God. Even if we were to apply it to faith, Paul does not say that they had to receive it whether they wanted to or not. But the context of Paul's words is one of forbidding party spirit and was surely not intended to be applied to basic repentance. Would Paul really have concealed such an important teaching as faith being an irresistible gift, in such a general statement against party spirit?

(2) Ephesians 2:8, 9—"**For by grace have you been saved through faith; and** *that* **not of yourselves: it is the gift of God: not of works, that no man should glory.**"

Augustine cites this and adds: "That is to say, And in saying through faith, (I meant) even faith itself is not of yourselves, but is God's gift."[57] Augustine's idea is that the word *that* (italicized above) refers back to the word *faith* in the previous phrase, meaning that faith itself is "not of yourselves." This sounds plausible, but there are a major and a minor reason why anyone reading Greek could not accept it. The minor reason is that, if it were true, then the words following, "not of works lest any man should glory," would also refer to faith. But Paul always set works and faith in antithesis, and for him to say "faith is not of works" would be very strange.[58] The major reason is that the Greek precludes the interpretation. The words *faith* and *grace* are both feminine in gender, but the word *that* (italicized above) is neuter. If the latter had been intended as a simple reference back either to faith or to grace, Paul would certainly not have used the neuter form (*touto*) but the feminine form (*haute*) which is quite different. The best interpretation that the Greek would seem to allow is for the phrase in verse 8, "for by grace have you been saved through faith," to be regarded as a similar type of parenthesis to that in verse 5: "by grace have you been saved"—which many versions[59] put in brackets. This would imply that the word *that* refers back to the whole process described in verses 4-7 of God quickening us and raising us together with Christ to show his grace to us in the heavenly places. None of this, Paul says, is through works, but is a gift of God. Whether or not this is his precise meaning, certainly no one who read the Greek could see any suggestion in this passage that the beginning of faith is an irresistible gift.[60]

(3) The few other verses are mainly from the LXX, where its translation is unsupported by the Hebrew. Thus, e.g., Esther 5:1[61]; Job 14:4, 5[62]; Proverbs 8:35[63]; and Proverbs 21:1[64] are cited.

Augustine himself realized the inconclusiveness of the "proof-texts" he cited, and appealed rather to his whole system than to specific verses to support his case. Before looking at his system we might ponder one question. In Paul's writings there are doubtless "some things hard to be understood." Yet when an idea is simple to state, it is found stated most clearly. That salvation is not earned but is a gift is stated most clearly by Paul. But the idea that faith is itself an irresistible gift is also very simple to state. Why (if he really believed it) did Paul not state it with equal clarity? Augustine thought he saw such a clear statement in Ephesians 2:8, but the early church read the original Greek in which Augustine's interpretation was impossible—and so saw no such thing. Why then was Paul so vague on this question if he really believed what Augustine later taught?

Augustine's main (and repeated) line of argument from his system may be briefly summarized as follows: All Christians agree that babies are baptized to regenerate them into Christ's body (the Catholic church). This shows, first, that they are born under the guilt of sin committed in Adam. It shows, second, that the determination of who should be regenerated does not depend on the will of those selected. What is true of babies is true also of adults. God selects some to be regenerated on some basis known only to him; it is not dependent on their own wills.

Let us now look in more detail at some of the aspects of this system.

ORIGINAL
SIN

Augustine's distinctive views on original sin form a useful starting point for considering his system. The early church never doubted the seriousness of the fall or of Adam's sin, but Augustine gave an entirely different interpretation to it. He taught that when Adam sinned, all his descendants sinned *in him* and so shared in the guilt of the act. The main support that Augustine found for this was in the Latin version of Romans 5:12, which reads: "By one man sin entered the world, and death by sin; so death passed upon all men, for *in him* all men sinned."[65] Augustine repeatedly referred to this verse and thought it plain and unambiguous. The problem with it is that the Latin translation renders the Greek phrase *eph' ho* as "in him," which is an impossible rendering. Sanday and Headlam, one of the great modern textual authorities on Romans, wrote: "Though this expression (*eph' ho*) has been much fought over, there can now be little doubt that the true rendering is 'because.'" They will allow no other reading, and note that in classical writers the phrase means "on condition that." They also consider the suggestion that the apostle meant to imply: "because all sinned in Adam." But they rightly object to this: "The objection is that the words supplied are far too important to be left to be understood. If St. Paul had meant this, why did he not say so? The insertion of *en Adam* would have removed all ambiguity."[66]

Romans 5:12 neither says nor implies that all sinned in Adam. The verse appears to support Augustine only if taken in his Latin mistranslation. When we look further on to Romans 5:18 we do indeed find the words: "as through one trespass the judgment came to *all men* to condemnation." Augustine often cited this, but it surely cannot mean that condemnation spread automatically to all men irrespective of their own acceptance of the sin principle which Adam released in the world. If we took it thus, then how could we interpret the words that immediately follow: "even so through one act of righteousness the free gift came unto *all men* to justification of life"? Paul deliberately parallels the two clauses by saying: "as . . . even so . . ." If the first meant automatic condemnation then surely the second must have meant automatic salvation for all men? Augustine's explanation that: "as the one embraces all men whatever, so the other includes all righteous men"[67] is simply a forcing of the apostle's words. Clearly both condemnation and justification came unto all men, and the sense of "came unto" must be conditional rather than as something automatic.

Augustine's other main proof texts for his view of original sin were the apocryphal Wisdom 12:10, 11[68] and Ecclesiasticus 40:11[69]; the Septuagint (but not the Hebrew) of Job 14:4, 5[70]; and Psalm 51:5.[71] The last stated is the most plausible, but we should remember that it was written by David after Nathan had touched his shepherd-heart, and then pronounced "You are the man!"[72] Psalm 51 is the bitter cry of a man crushed with guilt and anguish, with those words "You are the man!" ringing in his ears. Are we to take his words as though they were sober theological pronouncements? Does verse 4 literally mean that David had not wronged Uriah but only God? Should we therefore use it to build up, say, a doctrine that we cannot sin against man but only against God? The answer to this may be obvious, but we should surely be no less unwilling to use verse 5 to defend an Augustinian theological doctrine of original sin. In any case, whatever it might be taken to imply about his parents, David says nothing of inheriting any guilt, nothing about sinning "in Adam." We might, incidentally, note that Augustine nowhere seems to face the difficulty of Romans 9:11, which says that before birth Jacob and Esau had done "neither good nor bad."[73]

Not only did Augustine have difficulty in finding supporting verses, but he also faced a crushing difficulty. He said that for Christians the guilt of sinning in Adam had been removed in baptism. Surely, therefore, a child born of two Christian parents had been forgiven "in them" just as he had sinned "in Adam"? Augustine's answer was twofold. First, "it is quite possible for parents to transmit to their children that which they possess not themselves."[74] Second, children are born in Satan's power because: "they are born of the union of the sexes which cannot even accomplish its own honorable function without the incidence of shameful lust."[75] Augustine taught that sexual intercourse from any motive other than procreation was a venial sin[76] and the act was *always* shameful since always tinged with passion.[77] Thus only Christ (he said) was born pure, since only he was conceived without sexual intercourse.[78]

INFANT BAPTISM

Augustine taught that in baptism a baby was forgiven the guilt of original sin. He said: "As nothing else is done for children in baptism but their being incorporated into the church, that is, connected with the body and members of Christ, it follows that when this is not done for them they belong to perdition."[79] A baptized baby would (he said) go to heaven if he died, but an unbaptized one to hell. Whatever Christians today believe about infant baptism, most of us surely reject this particular idea of baptismal regeneration.[80]

Before considering Augustine's arguments for the doctrine, we may note how important a keystone it was in his system, which came to dominate western Christianity. Although it may be logically more obvious to begin from original sin and argue to this idea of baptism, Augustine's actual practice was to begin from infant baptism and argue to original sin. Thus he based two important ideas on infant baptismal regeneration:

(1) since baptism has this effect it must remove guilt, so in the case of infants it must be the guilt of Adam's sin.[81]

(2) this gives an irrefutable example of regeneration being independent of anything in the person's own will.[82]

The first of these points has already been discussed. The second is important, for one of Augustine's main defenses of his doctrine that faith is an irresistible gift was the idea that babies were (involuntarily) saved at baptism. Thus he says: "Let them think what they like respecting the case of adults, in the case of infants, at any rate, the Pelagians find no means of answering the difficulty. Infants in receiving grace possess no will, from the influence of which they can pretend to any precedence of merit."[83]

This was a repeated argument in Augustine's later works, a mainstay of his new doctrines, yet it forced him into an unfortunate position over the status of baptized infants. As we consider this let us bear in mind his common acclamation as the restorer of simple Pauline faith.

The actual practice of infant baptism was universal in the Catholic church at the time, and Augustine brought no Scriptures to defend it. What he had to show was that it made the difference (if the baby died) of heaven and hell. For this he cited Mark 16:16—"**He that believes and is baptized shall be saved, but he that disbelieves shall be condemned.**" Of this verse he says: "Now who can be unaware that in the case of infants, being baptized is to believe, and not being baptized is not to believe?"[84] Yet, as he wrote to Jerome in A.D. 415, infants being baptized have no faith of their own. Thus we find the following comment, also on Mark 16:16—"For which reason in the church of the Savior infants believe by means of other people, even as they have derived those sins which are remitted them in baptism from other people."[85] Baptized babies, he said, "are rightly called believers because they in a certain sense profess faith by the words of those who bring them to baptism."[86] This much he stated clearly, but we also find him commenting thus: "Therefore an infant, although he is not yet a believer in the sense of having that faith which includes the consenting will of those who exercise it, nevertheless becomes a believer through the sacrament of that faith."[87] Augustine seems to use this idea of a "sacrament of faith" as a kind of halfway measure—enough to save the infant if he died young but not if he later disbelieved. How he derived it from Scripture and how it fits in with his other statements is not clear. Whatever he meant by it, he certainly implied elsewhere that infant baptism involved regeneration to life.

This brought him great difficulties. He had strongly argued that baptism was as valid if administered by a drunkard or a heretic as if by an apostle.[88] He had also argued that: "their regeneration is not prevented by the fact that this blessing has no place in the intention of those by whom they are presented for baptism."[89] Well, we may ask, if salvation is "by faith," then whose faith is it in such cases? Augustine would reply: "The presentation of the little ones . . . is not so much of those by whose hands they are borne up . . . as of the whole society of saints and believers."[90] The implication, therefore, is that a baby baptized by a drunken heretic is saved by the faith of the Catholic church who may know nothing of the event. This is part of Augustine's "restoration" of the simple doctrine of salvation by faith!

A further complication comes from Augustine's insistence that "the Catholic church alone is the body of Christ, of which He is the head and savior of His body. Outside this body the Holy Spirit gives life to no one."[91] The Donatists held "entirely the same beliefs" theologically as the Catholics, but Augustine thought them damned for not accepting the authority of the Catholic church. He repeatedly defended this view using 1 Corinthians 13, claiming that anyone separated from the Catholic fellowship did not have love.[92] Believing this, he had then to explain how it was that baptism by heretics wrought regeneration. One answer he gave was that: "their sins, which in that moment had been dispelled by the holiness of baptism, return immediately upon them, as though it were the darkness returning which the light has dispelled while they were passing through it."[93] How he would apply this to baby Donatists is not clear but he accepted in general that a man could have genuine regeneration, genuine piety, and even genuine faith, but without membership in the Catholic church, it could avail him nothing and he would go to hell. On this basis, of course, Augustine would have condemned two of his most famous followers, Calvin and Luther, for his arguments for the authority of the Catholic church were as valid in their times as in his.

Augustine even went so far as to state that a man could have the genuine "faith which works by love," could have a genuine and not a feigned righteousness, but then fall away and go to hell.[94] Perseverance, he taught, depended on whether or not God had chosen and predestined a man.[95] However much faith we have, however well we know that God has regenerated and justified us, until the day of our death (he implied) we do not know whether he has mercifully predestined us to heaven or has justly predestined us to hell. This is Augustine's teaching.

We now see how Augustine's main defense for his picture of faith as an irresistible gift is bound up in his whole system: original sin, infant baptismal regeneration, predestination, etc. To us today, the most influential of his ideas, even among those who have never read any of his works, may be those on predestination and election. Briefly, he viewed election as God's choice of who should be believers[96]; and "predestination is a preparation for grace, while grace is the actual endowment."[97] Thus election is God's selection of some (with no reference to their own wills) to be given final salvation; predestination is God's preparation for giving them an irresistible gift of faith and final perseverance. God could have chosen and predestined others also, but for undisclosed reasons has not done so. This is Augustine's teaching.

It is unfortunate that such interpretations of election and predestination are often accepted today as the true biblical ones (even by those who know nothing of Augustine). Instead of taking care to see whether the ideas are truly biblical, people often merely soften their implications by saying that, of course, such doctrines are only "one side to the truth." This is highly unsatisfactory, for it is far from obvious that Augustine's interpretations of these concepts are biblical. We have seen in section 15 how our election is "in Christ" since he is the elect One, but how[98] Augustine effectively ignores the phrase "in Him" in Ephesians 1. We also saw the confusion caused by applying to believers' election, words Jesus used of his choice of apostles. Augustine's view of predestination is no less dubious, for the Bible never applies the word to the initial reception of grace. In Scripture, predestination is a "setting out of a horizon" for *believers*, not a decree as to who should believe. Neither the biblical teaching on election of believers nor that on predestination lends support to Augustine's allegation that faith itself is an irresistible gift. We may only decide whether he or the early church was right by considering his system as a whole and deciding whether or not it is biblical.

Underlying the whole system of Augustine is a basic assumption that God's will is always and inevitably done, and that man can never resist it. We see this clearly if we consider some passages in a basic handbook of Christian faith that Augustine wrote after reaching maturity, the *Enchiridion*. The passage below begins with the assertion that although it may seem unloving for God to take up and save one baby, and let another go to hell, yet all will be revealed to us in heaven:

> *Enchiridion xxiv*: Then, in the clearest light of wisdom, will be seen what now the pious hold by faith, not yet grasping it in clear understanding—how certain, immutable, and effectual is the will of God, how there are things he can do but does not will to do, yet wills nothing he cannot do, and how true is what is sung in the Psalm: "But our God is above heaven; in heaven and on earth he has done all things whatsoever that he would." This obviously is not true if there is anything that he willed to do and did not do, or, what were worse, if he did not do something because man's will prevented him, the Omnipotent, from doing what he willed. Nothing, therefore, happens unless the Omnipotent wills it to happen. He either allows it to happen or he actually causes it to happen . . . Unless we believe this, the very beginning of our confession of faith is imperiled—the sentence in which we profess to believe in God the Father Almighty. For he is called Almighty for no other reason than that he can do

whatsoever he wills, and because the efficacy of his omnipotent will is not impeded by the will of any creature.

One may note two things in particular about this:

(1) Augustine's use of the type of emotional argument we considered in section 6: "Surely God would not be almighty if anything could happen against his will?"

(2) He further supported his argument with reference to a Psalm. But in fact this seems to be a mixed quotation from Psalm 115:3 and Psalm 135:6. The context of either of these is a comparison of our God as One who hears, feels, and acts, with other gods who have neither consciousness nor power. The psalmist's mind was far from dealing with the question of whether God allows men freedom to accept or reject his offer of free salvation. But this is how Augustine intends to apply it. Thus:

> *Enchiridion xxv*: Furthermore who will be so foolish and blasphemous as to say that God cannot change the evil wills of men, whichever, whenever and wheresoever he chooses, and direct them to what is good?[99]

He had, of course, to try to deal with Bible passages that flatly contradict this notion (such as those cited in section 6). It is interesting to see how Augustine, although a great thinker, entangled himself as he tried to explain these away.

> *Enchiridion xxiv*: But the Lord's language is clearer when, in the Gospel, he proves the unrighteous city: "How often," he says, "would I have gathered your children together, as a hen gathers her chicks, and you would not." This sounds as if God's will had been overcome by human wills and as if the weakest by not willing, impeded the Most Powerful so that he could not do what he willed. And where is that omnipotence by which "whatsoever he willed on heaven and on earth, he has done," if he willed to gather the children of Jerusalem together, and did

not do so? Or, is it not rather the case that, although Jerusalem did not will that her children be gathered together by him, yet, despite her unwillingness, God did indeed gather together those children of hers whom he would? It is not that "in heaven and on earth" he has willed and done some things, and willed other things and not done them; "all things whatsoever he willed, he has done."

One can only be amazed at his argument, which is:

(1) Jesus' words admittedly make it look as though God willed something but did not do it.

(2) But the words of Psalm 135 (115?) imply that if God wanted to gather them then he did so.

(3) Therefore Jesus' words must be interpreted to mean this, whatever they might appear to mean!

This seems to be rather a bad example of inverse exposition: starting with conclusions to be read into a text. Yet what else, given his presuppositions, could Augustine have made of this verse?

Enchiridion xxiv & xxvii: Accordingly we must now inquire about the meaning of what was said most truly by the apostle concerning God, "Who wills that all men should be saved." For since not all—not even a majority—*are* saved, it would indeed appear that the fact that what God wills to happen does not happen is due to an embargo on God's will by the human will. Now, when we ask for the reason why not all are saved, the customary answer is: "Because they themselves have not willed it." But this cannot be said of infants, who have not yet come to the power of willing or not willing. For, if we could attribute to their wills the infant squirmings they make at baptism, when they resist as hard as they can, we would then have to say that they were saved against their will . . . Accordingly, when we hear and read in Sacred Scripture that God "wills that all men should be saved," although we know well enough that not all men are saved, we are not on that account to underrate the fully omnipotent will of God. Rather, we must understand the Scripture, "Who will have all men to be saved," as meaning that no man is saved unless God wills his salvation: not that there is no man whose salvation he does not will, but that no one is saved unless he will it . . . Thus also are we to understand what is written in the Gospel about him, "who enlightens every man." This means that there is no man who is enlightened except by God.

Again we are amazed by his argument, which is:

(1) It looks as though God's will that all shall be saved is not done.

(2) But babies are saved at baptism against their will.

(3) The "fully omnipotent will of God" must not be "underrated."

(4) Therefore the words "God wills that all men should be saved" must really mean "Any men that God wills shall be saved, will be." We note again two emotional arguments: one from contemporary Christian practice, and the other the appeal to God's almightiness. We also note that this is another use of inverse exposition. In this case, however, he afterward threw in an alternative suggestion. He suggested that perhaps all men really meant all types of men. Such a meaning for the word *all* is, to say the least, rare. But Augustine picked out the most likely-looking illustration (Luke 11:42) out of over 1100 verses where the word is used—apparently not noticing that the Greek in Luke is singular but in 1 Timothy 2:4 is plural. But, in fact, Augustine did not much mind how we interpret the latter verse, so long as we do not allow it to contradict his basic presupposition. He added: "We are not compelled to believe that the Omnipotent has willed anything to be done which was not done."

The last section we will look at is:

Enchiridion xxvi: These are "the great works of the Lord, well considered in his acts of will"—and so wisely well-considered that when his angelic and human creations sinned (that is, did not do what he willed, but what it willed) he could still accomplish what he himself had willed and this through the same creaturely will by which the first act contrary to the Creator's will had been done. As the supreme Good, he made good use of evil deeds, for the damnation of those whom he had justly predestined to punishment and for the salvation of those whom he had mercifully predestined to grace. For as far as relates to themselves, these creatures did what God wished not to be done; but in view of God's omnipotence, they could in no wise effect their purpose. For in the very fact that they acted in opposition to his will, his will concerning them was fulfilled. And hence it is said that "the works of the Lord are great, well considered in all his acts of will," because in a way unspeakably strange and wonderful, even what is done in opposition to his will is not done without his will. For it would not be done did he not permit it (and, of course, his permission is not unwilling but willing).

What is Augustine saying here? He is not merely saying that God permits man to disobey his will, but then seeks to bring good out of this. Clement of Alexandria could well say something of this kind as we have already seen, but such an idea would hardly fit in with Augustine's theology. What he is saying is that God's will for sinners is accomplished in their disobedience of his will. (Perhaps in anticipation of our complete puzzlement at this, Augustine calls it "strange and wonderful.") But is this really a restoration of Pauline doctrine, or is there rather some connection with the rigid determinism that had always fascinated Augustine?[100]

The examples of inverse exposition quoted from *Enchiridion* are far from rare in Augustine. Another example, picked at random, comes from a letter to Boniface: "For the apostle says: 'Quench not the Spirit;' not that he can be quenched but that those who so act as if they wished to have him quenched are deservedly spoken of as quenchers of the Spirit."

We may also note his loose quotation from the Scriptures, from the Latin version without reference to the original language. We have already remarked on his attitude in this respect, but it is in marked contrast to men like Origen who conducted painstaking labors in the original language[101] or Justin Martyr who stood closest to New Testament Greek and also did research into Hebrew.[102] It is also in contrast to Augustine's contemporary, Jerome, whose scholarship was outstanding.

Compared with Jerome, Augustine's approach to Scripture was casual and unlearned. Yet, though Jerome's translation was adopted by the Catholic church, it was Augustine's new and distinctive theology that triumphed in Catholicism and thus in western Christendom. Why was this? What made his ideas so acceptable to the Catholicism of his day and of succeeding generations? We can hardly hope, in such a general book as this, to answer this question about which so many volumes have been written. One major factor, however, may be interesting to consider.

After the conversion and triumph of Constantine in A.D. 312 there was increasing persecution not only of pagans, but also of non-Catholic Christians. There were, indeed, temporary lulls, but the general development of the use of force to compel "heretics" to become Catholics is well shown by Verduin[103] whose research into this was carried out under the auspices of the Calvin Foundation. The slide into persecution was not, of course, without some protest from leading Catholics. Hilary of Poitiers protested poignantly against it. When in A.D. 385 Priscillian and his followers were executed on the orders of a synod, leading Catholics like Ambrose were horrified and totally dissociated themselves from the guilty ones.

When, therefore, Augustine came on the scene there was conflicting opinion over the use of persecution, though no leading church figure seems to have approved of it or defended it. In 396 Augustine himself wrote: "I would have no man brought into the Catholic Communion against his will."

Yet, as he later changed his ideas about the grace of God, so he changed also his ideas on the use of force. As he came to believe that God effects conversion against men's wills, and that God himself uses force in changing their wills from evil to good, so also he came to believe that it was right for God's servants to use force. By A.D. 408 he could write to a non-conformist who advocated freedom of conscience:

> You are of the opinion that no one should be compelled to follow righteousness; and yet you read that the householder said to his servants, "Whomsoever you shall find, compel them to come in." You also read how he who was at first Saul, afterwards Paul, was compelled by the great violence with which Christ coerced him, to know and embrace the truth; for you cannot but think that the light which your eyes enjoy is more precious to men than money or any other possession. This light, lost suddenly by him when he was cast to the ground by the heavenly voice, he did not recover until he became a member of the Holy Church. You are also of opinion that no coercion is to be used with any man in order to his deliverance from the fatal consequences of error; and yet you see that, in examples which cannot be disputed, this is done by God, who loves us with more real regard for our profit than any other can; and you hear Christ saying, "No man can come to me except the Father draw him.". . .[104]

Augustine here makes very clear the connection between the two major changes in his thinking between about A.D. 395 and 408. He often repeats this argument that in persecuting non-conformists the Catholics are but following the example of their Lord.[105] It is based, of course, on his new ideas about God's sovereign will. Having once come to this conclusion, Augustine was quite resolute in his advocacy of persecution, confiscation of possessions, and "fear of punishment or pain." To the Tribune Boniface he wrote: "Is it not part of the care of the shepherd when any sheep have left the flock . . . to bring them back to the fold of his master when he has found them, by the fear or even the pain of the whip, if they show symptoms of resistance?"[106]

Many destitute and persecuted Donatists, understandably desperate, committed suicide by setting fire to themselves. A Donatist minister named Gaudentius, under persecution and threat of death, said he would sooner burn down his church with himself and his flock in it than become Catholic. Threatened again with death he said that he did not seek martyrdom but was prepared for it: "only the hireling flees when he sees the wolf coming!" Augustine wrote to him explaining that this suicide impulse must be from the devil.[107] Then he said:

"If you suppose that we ought to be moved because so many thousands die in this way, how much more consolation do you think we ought to have because far and incomparably more thousands are freed from the great madness of the Donatist party . . ."[108]

It is true that it was the practical success of fear and pain, rather than any theological or biblical argument, that first led him to support persecution.[109] But, whatever caused the actual change in his view, without his new theological system it would have been very hard to justify it.

In the mature Augustine, therefore, the state church found not only the first Christian leader of importance to advocate the use of persecution against non-conformists, but they found the only Christian theologian of significance whose theological system would justify such persecution. It is therefore not really surprising that his new ideas made a rapid advance within the state church, that by 424 they dominated the Latin sector of it, and that by 431 they were adopted for western Christendom at the third Ephesian council.[110]

Verduin and others have shown how the arguments Augustine used to support persecution have been repeated throughout history by many of those who adopted other features of his system. They were used by the early Catholic church, by Luther and the Reformers, by Calvin and his associates at Geneva, and by the later Catholics to defend persecution of groups like the Huguenots. Farrar rightly comments: "Augustine must bear the fatal charge of being the first as well as one of the ablest defenders of the frightful cause of persecution and intolerance. He was the first to misuse the words, 'Compel them to come in'—a fragmentary phrase wholly unsuited to bear the weight of horror for which it was made responsible. He was the first and ablest asserter of the principle that led to the Albigensian crusades, Spanish armadas, Netherlands' butcheries, St. Bartholomew massacres, the accursed infamies of the Inquisition, the vile espionage, the hideous balefires of Seville and Smithfield, the racks, the gibbets, the thumbscrews, the subterranean torture-chambers used by churchly torturers who assumed 'the garb and language of priests with the trade and temper of executioners,' to sicken, crush, and horrify the revolted conscience of mankind . . . It is mainly because of his later intolerance that the influence of Augustine falls like a dark shadow across the centuries. It is thus that an Arnold of Citeaux, a Torquemada, a Sprenger, an Alva, a Philip the Second, a Mary Tudor, a Charles IX and a Louis XIV can look up to him as an authorizer of their enormities, and quote his sentences to defend some of the vilest crimes which ever caused men to look with horror on the religion of Christ and the Church of God."[111] Augustine himself may not have advocated using torture, but once the use of fear and pain were accepted it was a natural extension for his later followers to make.

There is, in fact, some parallel between the pagan emperor's treatment of Christians and the Christian Emperor Honorius' treatment of non-conformists (on Augustine's advice). The severity and barbarism of the tortures were, of course, incomparably greater under the pagans, but some principles are the same. Under the pagan emperors the Christians were accused of all kinds of immorality and crime. Augustine likewise accused groups like the Donatists of crimes—and insisted on identifying the whole movement with an extremist nationalist fringe group,[112] rejected by many Donatists. But totalitarian states from Nero to the present day have made such accusations against Christian minority groups, and they are seldom very accurate.

But the main point is that Augustine, like the pagans, was not suggesting that they should be tried for *specific* crimes, nor even for some vague charge such as "incitement to sedition;" he was advocating their persecution simply because they were not Catholics. Like Christians in the pagan era, they were persecuted for religious nonconformity, not tried for specific civil offenses. Moreover, Augustine's repeated plea that the Donatists had appealed to Constantine to depose a Bishop, hardly excuses his active persecution of a group who in his own time (and nearly a century later than Constantine) advocated freedom of conscience.

We should be clear, here, exactly what Augustine was advocating. Verduin explains how objection to the use of force in "converting" had been one of the main reasons for the Donatists splitting off from the Catholics.[113] In theology they were orthodox. Augustine himself says: "The greater part of them declare that they hold entirely the same belief regarding the Father and the Son and the Holy Ghost as is held by the Catholic church. Nor is this the actual question in dispute with them; but they carry on their unhappy strife solely on the question of communion.[114] The issue between us and the Donatists is about the question where this body is to be located, that is, what and where is the Church?"[115]

The people he sought to persecute would have been regarded by us as ordinary Christians—and they were persecuted solely because they rejected the authority of the Catholic church. They were never convicted of any civil crime, their sole crime was to reject this authority. We may, indeed, remember Jesus' words: **"Depart from me, you cursed, into the eternal fire which is prepared for the devil and his angels: for I was an hungered, and you gave me no meat: I was thirsty, and you gave me no drink: I was a stranger and you took me not in; naked and you clothed me not; sick, and in prison, and you visited me not . . . Inasmuch as you did it not unto one of these least, you did it not unto me."**[116]

Through the influence and advocacy of Augustine thousands of simple brethren of Christ were actually caused to be hungry, exiled strangers, homeless, in prison or in pain. How then may we reconcile the words of Jesus with Renwick's description of Augustine as "the greatest Christian of his age"? How may we understand Souter's description of him as "the greatest Christian since New Testament times"? Even one of our leading evangelists, a man whom God widely uses today, seems to have been affected by the common exaltation of Augustine. He recently wrote: "Augustine was one of the greatest theologians of all time . . . He became one of the great saints of all time."

On what are we to base our standards of greatness? Can Augustine be excused on the grounds that "he was only a child of his times"? It is difficult to do this, for leaders among his predecessors and contemporaries were outspoken against violence. Tertullian declared: "God has not hangmen for priests. Christ teaches us to bear wrong, not to revenge it." Lactantius wrote that religion could not be enforced, and words should be used rather than blows. The great Athanasius commented on Song of Solomon 5:2—"Satan, because there is no truth in him, breaks in with axe and sword. But the Savior is gentle, and forces no one to whom He comes, but knocks and speaks to the soul, 'Open to me my sister.'" Martin of Tours and Augustine's revered teacher Ambrose both reacted strongly against those who had executed the Priscillianists. Augustine's great contemporary Chrysostom said: "Christians are not to destroy error by force and violence, but should work the salvation of men by persuasion, instruction and love." In short, Augustine's whole background had been one of tolerance, and he himself was a champion of tolerance early in his Christian life. He abandoned this earlier tolerance to become the first great Christian thinker to advocate violence, fear, and pain to spread the gospel. Surely Augustine molded the times rather than the times Augustine.

The appeal to the times is little more convincing when applied to Augustine's later followers. Take, for example, Calvin. Verduin says that when Calvin had Servetus burnt over green wood (so that it took him three hours to be pronounced dead), "a cry of outrage resounded over most of Europe."[117] A pamphlet was written asking if Christ had now become Moloch to demand human sacrifice, or if we could picture Christ as one of the constables lighting the fire . . .[118] To this, Calvin's close associate Beza could only reply: "Of all the blasphemous and impudent gabs!"[119] An appeal to the times is not convincing.[120] It becomes still less convincing when we are told, often by the same apologists, that those like Calvin and Augustine were the most competent Bible scholars in history. Surely if Calvin could write a work hailed as the most systematic treatise on the Christian faith ever written, it is an insult to suggest that his moral teaching was not an integral part of his system but was based on some opinions of contemporary men. Surely if Augustine had the greatness of mind and strength of character to overturn all the Christian teaching of the first 300 years, it is absurd to excuse his advocacy of persecution on the grounds of a spirit in him of conformity. The tragic fact is surely that those who deny any power but God's, and hence reduce everyone including Satan to servants of God, may (if times are ripe) finish by using Satan's own weapons of fear, force, pain, and persecution. Although Augustine initially adopted persecution because of its practical success (and it was indeed practically successful), he himself directly linked it with his theological system.[121]

We have, in summary, to recognize the effect of Augustine's teaching on our thinking even today. Yet we must decide whether his teachings are truly a "restoration" of the Apostle Paul. As we have seen, his difference from the early church was not a simple one of faith versus works. The early Christian teachers were no less clear than Augustine that salvation was a free gift. His point of departure from them was in saying that faith itself was an irresistible gift.

We must decide for ourselves whether we believe that Augustine, or the Christians of the first three centuries, had the true Pauline doctrine. Our decision on this issue is going to affect our whole attitude to God and his conflict with evil. Is the conflict real? Are we really "wrestling," in Christ, against powers of evil? If we are using the weapons of Christ, then what methods does *he* use for warfare and touching men's souls?

These are not merely academic questions. They will have a practical effect on the methods we adopt and on the urgency with which we obey Paul's command to fight the good fight.

WORKS OF AUGUSTINE
REFERRED TO OR QUOTED

Abbreviation	Title and Approximate Date
Confessions	*Confessions* (400)
On Bap.	*On Baptism, Against the Donatists* (400)
On Gen. to Let.	*On Genesis to the Letter* (401-415)
Cath. Ep.	*Catholic Epistle Against the Donatists* (402)
For. Sins	*On the Merits and Forgiveness of Sins* (412)
Corr. Don.	*On the Correction of the Donatists* (417)
On the Gr. of Chr.	*On the Grace of Christ* (418)
On Orig. Sin	*On Original Sin* (418)
Marr. and Conc.	*Marriage and Concupiscence* (419)
Ag. Gaud.	*Against Gaudentius* (420)
Ag. Pel.	*Against Two Letters of the Pelagians* (420)
Enchir.	*Enchiridion* (i.e. "Handbook") (424-426)
Gr. and Freewill	*Grace and Freewill* (426-427)
Reb. and Gr.	*Rebuke and Grace* (426-427)
Pred. Saints.	*The Predestination of the Saints* (428-429)
Gift Pers.	*On the Gift of Perseverance* (428-429)

NOTES

1. Gwatkin gives various possible divisions—and in all of these the parties on both sides taught "free-will." Perhaps the most obvious breakdown is into language/culture:

Greek: Justin, Athenagoras, Clement, Origen

Latin: Tertullian, Jerome

Syriac: Tatian, Bardaisan

2. Standard works we have used include:

F. F. Bruce, *The Spreading Flame*

H. M. Gwatkin, *Early Church History to* A.D. *313*

L. Duchesne, *Early History of the Church*

J. Quasten, *Patrology* (vols. i and ii)

We have also quoted from the two Inter-Varsity Fellowship books:

A. M. Renwick, *The Story of the Church*

M. A. Smith, *From Christ to Constantine*

The second of these was only recently published, is attractively produced, and could serve as an introduction to the subject for readers who may know little of it.

Lastly, mention should be made of a classic history of the early

church, written in the early fourth century but still well worth reading:
Eusebius, *The History of the Church*

3. Smith, p. 78

4. Renwick, p. 29; Quasten, vol. i p. 196

5. This whole description is a semi-quotation from Renwick.

6. See the introduction in the Anti-Nicene Library, Quasten, vol. i p. 229, and Chambers Encyclopaedia.

7. Duchesne; see also Chambers.

8. Smith, p. 56. It is fair to say, however, that others have been more critical of Bardaisan, and we would by no means place as much weight on his views as on mainstream writers. We have included Syrian Christian writers to show that even fringe groups taught free-will. Only total heretics like Marcion and Manes rejected it.

9. Duchesne, p. 245

10. e.g., Duchesne

11. See Renwick, Bruce, and Chambers, and Britannica Encyclopaedia.

12. See, e.g., Gwatkin p. 202

13. Renwick, p. 41

14. Smith, p. 134

15. Eusebius, 42.5

16. Bruce, p. 213

17. Renwick, p. 45

18. Bruce, p. 259. Professor Bruce also defends Origen against a charge sometimes made of non-orthodoxy on the Trinity. Origen lived before the controversy on this came to a head, but was fundamentally different from Arius.

19. Renwick, p. 47

20. We have excluded from the list that great Christian, Gregory the Wonderworker, who was a great admirer of Origen and was as clear as Origen on the free-will of man.

21. See Duchesne, p. 360, and Chambers

22. Britannica

23. Britannica

24. Britannica

25. Bruce, p. 329; Renwick, p. 58

26. Calvin: *Institutes* Bk. 3 ch. xxii sec. 8.

27. *Pred. Saints* 8 & 16.

28. In about 395 A.D. Augustine confessed in a letter to Jerome his ignorance of the teaching of even so great a figure as Origen, a confession implicit also in another letter two years later. Neither does Augustine seem very familiar with the Latin Fathers, excepting Cyprian and Ambrose whom he often quotes. Cyprian (c. 200-258 A.D.) is probably the only major church figure of the first three centuries who does not state the doctrine of free-will clearly. But, nevertheless, in spite of his strong emphasis on divine grace, he nowhere stated Augustine's doctrines either. He did not say that faith was an irresistible gift, and his statements on the importance of grace are in general terms.

29. James 2:25

30. No Christian, of course, could quite put it like that. But to

circles who are prone to reject the early church position, James' emphasis on conduct is something of an embarrassment. Calvin rather woefully remarked that: "he seems more sparing in proclaiming the grace of Christ than it behoved an apostle to be." Luther stated his position thus: "Doctrine and life are to be distinguished the one from the other. With us conduct is as bad as it is with the Papists. We don't oppose them on account of conduct. Hus and Wyclif who made an issue of conduct, were not aware of this . . . but to treat of doctrine, that is really to come to grips with things." Verduin, who cites this in *The Reformers and Their Stepchildren*, shows how a truly Christ-like life was the mark of an Anabaptist. It is no wonder that Luther made his famous remark about James' epistle being an "epistle of straw." Yet surely this shows some lack of understanding of Paul in Luther, rather than in the Apostle James and the early church.

31. Matthew 25:31-46

32. *Apology* 1.xlvi

33. Not all Christians would agree with Justin that some may be saved through Christ but without hearing about him. But the view has been held by many orthodox Christians, such as Campbell Morgan and J. N. D. Anderson in our own times (see also section 20 of our former book, *That's a Good Question*). Augustine himself seems to accept such a view in *Pred. Saints* 17 and a letter to Deogratias of A.D. 409.

As to Justin's choice of Socrates: from Xenophon's *Memorablia*, we see in Socrates about the best instance in antiquity of a "natural theology" of the one true God who deserves worship and service.

34. *Dialogue* 40, 86, 90, 91, 97, 111, 131.

35. *Dialogue* 15, 16, 18, 24, 28, 43, 114, 137.

36. *Dialogue* 13, 24, 139.

37. *Dialogue* 26, 35, 40, 83, 95, 100, 109, 117, 133, 141.

38. *Dialogue* 13, 44, 54, 112.

39. *Dialogue* 12, 47, 95, 137.

40. *Dialogue* 117.

41. *Dialogue* 8, 44.

42. See Acts 6:9-10; 9:29; 17:2, 17; 18:4, 19; 19:8, 9; 24:25

43. Acts 17:28; the apostle quotes Epimenides (on whom see *Good Question*, section 20) and also Aratus. The quotation from Aratus is similar to a phrase in Cleanthes' famous hymn to Zeus.

44. 1 John 5:3

45. We have shown this for Clement of Rome and Justin, but it is equally true of other early Fathers; see, e.g., Irenaeus, *Ag. Heresies* 3.19; 4.29; Origen, *De Principiis* 3.2.

It is not only early church figures who are misrepresented in such ways. A similar process may be observed in connection with that great and gentle Reformation scholar, Erasmus. The revival of interest in the Greek New Testament was largely due to this remarkable man, and this in turn stimulated the many vernacular versions. Consistent with his work in this field were (1) his anxiety to see the Scriptures in the hands of the common people, (2) his rejection of the vagaries of scholastic philosophy as worthless to God, and (3) his emphasis on simple inner piety. Because, perhaps, of his emphases on the Christ-like spirit, the quality of inner spiritual life, and the fruit of the Spirit, he is often thought of as unconcerned with precision of doctrine or perhaps even unmindful of the necessity of grace. A much more realistic picture seems to be given by Professor Roland H. Bainton in *Erasmus of Christendom*. Bainton formulates a set of beliefs that Erasmus would have considered essential in a Christian: "the incarnation, the pledge of Christ's authority; the passion, the seal of our redemption; the resurrection, the token of our immortality; justification by faith, the ground of our hope; and the imitation of Christ, our obligation" (p. 227). Erasmus, like the early church, was quite clear that man could not earn his salvation and that the free grace of God was essential; but, also like the early church, he found in Scripture the teaching that man must respond by accepting God's proffered gift.

46. Letter to Anastasius, c. 412 A.D.
47. *Grace and Freewill* 10
48. *Pred. Saints* 7
49. *Reb. and Gr.* 10-16; *Pred. Saints* 7-16; etc.
50. *On Gen. to Let.* 11.10; *Enchir.* 98.
51. *Pred. Saints* 13
52. *Reb. and Gr.* 3
53. e.g., *Gr. and Freewill* 10; *Pred. Saints* 7
54. *Pred. Saints* 12
55. Romans 4:4, 5
56. John 6:29
57. *Pred. Saints* 12
58. See section 19.
59. Some form of parenthesis—dashes or brackets—are used by AV; RV; RSV; JB, and Phillips.
60. We do not, of course, in these present remarks, mean to deny that there is a sense in which Jesus came "to give repentance to Israel" (Acts 5:31) and that repentance was also "granted" to the Gentiles (Acts 11:18). In *All Of Grace*, C. H. Spurgeon wrote: "Repentance, as a natural feeling, is a common duty deserving no great praise . . . Jesus is exalted on high, that through the virtue of His intercession repentance may have a place before God. In this respect He gives us repentance, because He puts repentance into a position of acceptance, which otherwise it could never have occupied." It is undeniably true that unless God has given through Jesus the opportunity for repentance it would be useless if not impossible for anyone to repent. But Peter does not say that the gift is given to a select few, he says "to Israel," and his hearers would clearly have understood him to mean the nation as a whole. It is obvious, however, that it was not an *irresistible* gift, for not all of Israel accepted it. Likewise repentance is granted not merely to *"some* Gentiles" (as Augustine would have us believe) but to *"the Gentiles"*—though some did not accept the proffered gift (see also section 20 note 20).

Needless to say, the gift of faith mentioned in 1 Corinthians 12:9 is a gift of a special kind of faith to some believers; it is not at all connected with Augustine's doctrines.

61. *Gr. and Freewill* 42; *On the Gr. of Chr.* 1.25; *For Sins* 1.34
62. *On Orig. Sin* 2.37; *Marr. and Conc.* 2.50

63. *Enchir.* 9.32

64. *On the Gr. of Chr.* 1.24

65. He quoted this many times, e.g.: *For. Sins* 1.11; *Orig. Sin* 2.29; *Marr. and Conc.* 1.1; 2.8, 15, 24; *Ag. Pel.* 8

66. Sanday and Headlam, *Commentary on Romans*, pp. 133, 134

67. *For. Sins* 1.19

68. *Marr. and Conc.* 2.20; the reference in Wisdom, however, is not to mankind but to the Canaanites, and it says nothing whatever about sinning "in Adam."

69. *Enchir.* 17; this reference is also far from clear.

70. *On Orig. Sin* 2.37; *Marr. and Conc.* 2.50; *For. Sins* 1.34; the Hebrew of this verse (Job 14:4, 5) gives little support to Augustine.

71. *Enchir.* 46; *Marr. and Conc.* 2.50; *For Sins* 1.34

72. The story behind Psalm 51 is found in 2 Samuel 12.

73. In *On Orig. Sin* 2.36 Augustine referred to Romans 9:11— "Paul says most plainly that before they were born they did neither good nor evil." In this we agree. Yet Augustine elsewhere stated his theory most clearly: it is precisely that babies *did* do evil before they were born, in sining *in Adam*, and it is their personal participation in this sin that leads to their guilt. The extreme difficulty this presents is obvious, but Augustine simply avoided facing it by following his reference to Romans 9:11 with vague phrases like "the bond of ancient debt" (of Adam's sin). This is highly unsatisfactory—but what else could he do?

74. *For. Sins* 3.17

75. *Marr. and Conc.* 2.15

76. *Marr. and Conc.* 1.9, 16, 17

77. *Marr. and Conc.* 1.5; 2.37; *On Orig. Sin* 2.42

78. *Marr. and Conc.* 1.24

79. *For. Sins* 3.7

80. Those in the Church of England, for example, practice infant baptism, but the 39 Articles of the Church of England pointedly exclude any reference to infant baptismal regeneration.

81. Augustine's customary argument (e.g., in *Marr. and Conc.* 1.24) was that baptism and exorcism of infants was to deliver them from Satan and free them from sin. Since they had no sin of their own (he argued) it must be from original sin.

82. e.g., *Pred. Saints* 23; *Gr. and Freewill* 44; *Marr. and Conc.* 2.47

83. *Gr. and Freewill* 44. Note that the issue is phrased in terms of preceding *merit* (as was customary in Augustine) which entirely begs the question of whether faith is a "merit" or not.

84. *For. Sins* 1.40. Augustine specifically denied any "middle place" for babies who die unbaptized (*For. Sins* 1.55), saying that someone "can only be with the Devil who is not with Christ." He used such descriptions of babies without baptism as "in darkness" (1.35, from John 12:46); "destined to perish" (1.62, from John 3:16); and "condemned" (1.62, from John 3:18). It seems hard, therefore, to take him other than to mean that they go to hell.

85. *Ag. Pel.* 40

86. *For. Sins* 1.25; also *Marr. and Conc.* 1.22

87. This is in a letter to Boniface, A.D. 408, section 10.

88. In a letter to Vincentius, 48

89. To Boniface, 5
90. To Boniface, 5
91. *Corr. Don.* 50
92. A letter to Donatus, A.D. 416, to Theodorus, A.D. 401; *On Bap.* 1.9; 4.17; *Corr. Don.* 50, etc.
93. *On Bap.* 1.19; also 3:18
94. *Pred. Saints* 26; *Gift Pers.* 1; *Reb. and Gr.* 10
95. *Reb. and Gr.* 14
96. *Pred. Saints* 34
97. *Pred. Saints* 19; also *For. Sins* 2.43
98. See section 15 note 3.
99. The same entanglements are reflected in that great Reformation figure, Luther. Luther was one of the greatest minds of his age, but his adoption of Augustine's philosophical ideas about God's sovereignty led him to the following position:

"Common sense and natural reason are highly offended that God by His mere will deserts, hardens, and damns, as if He delighted in sins and in such eternal torments, He who is said to be of such mercy and goodness. Such a concept of God appears wicked, cruel and intolerable, and by it many have been revolted in all ages. I myself have more than once been offended to the very depth of the abyss of desperation, so that I wished I had never been created.

There is no use trying to get away from this by ingenious distinctions. Natural reason, however much it is offended, must admit the consequences of the omniscience and omnipotence of God."

Part of the consequences are that when these philosophical concepts are placed side by side with the Scriptural teaching on God's mercy and desire that the wicked should repent rather than be destroyed, the result is plain contradiction (though it may be called paradox). Luther draws the only possible conclusion:

"If it is difficult to believe in God's mercy and goodness when He damns those who do not deserve it, we must recall that if God's justice could be recognized as just by human comprehension, it would not be divine. Since God is true and one, He is utterly incomprehensible and inaccessible to human reason. Therefore His justice also must be incomprehensible."

If this position were taken seriously the results could be catastrophic. The surest test of whether an interpretation of a Scripture passage is correct, is to see whether it is consistent with other parts of Scripture. But if we were to accept that there is a fundamental inconsistency (whatever form of words we cloak this in) in God's revelation of himself to us in Scripture, then this test would be quite improper. Any teaching would have to stand or fall on its own, without having to be consistent with any other teaching. Such a relativistic position would seem strange for anyone who fully accepts the authority of the Bible, and would be impossible to reconcile with the writings of Paul. Paul continually uses reasoning throughout the arguments in his epistles, scattering them with words like hence, therefore, since, and so on. Would he have bothered to argue so logically if, in fact, his whole doctrines were fundamentally inconsistent?

Augustine was fond of quoting Romans 11:33—how **unsearchable** are his judgments, and his ways past tracing out! For who has known the mind of the Lord? This was Augustine's stock citation when he asked himself why God should damn those he could have saved, or why he should allow truly righteous men to fall from grace and go to hell. The citation is, unfortunately, a misleading one. The implication in this passage of Paul is not that God is always incomprehensible, but that no one can advise God or guess his plans before he reveals them. It is just such a revelation that Paul has outlined in the previous chapters (9-11) of Romans. When we consider 1 Corinthians 2, we find a similar question in verse 16: who has known the mind of the Lord, that he should instruct him? But now Paul specifically replies: But we have the mind of Christ. The whole point is that God *has* revealed the deep things of his Spirit (1 Corinthians 2:10). It is true that the natural man cannot understand them (v. 14), but the man willing to be taught by the Spirit does understand God's revelation. In the mind of Christ we do understand God's mind—it is not some enigma to be revealed in heaven. Indeed, as spiritual men, we "compare spiritual things with spiritual" (v. 13). The language resembles 1 Corinthians 14:29; we are to "weigh up" different revelations, for anything that is of God is consistent with all his other revelation. Paul is saying that natural reasoning is inadequate; we must strive for spiritual understanding. But spiritual understanding is certainly not the same as total incomprehension.

100. Smith says: "The rigid fatalistic determination of Manichaeism was to appeal to the young Augustine" (p. 158). This idea of God's will always being done was very strong indeed also in Roman Stoicism, the philosophy that had great appeal to the "Roman" mind.

101. Origen's thoroughness is shown in a letter to Africanus, even though we may disagree with him on the particular issue.

102. We see in the *Dialogue* that Justin had compared the LXX with the Hebrew.

103. Verduin: *The Reformers and Their Stepchildren* (Paternoster). Another interesting book on this subject is Broadbent's *The Pilgrim Church* (P. & I.).

104. Letter to Vincentius, 2.5

105. e.g., *Corr. Don.* 21, 23; letter to Vincentius 5 (A.D. 408); letter to Donatus 3 (A.D. 416).

106. *Corr. Don.* 23

107. Augustine cited Matthew 17:15.

108. *Ag. Gaud.* 1.29; see also the letter to Boniface.

109. He wrote to Vincentius that his former opinion "that no one should be coerced into the unity of Christ" was overcome "not by the words of those who controverted it, but by the inconclusive instances to which they could point."

110. It has sometimes been suggested that Augustine's emphasis on baptism and grace rather than responsibility appealed to times in which the unruly "mob" had become Christian. This may be unfair to Augustine, who certainly insisted that Christianity involved some standards of behavior. Nevertheless his strong insistence that "tares" and "wheat" should be left together in the church did make it simpler for state churches to operate. It also meant that he was afraid of his own flock (see letters to Aurelius, A.D. 392, Albina, A.D. 411).

In a letter to Albina in 411 he described an incredible incident of unruly behavior of his flock, in which he himself had played a dubious role and for which he showed no apparent surprise or remorse.

111. Farrar: *Lives of the Fathers* p. 536

112. Augustine himself belies this accusation in his letters to leading Donatists. See, e.g., letters to: Maximin (A.D. 392); Emeritus (A.D. 405); a debate with Fortunius (recorded in a letter of A.D. 398); *Corr. Don* 4.16; and his letter to the Rotagist Vincentius.

113. Verduin, *The Reformers and Their Stepchildren*, ch. 1

114. *Corr. Don.* 1

115. *Cath. Ep.* 2.2

116. Matthew 25:41-45

117. Verduin, p. 55

118. Verduin p. 55

119. Verduin p. 55

120. An example of inconsistency in such an appeal is found in the book *The Man God Mastered* by Cadier (IVP). This first tells us: "For Calvin, the death penalty could be the only possible one for a zealous denier of fundamental doctrines such as the Trinity and infant baptism." Cadier then tells us that Calvin wanted Servetus executed rather than burned—though he omits to tell us the reason for this was that execution would have made it appear that Servetus was killed on a civil charge rather than a religious one (see Verduin p. 52). In excuse for Calvin we are told: "it was the opinion of all the men of the times apart from Castellion" that such extreme heresy as that of Servetus was more deserving of severe punishment than any civil crime (p. 153). Yet later we are told: "protests arose on all sides" (p. 162). Who made these protests if it was nearly everyone's opinion that such punishment was justified?

121. The tendency of Augustine's theology to coincide with persecution of dissenters is reflected in other ages also. An outstanding example in the time of the Reformation is seen in the difference between Erasmus and Luther. Their main point of difference was precisely over the correct meaning of predestination, election, etc. On this issue the early church view was represented by Erasmus (who quoted them in this respect), and the view of Augustine was adopted by Luther (who copied many of Augustine's proof-texts and arguments). Yet, again, while the Lutherans persecuted the non-conformists, Erasmus eloquently pleaded for tolerance, and said that the weapons of Christ should be gentle reproof and verbal demonstrations of error. While Luther denounced all popes as anti-Christs, Erasmus tried to act as a mediating influence between warring parties of Christians, accepting as true believers those in any denomination with genuine spiritual experience. Erasmus might accept much of Luther, and said: "I have said that our salvation depends not on our desert, but on God's grace. I highly approve of Luther when he calls us away from frail confidence in ourselves . . . Our hope is in the mercy of God and the merits of Christ." Erasmus, like the early church, believed that salvation was a gift—but he rejected the Augustinian doctrines both of faith as an irresistible gift, and of the use of force in persecution as simply following God's example (see also note 45, and Bainton's book on Erasmus).